A TALE OF TWO CITIES

A TALE OF TWO CITIES

THE 2004 YANKEES–RED SOX RIVALRY AND THE WAR FOR THE PENNANT

TONY MASSAROTTI AND
JOHN HARPER

THE LYONS PRESS
Guilford, Connecticut
An imprint of The Globe Pequot Press

The Lyons Press is an imprint of The Globe Pequot Press.

10 9 8 7 6 5 4 3 2 1

Printed in the United States of America

Designed by Sheryl P. Kober

ISBN 1-59228-704-2

Library of Congress Cataloging-in-Publication Data is available on file.

JOHN HARPER

To Liz, Matt, and Chris,
who have accompanied me on many a
road trip to Fenway Park, and even lived
to tell about sitting in the bleachers.

TONY MASSAROTTI

For Natalie and Alexander

TABLE OF CONTENTS

ACKNOWLEDGMENTS: JOHN HARPER

I WOULD LIKE TO THANK TOM MCCARTHY, OUR EDITOR AT THE Lyons Press, for his belief in this project and his guidance along the way.

Also: *Daily News* sports editor Leon Carter, and fellow *Daily News* baseball writers Bill Madden, Anthony McCarron, Sam Borden, and Christian Red for their help with information and insights regarding the Yankees.

Also: Tom Verducci of *Sports Illustrated* and Michael Kay of the YES Network and Bob Klapisch of the *Bergen Record* for their cooperation with interviews and Yankee insights.

ACKNOWLEDGMENTS: TONY MASSAROTTI

IN 12 YEARS COVERING THE BOSTON RED SOX, WRITING A BOOK always has been a goal. But in between the idea and the final product, a host of people helped make this project a reality.

Thanks largely to the efforts of anyone who wrote a single word about the Red Sox for either the *Boston Herald* or the *Boston Globe*, the research throughout this process was not nearly as difficult as it could have been. Either the papers or the specific reporters are credited at various points throughout this book, and it should be stressed that, in many cases, generic terms like *Herald reporter* were used in place of first-person pronouns. Some of the attributed quotes were made to groups of reporters at a given time; others came in far more private and intimate, one-on-one settings.

Ultimately, the reality is that baseball in Boston was covered almost as well as it was played in 2004, which speaks to the persistence, skill and dedication of the many reporters who set foot in Fenway Park.

As for the *Herald*, in particular, no measure of thanks could be enough for the many people who offered their support. Owner and publisher Pat Purcell helped market the book almost exclusively as a courtesy, putting us in the capable hands of promotional whiz Gwen Gage. Executive sports editor Mark Torpey offered to run excerpts and trusted that the book would not become a distraction; assistant sports editors Hank Hryniewicz, Joe Thomas, Mark Murphy, and Nate Dow have served as valuable sounding boards and resources.

And, of course, an unheralded cast of copy editors has provided a safety net and served as a needed grounding device.

Thanks, too, to the *Herald* library staff headed by John Cronin. Thanks especially to Al Thibeault and Chris Donnelly, who have been great resources over the years and, at select times, during this project. Each of you has been patient and responsive, which makes any research so much easier.

Of course, were it not for the performance and assistance of the 2004 Boston Red Sox, this book would have been impossible. Glenn Geffner and the entire media relations department have responded to any and all requests, no matter how specific, peculiar, or downright ridiculous in nature. And aside from being quite cooperative and understanding of the media's needs and wants, owners John Henry and Tom Werner, president Larry Lucchino, manager Terry Francona, and general manager Theo Epstein (as well as the latter's entire baseball operations staff) have remained committed to maintaining Boston's place as a perennial playoff contender, which makes watching the Red Sox and writing about them an infinitely easier and more enjoyable task.

That said, several colleagues offered their help for this book, and longtime *Worcester Telegram* reporter Bill Ballou and *Boston Herald* teammate Michael Silverman sacrificed time to read and review select chapters. Many others knowingly or unknowingly inspired thought through discussions, though, as always, specific thanks are directed toward the regular members of the traveling party, a group that includes Sean McAdam and Steve Krasner of the *Providence Journal*, Gordon Edes and Bob Hohler of the *Boston Globe*, Jeff Horrigan of the *Herald* and Dave Heuschkel of the *Hartford Courant*.

Finally, a very special thanks to The Lyons Press and to editor Tom McCarthy, who embraced this idea from the very beginning and remained patient, optimistic and unwavering in his support throughout. And thanks, too, to John Harper of the *Daily News*, whose easygoing nature made him a pleasure to work with and whose reputation and abilities speak for themselves.

Even if he is a New Yorker.

INTRODUCTION

IN RETROSPECT, THE END WAS MERELY A BEGINNING.

But when Aaron Boone's home run landed like a final cannonball in the left field seats at an ecstatic Yankee Stadium in the earliest moments of October 17, 2003, no one could have imagined the impact or the aftershocks. No one could have imagined that the deflated Boston Red Sox would emerge more resolute than ever and assemble a team that even their most fatalistic of fans believed would finally topple the hated New York Yankees. No one could have imagined that Boone would soon go from immortal to invalid, the result of an off-season knee injury sustained while playing, of all things, basketball. And no one could have imagined that the loss of Boone would trigger a series of events that delivered to New York the widely regarded best player in baseball, the great Alex Rodriguez, whom the Red Sox had steadfastly pursued for a series of weeks, a chase that forever alienated their own franchise shortstop, the gifted Nomar Garciaparra.

Looking back, no one could have imagined any of that.

Yet, anyone whose heart rate climbed with Boone's long ball surely expected the drama to continue in some fashion. Millions of emotionally spent fans in the two respective cities, from Rudy Guiliani in New York to Ben Affleck in Boston, were sure there would be no backing down from either side after their epic playoff series. Not after the stakes had been raised so pointedly on each side. The history between the two teams goes back to the sale of Babe Ruth, and surely it reached a climax of sorts when Bucky Dent hit his storied home run in a 1978 playoff game that brought thrill to New York, agony to Boston. But Red Sox president Larry Lucchino launched an unprecedented era of cutthroat competition between the two franchises in January of 2003 when he off-handedly labeled the Yankees the "Evil Empire" in a frustrated response to the Yankees—and owner George Steinbrenner, in particular—outbidding the Red Sox for the talents of Cuban pitcher Jose Contreras.

If Steinbrenner always has been consumed with beating the Red Sox, Lucchino's jab turned the Yankees owner's grim determination into a crazed obsession. Indeed, to acquire Boone, Steinbrenner had overruled his front-office executives, insisting they make the deal with the Cincinnati Reds at the July 31 trading deadline (even if it meant giving up a prized pitching prospect) simply because he wanted to prevent the Red Sox from acquiring Seattle Mariners pitcher Freddy Garcia in a rumored three-way deal that would have sent Boone to Seattle. Meanwhile, Lucchino's ownership group, which bought the team in 2002, proved to be the first in Boston willing to stand up to the bully in New York and take him on verbally as well as financially. It made for fascinating backroom intrigue, above and beyond the thrills the teams produced on the baseball field. And so, in living rooms and barrooms from Cape Cod to Coney Island, from the tiniest outposts in New England to the crowded suburbs of metropolitan New York, it heightened the level of intensity surrounding the most famous rivalry in sports.

This is where we come in, a couple of newspaper guys to tell the tale of two cities in the truest spirit of the rivalry, shouting at each other from opposite sides of the press box—Massarotti from Boston, Harper from New York. Each has deep baseball roots and viewpoints shaped by a lifetime of living on opposite ends of the endless debates—or raging arguments—between Beantown and Big Apple sports fans.

Massarotti is a Boston guy through and through. He grew up in nearby Waltham, Massachusetts, rooting for his beloved Sox, wearing his Fred Lynn jersey as a kid, playing shortstop in high school and then for two years at Tufts University. Like most of the Boston writers, he thinks his New York counterparts have more Steinbrenner in them than they know—loud, overbearing at times, contentious, and reveling in Yankee chaos so they can flex their back-page muscle and make a name for themselves. Harper, meanwhile, grew up in North Jersey imitating Bobby Murcer's left-handed swing and Gene (Stick)

Michael's sleight-of-hand as the master of the hidden-ball trick, in the rare era when there weren't many other reasons to watch the Yankees. He came to know Boston fans all too well at the University of Bridgeport (Connecticut), even came to embrace a handful of them as teammates on the baseball team, and came away convinced the only thing they love more than the Red Sox and Celtics is cold beer. Like most of the New York writers, he's convinced the Boston scribes all still secretly live and die with the fate of the Sox and take it personally when the home boys lose, then let 'em have it with the viciousness of a jilted lover.

We're friendly enough, since it's not like we're competing on the same beat. Yet there's always an unspoken wariness between us when the Sox and Yanks are playing, as if the rivalry extends all the way to the press box. The first thing Massarotti said when the teams got together for a spring training game last March, for example, was how he was glad A-Rod didn't wind up with the Red Sox because the guy is the biggest phony in the game. Harper rolled his eyes in response, sure that his colleague was rationalizing like the rest of Boston, devastated that A-Rod somehow wound up a Yankee after the Sox chased him all winter. Harper responded that A-Rod was the best thing to happen to New York reporters in the button-downed Yankee clubhouse since David Cone retired—the new guy has already offered more insight and quotable answers than the ever-standoffish Derek Jeter has in his entire career, he said—and who cared if it was a calculating attempt to cultivate good press? Massarotti shook his head and thought: *Typical New York attitude, all about headline potential over substance.*

From those polar opposite viewpoints the idea for this book was born. It was March 2004 when we agreed to chronicle the Red Sox and Yankees throughout the approaching season, and it was our hope that fate (not to mention combined payrolls totaling $315 million) would deliver both teams back to the American League Championship Series. What we received was a great deal more: a stirring Red Sox comeback—arguably the greatest turnaround in the history of team sports—and Boston's first baseball championship since 1918, a truly historic feat accomplished in unprecedented fashion.

On those occasions where our parallel storylines intersected in the head-to-head meetings between Boston and New York, we invoked editorial license. Our idea was to go beyond the hows and whys of wins and losses, to capture the passion the rivalry generates in the two cities. And with that in mind, we turned the chapters on the head-to-head meetings into more opinionated forums, affording us the opportunity to have a little fun, incite one another with caustic jabs, and mock the opposing teams and their followers.

If anyone gets offended, well, isn't that, too, part of what this rivalry is all about?

Our idea, after all, was to put readers in the middle of the game by providing a look from the inside—what it's like to cover these teams and deal behind the scenes with a temperamental superstar such as Pedro Martinez or an outrageous owner such as George Steinbrenner. In doing so, we present an up-close portrayal of the disparate personalities of the two ballclubs, the Red Sox with their frat-house approach to bonding and their free-spirit hairstyles, the Yankees with their corporate manner and their solemn pursuit of the championship their owner demands for his money.

Along the way we see how the Yankees look down their noses at what they consider childish and sometimes unprofessional antics of the Red Sox, and how the Red Sox giggle at the Yankees' all-business approach they believe is born from a fear of incurring the wrath of Steinbrenner. It all contributes to a genuine dislike for one another that has percolated for years around Pedro's brush-back or head-hunting tactics, depending which side you take, and then erupted in 2004 when Jason Varitek and A-Rod set off a brawl that, by baseball standards, was remarkably vicious on both sides.

Six straight seasons of the Yankees finishing first, the Red Sox second, in the AL East provided the backdrop for growing hostility. And when Boone hit his Game 7 home run, he not only denied the Sox the chance to win their first world championship since 1918, but set the wheels in motion almost immediately for the fireworks between the teams in 2004. For a while Boone's home run prolonged a familiar history between the teams, both the Yankees and the Red Sox entering the off-season looking for what they considered a missing piece to a championship. The Sox felt with just a little more pitching they would have put the Yankees away; the Yankees, meanwhile, felt they needed more offense after losing to the young and powerfully armed Florida Marlins in the World Series. In truth, what the Yankees may have needed most to win the World Series was a week off to recover from the emotionally draining series with the Red Sox.

In rallying from a 5–2 deficit in the eighth inning to survive Game 7 against the Red Sox, the Yankees had called upon all of the grit and willpower that had helped them win four championships during the Joe Torre era. By any measure, however, they had been fortunate to pull off such a comeback and finish off a Red Sox team that had played them dead even all season. Prior to Boone's decisive blow, in fact, the Red Sox and Yankees were exquisitely matched. Entering the fateful 11th inning of Game 7, the teams had scored precisely the same number of runs over 64 innings in the series. The seventh game was a record 26th meeting between the clubs that season, the Yankees holding a 13–12 edge in victories at the time. And there was the belief in both organizations—in both cities, really—that the Red Sox finally were every bit as good as their counterparts.

As Red Sox pitcher Derek Lowe said in a somber Boston clubhouse in the aftermath of Game 7: "If we played 100 times, I think we'd win 50 and they'd win 50."

The Yankees might have believed that, too, but they were sure they had the championship character to win the games that counted most. Indeed, they had come to believe in the October magic that has defined them since Derek Jeter came along in 1996.

"Derek told me the ghosts would show up eventually," a breathless Boone said after his heroic home run. "When I joined the Yankees this is the kind of thing I thought I could be part of. This is the perfect ending."

So, after the 2003 season, both the Red Sox and Yankees entered the off-season seeing ghosts. To the Yankees those ghosts took the form of aura and mystique, the friendliest of supernatural forces. To the Sox they took the more full-figured form of (who else?) Babe Ruth and the countless spirits who made up his legacy. Some things, it seemed, never changed.

Along the way, the storied rivalry continued to grow by the minute.

In New York and Boston, after all, the baseball season never really ends so much as a new one begins.

HITS . . . AND A MISS—RED SOX

IN BOSTON, AS ALWAYS, A BRIEF MOURNING FOLLOWED THE FATEFUL NIGHT.

John Henry had been the principal owner of the Red Sox for less than two years when the 2003 season concluded, and New York Yankees third baseman Aaron Boone's home run in Game 7 of the 2003 American League Championship Series provided Henry, especially, with a crash course in Red Sox heartache. After an extraordinary 2003 baseball season in which his Red Sox had demonstrated remarkable grit, determination and fight, Henry's team was on the verge of toppling the mighty New York Yankees, extinguishing years of anguish, ending years of self-doubt. The Red Sox led the Yankees by a 5–2 score entering the eighth inning of decisive Game 7 when it all went so wrong. The Yankees rallied to tie the score against Sox ace Pedro Martinez, forcing the game into extra innings, ultimately advancing to the World Series when Boone led off the bottom of the 11th inning with a solo home run against Sox knuckleballer Tim Wakefield, who in one pitch went from the Most Valuable Player of the series to a most unfortunate, undeserving tragic figure.

As for Henry, he had owned the Florida Marlins prior to purchasing the Red Sox. Slightly more than a week after the Red Sox were eliminated from the postseason, it was Henry's old Marlins who would defeat the emotionally-drained Yankees in six games of the 99th World Series. Florida's victory came one year after a World Series win by the Anaheim Angels, the team Henry nearly had purchased before buying the Red Sox in the spring of 2002.

Had Henry cared even the slightest bit, he might have acknowledged the irony amid all of that in an e-mail he sent during the World Series:

> As much as I love some of the Marlins' players and root for them to win, I have no interest in watching this series. The only interest I currently have in baseball is to prepare for next season. The supportive communications I have received from fans has been shocking and has stirred me greatly—emotionally.
>
> Initially, I thought New Englanders would just finally throw up their hands. But their level of commitment and resolve is astonishing and deserves our full attention to moving this franchise forward without a break. It shows you how little I know about the toughness of this region. And it shows me how tough I need to be in making sure that we accomplish our goals.
>
> So I'm riding their "wave," so to speak. They've given me the energy to move forward without having to get away from it all. I thought I would have to get away from it all to recharge and start again. But they have refocused me. And I can tell you that Theo [Epstein, the team's general manager] and Larry [Lucchino, president] did not take a one-day or even a half-day break this week. I don't think they needed an external force to recharge themselves. This franchise is in very good shape with these two leading it.
>
> How amazing is it that even the angriest/saddest/most broken-hearted fans offer thanks and remain determined to see this team prevail? It's astonishing. I'm not listening to the radio, so maybe things are different there. I just know what comes directly to me.
>
> There isn't anything I wouldn't do for these people. You know, there isn't anything these people wouldn't do for the Red Sox. We owe them.

In that e-mail, the Red Sox battle plans for the 2003–04 off-season effectively were hidden.

In Boston, heads soon began to roll.

And so, beginning with the dismissal of manager Grady Little on October 27—two days after the Marlins defeated the Yankees in the sixth and final game of the World Series—the Red Sox put into motion a series of events that would have both repercussions and rewards. Little was fired and replaced, eventually, with the younger and more polished Terry Francona, whose only previous managerial experience had been an enormously unsuccessful four-year stint with a wretched Philadelphia Phillies team. Slugger Manny Ramirez was placed on release waivers with the slim hope that someone would claim both the player and the approximately $100 million remaining on his contract. And the estimable Alex Rodriguez, then of the Texas Rangers and soon to be named the Most Valuable Player in the American League, was pursued as part of a master plan in which the Sox would dispose of both man-child Ramirez and wonderboy shortstop Nomar Garciaparra, with whom team officials were grappling in contract negotiations and whom Sox officials found to be extraordinarily difficult.

For Henry, in particular, the decision on Little was an easy one. A mathematical genius who devised formulas to forecast futures and commodities markets, Henry was a painstaking, methodical thinker and a certified problem-solver. He preferred to deal with reporters via e-mail rather than in person because it allowed him to first ponder a response, then present it. John Henry did not like snap decisions and he approached baseball with the same kind of philosophy, which placed him at the opposite end of the spectrum from someone like Little, a North Carolina native and one-time cotton farmer who spoke with a drawl and effectively said what was on his mind.

In fact, shortly after being hired during the spring of 2002, when he sensed that a reporter was having difficulty with what would be perceived as a tough question, Little eased the tension with one of his greatest gifts.

Humor.

"If you don't hurry up and get to the point," said the manager, "I'm going to pee my pants."

Alas, the contrast between the owner of the Red Sox and the team's manager was striking.

Grady Little didn't want or need e-mail to communicate and he dealt with life as it came.

Approximately two years later, following Little's decision to stick with ace Pedro Martinez rather than turn the game over to his relief corps during the New York Yankees' game-tying rally in the eighth inning of unforgettable Game 7, many critics argued that Little, in fact, had *soiled* his pants at the most critical moment of the 2003 season. Much to the dismay of Sox ownership and management—Henry, in fact, wanted to fire Little four months earlier—Little went with his gut and bypassed the hard data that suggested he turn the game over to set-up man Mike Timlin and closer Scott Williamson, whose names became to Red Sox fans part of an infuriating off-season refrain. *Timlin in the eighth, Williamson in the ninth.* The problem was that Grady Little did not know the lyrics to the song, though that was hardly unusual among managers, who often made their biggest decisions by simply placing their fate into the hands of the players they trusted most.

Regardless of what the formula called for or whatever coddling Pedro Martinez needed off the field, Grady Little trusted Martinez implicitly when it came time to get somebody out. Little was in his second season as Red Sox bench coach to former Red Sox manager Jimy Williams when Martinez first came to the Red Sox in 1998, and he remained at Williams' side when Martinez went 23–4 during a historic 1999 campaign during which Martinez won the first of his two Cy Young Awards in Boston. Little was at Williams' right hand, too, when a wounded Martinez emerged from the bullpen in decisive Game 5 of the 1999 AL Division Series against Cleveland to pitch six no-hit innings and propel the Red Sox into the next round of the playoffs.

Under the direst of circumstances, Grady Little had seen Pedro Martinez succeed.

And so come Game 7 of the 2003 AL Championship Series, Little was not about to trust anyone else.

Of course, the Yankees rallied against Martinez and eventually won Game 7, and 10 days later the axe fell on Grady Little, who became to the 2003 Red Sox what tragic figure Bill Buckner was to the 1986 team that blew the World Series against the New York Mets.

A scapegoat.

And an easy target.

In fact, Grady Little's tenure in Boston was largely successful, though too many people did not see it that way. Hired during the spring of 2002, Little guided the Red Sox to 93 wins in his first season, 95 in his second and final campaign. He came within five outs of going to the World Series. And while most everyone focused on Little's decision to stick with Martinez—rest assured that the manager similarly would have been vilified had he gone to his bullpen and lost, despite contentions to the contrary by Red Sox fans blinded with anger—most ignored the fact that Little deftly managed a clubhouse with an array of egos and personalities. That never was more evident than during the days leading up to the 2003 All-Star break, when Ramirez failed to show up for the finale of the season's first half—Ramirez told Little his mother was sick, an excuse that caused even Ramirez' teammates to privately chuckle—and ace Pedro Martinez was allowed to go home a day early while the rest of his teammates played on.

Empowered with big contracts and years of enabling, players like Manny Ramirez and Pedro Martinez did what they wanted when they wanted, and there really wasn't much that someone like Grady Little could do about it. Most fans loved managers who portrayed themselves as disciplinarians while kicking the dirt and tossing their caps, but those managers typically had a short shelf life and succeeded only with younger, moldable teams. Grady Little, on the other hand, had a team of veterans with a big payroll. The object was to win.

He *needed* them.

"Let me ask you something," Little said to a *Boston Herald* reporter while sitting in his office at Detroit's Comerica Park on the day that Ramirez went AWOL and Martinez was granted a leave. "If someone gives you a dog and that dog has a habit of peeing on the floor, can you change them? Is that your fault?"

The answer, of course, was no.

Still, Little had reason to be optimistic at the midpoint of the 2003 season, during which the omens were promising. Despite the disappearance of Ramirez during the Sox' weekend trip to Detroit, the Red Sox entered the All-Star break on pace for 96 victories and Little had won big at the local casino, twice hitting sizable payoffs on the $5 slot machines. The Red Sox were playing well on the whole, and Little was not the type to get bogged down with the particulars when things generally were going well. So while the media was kicking up a storm about the absence of Ramirez and Martinez, Grady Little simply went about his business and filled out his lineup card everyday, making molehills out of mountains and genuinely believing that the 2003 Red Sox were going to win the World Series.

When they failed—and when he was identified as the culprit—he was left with a bitter taste in his mouth.

"I'm prepared for the likelihood [of being fired]. . . . I'm not sure that I want to manage that team," Little told *Boston Globe* reporter Gordon Edes from Little's home in North Carolina roughly a week after the Yankees eliminated the Red Sox and just before Little was officially dismissed. "If they don't want me, fine, they don't want me. If they want me to come back, then we'll talk and see if I want to come back up there. That's the way I feel about it.

"All I know is, when I left there, there was some hesitation. That's all I need to know," Little continued. "If Grady Little is not there, he'll be somewhere. Right now I'm disappointed that evidently some people are judging me on the results of one decision I made—not the decision, but the results of the decision. Less than 24 hours before, those same people were hugging and kissing me. If that's the way they operate, I'm not sure I want to be part of it."

Concluded Little: "Just add one more ghost to the list if I'm not there, because there are ghosts. That's certainly evident when you're a player in that uniform."

Or, for that matter, a manager.

And as the end of the 2003 season proved, particularly in an impassioned baseball town like Boston, people always needed someone to blame when things did not turn out as hoped.

The firing of a manager—and the subsequent search for and hiring of a new one—would normally serve as the major off-season story in a baseball-crazed town like Boston, but the swap of Little for Francona ultimately became an afterthought in the following weeks and months. Instead, the prevailing drama of the winter began with the curious choice by Red Sox officials to place Ramirez on waivers, exposing him to the other 29 teams in baseball as if he were a piece of old furniture placed on a neighborhood curb. The decision was as much a reflection on the game's economic state as it was on Ramirez, whose childish nature pushed Sox officials to their breaking point late during the 2003 season. At one point, in fact, Ramirez failed to report to Fenway Park to meet with team medical officials during a critical weekend series with the Yankees, inspiring the club to send team doctor Bill Morgan to Ramirez' residence at the Ritz-Carlton hotel. When Morgan got there, a gleeful Ramirez welcomed Morgan and acted as if nothing were wrong, further adding to the riddle that was the great Manny Ramirez.

In Red Sox circles, there became a simple way to explain Ramirez' unpredictable actions.

It was just *Manny being Manny.*

And so eventually, at the onset of an off-season during which Ramirez' agent, Jeff Moorad, would somehow go from publicly stating that Ramirez wanted to play for the Yankees (the audacity!) to suggesting that Ramirez "would be disappointed if he were traded at this point," Red Sox officials chose to be proactive. Yes, Manny Ramirez was a gifted hitter, Sox officials believed, but, no, he was not worth the average annual salary of $20 million (for five more years!) that resulted from the eight-year, $160 million contract he signed *before* John Henry and his partners purchased the team.

In Ramirez, Henry and his partners believed they had inherited a problem.

Consequently, they tried to dump him on someone else, placing the player on release waivers on October 29, less than two weeks after Boone's decisive home run in Game 7 of the American League Championship Series.

At that point—and although the Red Sox and Texas Rangers already had engaged in some discussion about the extraordinarily gifted Alex Rodriguez, who was named the American League Most Valuable Player shortly after the conclusion of the World Series—the entire baseball world saw the makings of a blockbuster deal: What about Ramirez for Rodriguez, the latter of whom was eager to leave Texas? Like Ramirez, Rodriguez has signed a monumental contract during December 2000, baseball's Winter of Recklessness. It was during the 2000–01 off-season, after all, that Rodriguez, Ramirez, and then-free agent Mike Hampton signed the three largest contracts in baseball history for the staggering total of $533 million. Yet just three years later, between the 2003 and 2004 seasons, Hampton already had been traded from the team with which he signed (the Colorado Rockies) while the Red Sox and Rangers openly peddled Ramirez and Rodriguez, a blunt admission that all three clubs were regretful of the rash decisions they had made.

So, like the Red Sox, the Texas Rangers wanted to rid themselves of a hefty contract following a disappointing finish to the 2003 campaign, though the depths of frustration in Texas and Boston were entirely different. During Rodriguez' three seasons with the Rangers, Texas won, in order, 73, 72, and 71 games, meaning the Rangers actually were getting worse while posting three consecutive last-place finishes within their division. So because Rodriguez' deal was longer than that of Ramirez—ten years as opposed to eight—and because Rodriguez was being paid more—an average of $25.2 million compared to $20 million—*and* because both deals were back-loaded, the Rangers could save approximately $85 million over six years by trading Rodriguez for Ramirez, a trade that would have swapped the two biggest contracts in baseball history totaling a stunning $412 million. All of that gave the clubs a solid foundation from which to deal, though, from the standpoint of the Sox and Rangers, there still were significant financial hurdles to overcome to bring the megatrade to fruition.

For the Red Sox, there was, also, one glaring conflict:

Alex Rodriguez played shortstop, the same position as the team's homegrown franchise player, Nomar Garciaparra.

So, while Sox officials pursued an array of off-season changes and improvements that ultimately included the acquisitions of starting pitcher Curt Schilling (in a trade with the Arizona Diamondbacks) and closer Keith Foulke (a free agent from the Oakland A's), the pursuit of rock star Rodriguez became a focal point in the eyes of the team and the public. The Red Sox knew that Rodriguez, too, came with certain drawbacks—in Texas, Rodriguez was perceived as being both high maintenance and me-first—and there were even incidents during the 2003–04 off-season that suggested Rodriguez came with his share of complexities and needs. Roughly two weeks before spring training, in fact, Rodriguez would agree to a morning interview on the CNBC program *Squawk Box*, inviting the network into his home to conduct the segment. The player ultimately missed the scheduled interview, and when CNBC pressed him for an explanation, Rodriguez told employees of the network that he had trouble deciding which pair of pants to wear.

Nonetheless, the Red Sox found it far more palatable to pay Alex Rodriguez $25 million a year than to pay Manny Ramirez $20 million, something that was especially true given the team's fruitless contract negotiations with Garciaparra, whom they believed they would lose to free agency, anyway. So while moving both Ramirez *and* Garciaparra would dramatically alter the composition of a Sox team that came within five outs of its first trip to the World Series since 1986, club officials felt that such a maneuver would better position them for the long term as well as the short.

As a result, the Sox requested and received permission from commissioner Bud Selig for Henry to meet with Rodriguez, a highly unusual development given that a meeting otherwise would have violated baseball's rules for tampering. And while the Red Sox would say later that their pursuit of Rodriguez came only after they had disclosed their intentions to Garciaparra, their actions at the time were nonetheless curious. When contacted by a *Boston Herald* reporter about a meeting between the Red Sox and Rodriguez, both Henry and general manager Theo Epstein expressed concerns that the reporting of such information would alienate their existing shortstop. ("Number 5 won't be too happy about that," said Epstein, referring to Garciaparra by the player's jersey number, "but you've got to do what you've got to do.") And Selig, who authorized the meeting, denied any knowledge of a rendezvous between the owner and player when similarly questioned.

"If that has happened," said the commissioner, "I don't know anything about it."

Hence, the conspiracy theorists had more than their share of ammunition.

There *was* a meeting, after all.

And officials with the Red Sox, Rangers, and Major League Baseball all knew about it.

Eventually, so would Garciaparra, who was on his honeymoon with women's soccer star Mia Hamm when the story broke. And while Garciaparra's agent, Arn Tellem, told a *Boston Globe* reporter that the meeting between Henry and Rodriguez was a "slap in the face" to his client, the shortstop simultaneously returned a call to the *Herald*, completing a full-scale counterstrike in Boston's two major newspapers. A day later, Garciaparra also would call in to Boston's top-rated all-sports radio station, WEEI, telling Red Sox fans that he felt jilted and unappreciated, though, of course, that was only his side of the story.

In fact, the relationship between Nomar Garciaparra and the Red Sox had long since been deteriorating. And as Red Sox fans had learned previously during the departures of homegrown players Roger Clemens and Mo Vaughn, assigning blame in a divorce—particularly one involving the Red Sox and one of their star players—was an impossible task.

"I think I'm kind of like the fans are. If you were a fan looking at this, you might think, 'Are they really considering this option?'" Garciaparra said. "I've always respected the uniform that I've worn. It's been the only uniform I know and it's the only uniform I want to know for my entire career. That's basically how I feel.

"What I'd like to say is that I know there's always been this speculation that I'm unhappy [in Boston]. I've heard it and read it—that I want to go home [to California] and I'm unhappy—and I don't know where that comes from," Garciaparra continued. "No words have ever come out of my mouth—publicly or privately—that I don't want to be there. I also believe that my actions have shown I don't want out of there. I go out there and play hard and give it my all, day in and day out, not just on the field, but off. I have a [charitable] foundation there. I'm coming back in January to do my 10th hitting camp, I think."

Concluded the Red Sox shortstop: "Before we got married, my wife and I purchased a new home [in the Boston area]. If you look at all that, I wouldn't do all that stuff if I wanted to leave."

Just the same, there were those in Boston who doubted the shortstop, a faction that included even some of Garciaparra's teammates. The Ramirez-for-Rodriguez trade became such a certainty at one point—the Red Sox had principally agreed on a conditional trade of Garciaparra for Chicago White Sox outfielder Magglio Ordonez to accommodate Rodriguez at shortstop—that overly talkative Sox first baseman Kevin Millar said during a television interview that, yes, he would rather have Rodriguez on his team than Garciaparra. Millar believed he was merely being honest at the time, but the remark ultimately would blow up in his face when the Rodriguez deal fell apart, leaving the Red Sox with both a left fielder (Ramirez) and a shortstop (Garciaparra) who had every right to feel unwanted while being asked to fill the Nos. 3 and 4 positions in the Boston batting order.

In some ways, it seemed, Red Sox officials had succeeded only in taking the heart of a 2003 lineup that led baseball in runs scored and set a major league, single-season record for slugging percentage (breaking a mark previously held by the immortal 1927 Yankees), and stomped on it with sharpened spikes.

Still, Millar's remarks were revealing if for no reason other than this: even inside the Red Sox clubhouse, there were those who did not understand Nomar Garciaparra. Millar was most certainly among them, though that was hardly surprising given the differences in their abilities and personalities. Undrafted by the major leagues out of high school and college, Millar began his career in the independent Northern League, from where he was signed by the Florida Marlins late in 1993. Millar subsequently climbed his way through the Florida system for one reason and one reason only—he could hit—and ultimately had agreed to play for a more lucrative contract in Japan when the Red Sox unexpectedly and unconventionally disrupted the process by claiming him off waivers following the 2002 season. The chance to play for an organization like the Red Sox prompted Millar to rethink his position on Japan, inspiring the player and his agents—likeable twin brothers Sam and Seth Levinson—to concoct an amusing, far-fetched story about how Millar suddenly had reservations about playing overseas with America recently having launched the war on Iraq.

So, after a long and strange trip through the independent leagues, minor leagues, Florida, and, nearly, Japan, long shot Kevin Millar ended up in baseball-crazy Boston, a place that someone like him only dreamed about.

As for Garciaparra, his arrival in Boston was anticipated from the moment the Red Sox selected him with the 12th overall selection of the 1994 draft. Unlike the nothing-to-lose Millar, Garciaparra was a *first-round pick.* There was *expectation* for him. And after a minor-league career that included really just one full season, Garciaparra effectively arrived in Boston in time for the 1997 campaign, during which he had one of the greatest rookie years in the history of major league baseball. In his first four seasons as a major leaguer, Garciaparra unanimously won the American Rookie of the Year award, finished second in the AL Most Valuable Player award voting, and became the first right-handed hitter to win consecutive AL batting titles since New York Yankees great Joe DiMaggio in 1939–40. He accomplished all of that before the age of 28, adhering to a rigid routine from which he never strayed, so structured that even his teammates saw those eccentricities as the crutches on which Garciaparra leaned.

Nomar Garciaparra was not obsessed with baseball so much as he was obsessed with succeeding. Consequently, few players placed as much pressure on themselves.

And it showed.

"It's just weird to see a guy have that many superstitions and have that much ability," former Red Sox designated hitter Reggie Jefferson, who once occupied the locker adjacent to Garciaparra's, said during Garciaparra's rookie season of 1997. "It would be one thing if he didn't have the ability, but he does the same routine every day. You hope someday he realizes it's the ability, it's not what you do."

Still, regardless of *why* he had succeeded in his career, Nomar Garciaparra now was confronted with an unusual situation.

His team had better options.

Amid all of that—the firing of Little, the hiring of Francona, the pursuit of Rodriguez, the attempted abandonment of Ramirez, and the alienation of Garciaparra by Sox management and players alike—overshadowed, too, were the acquisitions of Schilling and Foulke, whose arrivals in Boston ultimately were the most significant developments of the off-season. In falling to the Yankees both during the 2003 regular season and playoffs, the Red Sox demonstrated two areas of weakness that ultimately led to their downfall: the absence of one more reliable starting pitcher and the need for a proven closer. Red Sox officials believed that a better game manager, too, was on that list, so by the time the Sox had completed the trade for Schilling and signed Foulke, the club had added Francona, a big-game starting pitcher and a steady closer to a club that had won 95 games and reached Game 7 of the AL Championship Series.

None of those additions was more important than Curt Schilling.

A 36-year-old veteran of 16 major league seasons at the conclusion of the 2003 campaign, Schilling's career actually began with the Red Sox, who originally drafted him in 1986. He was traded three times before the age of 26, the final occasion coming in April 1992, when he was dealt from the Houston Astros for pitcher Jason Grimsley, a deal that awakened Schilling to the reality that he was regarded as a chronic underachiever, another misguided talent with a million-dollar arm and a five-cent head, like Nuke Laloosh in *Bull Durham*. Schilling subsequently resurrected his career with the Philadelphia Phillies, for whom he pitched the next nine years, helping the Phillies reach the 1993 World Series and establishing his place, finally, as one of the more durable and potentially dominating right-handed pitchers in baseball.

Nonetheless, Schilling came with flaws, many of which were on display throughout his career. Regarded by many in baseball as a relentless self-promoter, Schilling was once niftily categorized in the most succinct terms by Phillies general manager Ed Wade, who described Schilling as "a horse" every five days, but "a horse's ass" the remaining four. Such an assessment could speedily make its way throughout Major League Baseball, which, in the end, was like any other industry, be it decorated with smokestacks or scoreboards.

Baseball was a small circle. Word got around. People developed reputations early on and spent much of their careers either living up to them or trying to shed them, and in the case of the talented but loose-lipped Schilling, he was trying to do both at the same time.

Curt Schilling was both bright and talented.

And all too frequently, he inexplicably felt the need to tell people about it.

Because Schilling had the right to reject a trade from the Arizona Diamondbacks to Boston, the pitcher bargained for—and received—a two-year contract extension from the Red Sox worth $25.5 million that he negotiated along with his wife, Shonda. Though he once delegated his contract negotiations to an agent, Schilling decided late in his career that he could bargain for himself, though the decision often seemed inspired by Schilling's undying need to prove something more than a desire to save the estimated 4 percent he would sacrifice from his earnings. So Schilling became his own agent. He prepared for each game by analyzing video, poring over statistics, and even keeping notes, the latter of which he often did in the dugout, where teammates, opponents, television cameras, and reporters could see him hard at work. He often seemed to seek credit for everything he did or accomplished, something that was easily translated for anyone who cared to notice.

"When the paper comes out, there's a *W* or an *L* next to my name," Schilling said in the trophy room of his Arizona home shortly after being traded to the Red Sox. "I've never read a boxscore where the catcher or the pitching coach got a win or a loss. That's *my* game. That's what they pay me for."

And then there was this: "I don't get mad at errors. Errors present a challenge to me. But the one thing I will not tolerate is someone not being [mentally] into the game."

Such remarks might have been perceived as perfectionism on many fronts, but they also revealed a self-importance that was impossible to ignore. Curt Schilling believed that *he* gave maximum effort. He believed that *he* often won or lost. He believed that teammates needed to match *his* level of intensity and preparation, and he seemed to have little understanding that no team in baseball could possibly function in harmony if each of the 25 players believed that the other 24 were required to live up to his standards.

As Curt Schilling was in the process of introducing himself to both Boston and the Red Sox, it was not hard to understand why there were questions about how he would fit into a Red Sox clubhouse where, in 2003, camaraderie had been one of the greatest assets. And while baseball was a game in which players could focus on themselves and still help the team cause—this was especially true of starting pitchers, who frequently adhered to their own programs, anyway—players always had cast a disapproving eye at teammates who were not in it for the greater good, who were not really *team*mates, who were more focused on themselves than on the group.

For the Red Sox, the good news was that Francona knew all about this, having managed Schilling in Philadelphia from 1997 to 2000. In fact, he and Schilling got along wonderfully, a fact that many believed also influenced Schilling's decision to agree to a contract extension with the Red Sox, though the club had not yet officially named Francona manager at the time. (The decision, however, was largely a foregone conclusion.) In any case, by the middle of January, when Francona attended the annual Boston Baseball Writers dinner along with a host of Red Sox players and representatives, there were questions about Curt Schilling that were obvious.

"You're going to want to tell him to shut up every once and while," Francona told Sox players Millar and Tim Wakefield during the event. "But he's a good guy."

"I don't care about that," Wakefield said. "I just want to know if he'll do the same work everyone else does."

Replied the manager: "Yes."

Indeed, for all of the criticisms of Schilling as a clubhouse nuisance, there was no disputing his commitment to pitching. Even late in his career, after baseball had transformed into a mishmash of middle relievers, setup men, and left-handed specialists, Schilling was that rarest of commodities: a pitcher who conditioned himself to go the distance. Though freak injuries limited him to just 24 games in 2003, Schilling had averaged 258 innings pitched during the 2001–02 seasons, an *average* of better than seven innings per start. So, during an age when many pitchers were becoming more and more content to last through merely the sixth inning, Schilling still was pitching into the eighth, in his mid-30s, which was as much a testament to his competitiveness as it was to his work ethic.

And make no mistake, for all of Curt Schilling's imperfections, he was an extraordinary competitor. As part of his contract with the Red Sox, Schilling proposed incentive clauses that emphasized his willingness to take on the challenge that many players were unwilling to take. Presented with the opportunity of playing for the Red Sox or New York Yankees late in their careers, many players often chose New York simply because they believed it was their best chance to win a championship. That reality was what drove Roger Clemens, for instance, to force a trade from the Toronto Blue Jays to the Yankees between the 1998 and 1999 seasons. And two years later, following the 2000 campaign, free-agent pitcher Mike Mussina similarly chose New York over Boston, opting to become part of the Yankees dynasty instead of the man who might have toppled it.

To those players, the strategy was obvious.

If you can't beat 'em, join 'em.

Schilling, for his part, did not see it that way, electing the far more difficult path, though it should be noted that he already had won a world championship, with the Diamondbacks in 2001, when he and fellow ace Randy Johnson shared honors as the Most Valuable Player of the Series in a riveting, seven-game defeat of Clemens, Mussina, and the Yankees. Schilling understood quite well that the Red Sox wanted him to duplicate the feat in Boston, a fact that ultimately led him to propose revolutionary incentives during the course of his contract negotiations with the Red Sox:

Were the Red Sox to win the World Series at any point during Schilling's contract with the team, his salary for the subsequent season would increase by $2 million. Additionally, the contract would be extended by a third year, through 2007, at a salary of $13 million. All in all, Curt Schilling could earn as much as an additional $19 million during his contract with the Red Sox depending on how many world titles the team won during his career in Boston, and he could earn a minimum of $15 million if the Red Sox could win even one title, their first since 1918.

For all involved parties, that made things quite clear.

"They didn't bring me here to pitch well. They brought me here to put one of those on their mantle," Schilling said at his Arizona home in December 2003, pointing to a replica of the 2001 World Series trophy that decorated his war room. "If that doesn't happen, to me, this contract would be a failure."

As always, Curt Schilling spoke as if he had something to prove.

In the end, for all of the encouraging changes that took place during the months between Aaron Boone's home run and the start of Spring Training 2004, the off-season in Boston concluded in the same heartbreaking fashion it began.

Frustrated by their inability to consummate a deal for Rodriguez after negotiations that reached the levels of Sox owner Henry and Texas Rangers owner Tom Hicks, the Red Sox went to the Major League Baseball Players Association in mid-December with a proposed restructuring of Rodriguez' contract that could have made the deal work from their perspective. Union deputy Gene Orza promptly rejected the proposal, inspiring Sox president and longtime union oppositionist Larry Lucchino to term the Rodriguez pursuit "dead," and, seemingly, putting an end to a never-ending saga that dominated sports talk in Boston throughout the winter, even as the New England Patriots were rumbling toward their second Super Bowl championship in three years.

In subsequent days and weeks—and in both Boston and Texas—the spinsters worked full-time. After Hicks stated with certainty on December 23 that Rodriguez would be with the Rangers on Opening Day 2004, the Rangers conducted an unusual press conference roughly one month later (on January 25) in which Hicks, general manager John Hart, and manager Buck Showalter named Rodriguez team captain. Rodriguez, too, played an active role in the dog and pony show, telling an assembled media contingency, "I definitely think I'm going to be here for a long time," and "I'm probably pretty sure it will all work out for the best," an obvious attempt at damage control given that the sides were unhappily stuck with one another after so actively working to facilitate a separation.

Alex Rodriguez and the Texas Rangers were joined at the hip.

Or so it seemed.

What took place subsequently stunned baseball followers, particularly in New England, where Red Sox officials mistakenly had lulled themselves into thinking the Rangers had no place but Boston to send the dissatisfied Rodriguez. That all changed when third baseman and Game 7 hero Boone (of all people!) injured his knee playing basketball, unexpectedly placing the Yankees in the market for an infielder. New York naturally focused on third basemen until the idea of pursuing another *shortstop* dawned on them, leading to a new chapter of Rodriguez talks and producing a swift resolution that delivered Rodriguez to the Yankees (for multitalented second baseman Alfonso Soriano and cash considerations the Red Sox had not matched) and leaving embarrassed Red Sox officials with their pants resting messily around their ankles.

As New Englanders often were wont to do, the Red Sox and their followers subsequently focused not on what they had but rather on what they did not. With the news that Rodriguez was heading to New York, word quickly spread throughout baseball that the Red Sox desperately appealed to both Rodriguez (to reconsider the trade) and commissioner Selig (to reject the deal) in a last-gasp attempt to thwart the Yankees. Rodriguez' subsequent arrival in New York—this time, too, there was a dog and pony show—featured remarks in which Rodriguez respectfully cited Sox owner Henry and general manager Epstein, an obvious and backhanded swipe at Lucchino, whom both the player and his agent (Scott Boras) felt was largely responsible for the acrimony that grew out of the negotiations between the Red Sox, Rangers, Rodriguez, and the Major League Baseball Players Association.

Whoever was to blame, there was no disputing the impact of the deal in Boston:

The Red Sox looked bad.

And where the Sox had fruitlessly worked for weeks, the Yankees had swooped in with conviction and, in no uncertain terms, closed the deal.

Making matters worse, however, was the astonishing dexterity with which Red Sox officials backpedaled. In haggling with the Rangers throughout negotiations for Rodriguez, Red Sox officials had held their ground based on the assumption that the Rangers had no other suitors. Yet as soon as the Yankees entered the picture, the Sox suddenly seemed willing to make concessions and financial sacrifices that club officials previously had said were impossible, offering evidence that Red Sox officials, like many of their fans, suffered from an inferiority complex and an obsessive-compulsive disorder when it came time to confront their accomplished rivals from New York.

In retrospect, even Selig seemed somewhat distraught at the outcome of the Rodriguez sweepstakes, only fueling theories in New York that the commissioner had a bias toward the Red Sox—and, more specifically, against the Yankees—in an attempt to make the economic landscape in baseball far more level. With the Rodriguez acquisition, New York's 2004 payroll projected to be in the range of $185 million, a number roughly seven times that of the expected payroll of the Tampa Bay Devil Rays, who also played in the American

League East. New York's estimated payroll, in fact, was more than 40 percent greater than that of the *Red Sox*, who prepared to enter spring training with a projected $130 million payroll that was the second highest in all of baseball.

Nonetheless, a reluctant Selig had no choice but to give the deal his formal stamp of approval.

"I am very concerned about the large amount of cash consideration involved in the transaction and the length of time over which the cash is being paid," Selig said in a statement. "I want to make it abundantly clear to clubs that I will not allow cash transfers of this magnitude to become the norm. However, given the unique circumstances, including the size, length and complexity of Mr. Rodriguez' contract and the quality of talent moving in both directions, I have decided to approve the transaction."

Left with that reality, the Red Sox seemed stunned. At one point, Sox officials seemed so concerned with the fallout from the Rodriguez deal that team officials privately acknowledged select members of the media who took the stance that Rodriguez' ultimate impact on the Yankees, Red Sox, and 2004 American League East would not be nearly as great as the Red Sox feared. Lucchino, for one, seemed especially grateful—"Your stance on this has been duly noted," the club president told one reporter—and even the typically reserved Henry seemed frustrated and embarrassed, as if he recognized that the Red Sox had missed an opportunity, allowing the Yankees to sneak in under Boston's nose and grab perhaps the best player in baseball.

While it was not completely out of character for Henry to vent his frustration—in December, the owner shot back at Garciaparra and agent Arn Tellem by calling Tellem's campaign against the club the "height of hypocrisy"—Henry this time seemed much more like a sore loser, which, quite honestly, he was.

The Red Sox missed the boat and they knew it.

"It will suffice to say that we have a spending limit and the Yankees apparently don't," Henry sourly wrote in one of his trademark e-mails. "Baseball doesn't have an answer for the Yankees. Revenue sharing can only accomplish so much. At some point it becomes confiscation. It has not and will not solve what is a very obvious problem. More often than not, $50 million, on average, will not allow a MLB franchise to field a highly competitive team. Every year there will be an exception, but that is really the baseline number. So what has meaning are the dollars spent above $50 million. Most clubs can perhaps afford to spend $10 million to $25 million above that figure trying to compete. A few can spend as much as $30 million to $60 million above that. But one team can and is spending $150 million incremental dollars, and at some point owners and players say to themselves, 'We can't have one team that can spend 10 dollars above the baseline for every incremental dollar spent by an average team.' One thing is certain: the status quo will not be preserved."

Added the owner of the Red Sox, who met with Rodriguez during the courting process: "Personally, I am very happy for Alex. He very much wanted to play in games that have meaning. This year he will get that chance. We will be ready as well."

Apprised of Henry's remarks, Yankees owner George Steinbrenner seemed rightfully amused. Steinbrenner did not point out that the Red Sox had a projected payroll of $130 million that ranked second only to New York, but he did not have to. That fact spoke for itself. At the end of the day, the Red Sox were able to outspend every team in baseball but one, and it just so happened that the one was the Yankees, against whom the Sox were invariably measured, in the shadow of whom Sox officials, too, made the inexcusable blunder of feeling inferior.

It is one of the first rules of competition, after all.

If you believe your opponent is better than you, your opponent will be.

"We understand that John Henry must be embarrassed, frustrated and disappointed by his failure in this transaction," Steinbrenner said in a statement. "Unlike the Yankees, he chose not to go the extra distance for his fans in Boston. It is understandable, but wrong that he would try to deflect the accountability for his mistakes on to others and to a system for which he voted in favor. It is time to get on with life and forget the sour grapes."

Yes, the Yankees had Alex Rodriguez.

And the Red Sox did not.

In the wake of Rodriguez' arrival in New York, Red Sox players took a noticeably different approach from their owners and bosses, choosing instead to ultimately recognize Rodriguez for what he was: One player on one extremely talented Yankees team.

Nothing more.

"Nobody said it would be easy and George [Steinbrenner] is going to do whatever it takes to stop us," said Red Sox relief pitcher Alan Embree. "I think [the A-Rod trade] is kind of exciting . . . [because] they're worried about us. They know we have a very good ballclub."

Said backup catcher Doug Mirabelli: "I think there's definitely respect for the Red Sox there, but I don't know if they'd admit that. They know they've got a fight on their hands every time they play us, regardless of who they've got on their team.

"Look, A-Rod would help any team," Mirabelli concluded. "But, still, on paper, the Red Sox are right where they need to be."

At the conclusion of the circus that was the off-season between the 2003 and 2004 baseball seasons, many people had overlooked that fact.

Red Sox players had not.

They were looking forward to playing baseball in Boston.

And they were looking forward to a fight.

REELING IN A-ROD—YANKEES

BRIAN CASHMAN WAS VACATIONING WITH HIS FAMILY ON THE island of Anguilla in mid-January, 2004, having dinner one night when his cell phone rang. He knew it had to be important because he had rented a cell phone in Anguilla that would work on the island, and only a few Yankee people had the number. But the general manager wasn't prepared for what team president Randy Levine began telling him in a panicked tone: Aaron Boone's agent, Adam Katz, had called to say that Boone had injured his knee playing in a pickup basketball game, and was probably out for the year. Cashman immediately began thinking of whom the Yankees might be able to acquire at this late date, with virtually all premium free agents signed for the 2004 season, to play third base. At the time, he never considered the idea of Alex Rodriguez.

"It seemed too far-fetched," he would recall months later.

A-Rod's future had been the talk of the baseball off-season, of course, as the Texas Rangers and Boston Red Sox very publicly tried for weeks to make the finances work in a proposed trade of Rodriguez for Manny Ramirez. Privately the Rangers had offered the Yankees the chance to make a deal for A-Rod, as well; Texas GM John Hart had called Cashman around noon on Sunday, October 26, barely 12 hours after the Yankees' season ended in disappointment, as they lost Game 6 of the World Series to Josh Beckett and the Florida Marlins. Cashman was a bit stunned when Hart told him that he and Texas owner Tom Hicks were in New York, at the St. Regis Hotel, and ready to talk about trading the reigning American League MVP.

"Do you want to come down tonight and talk about it?" Hart asked Cashman. Hart then volunteered that the Red Sox brass was flying in and had an eight o'clock appointment, knowing such news would set off alarms for Cashman. Still, the Yankees' GM felt he needed time to recover from the Series, and told Hart, "I need a day to catch my breath."

The next day Cashman and other Yankee executives discussed the idea of making a play for A-Rod and, with George Steinbrenner's approval, decided they weren't willing to move Derek Jeter from shortstop. Since A-Rod at the time wasn't even considering switching positions, the Yankees told the Rangers they weren't interested.

Two months later, as Cashman received the news about Boone, he still believed the Red Sox would find a way to work out the deal for A-Rod. So he frantically began searching for a third baseman, making calls that night. His first priority, however, was to try to make sure the Boone news didn't become public. If other clubs knew the Yankees needed a starting third baseman, Cashman would have no leverage in trade talks. So, after first returning to his dinner with family members and telling them he now needed a third baseman, a frightening thought occurred to him. By coincidence Tyler Kepner, the *New York Times*' Yankees beat reporter, was vacationing at the same island resort as Cashman that very week, and the GM worried that Kepner might somehow overhear him or someone he'd just told about Boone's injury.

"We had a lot of family there with us," Cashman recalled. "After I told them about Boone, I remembered that Tyler was staying there. So I told everybody, 'Please don't talk about this, around the pool or anywhere else.' Tyler's a good guy, but I knew I would be racing against the clock, trying to find a third baseman, and if word got out about Boone, it would make it that much tougher."

As it turned out, the Yankees managed to keep Boone's injury quiet for two weeks. But Cashman began working the rented cell phone immediately. He talked trade with a handful of fellow GMs as casually as possible, feeling them out about trades, indicating the Yankees were looking for an extra infielder or were considering trading Alfonso Soriano—allowing them to assume the Yankees would move Boone to second if they traded Soriano. Among others, Cashman talked to the White Sox about Jose Valentin, a shortstop with power who could move to third, and the Dodgers about Adrian Beltre, a third baseman who went on to have an MVP-type season.

"I was doing a lot of bullshitting," Cashman said. "I didn't lie about anything. I just didn't tell anyone why I wanted a third baseman. There's nothing wrong with that. That's part of the horse trading business."

Cashman couldn't make a deal, however, and finally, about two weeks after getting the news on Boone, the thought struck him as he was driving to his home in Connecticut from Yankee Stadium one night: what if A-Rod would consider playing third? By then, late January, A-Rod's potential move to the Red Sox appeared dead, after the Players' Association refused to allow him to restructure his historic $252 million contract to the club's liking. So Cashman called Texas GM Hart that night and told him what he was thinking: A-Rod for Soriano. Hart was hesitant, at least partly because he didn't want to have another potential A-Rod trade dragged through the mud of public opinion for days and days, as was the case with the Red Sox.

"Oh, no," Hart said to Cashman. "You're not going to do this to me, are you?"

Cashman persisted: "John, trust me. This won't get out. I haven't told anybody about this. It's just me and you. I give you my word."

It was true, Cashman hadn't mentioned his idea to anyone in the organization, or even his wife. With a chuckle he would recall during the summer how his wife had confronted him after overhearing a conversation he was having with Hart at home one night, more than a week after the two GMs had begun discussing the idea.

"She was like, 'You're talking about getting Alex Rodriguez?'" Cashman remembered. "I hadn't told her. I didn't tell anybody."

Hart was just as discreet, as he and Cashman talked daily, working through a process that Cashman later likened to "climbing Mt. Everest." Hart offered Cashman the opportunity to pitch his idea personally to superagent Scott Boras, who would then take it to A-Rod. Cashman, leery of dealing with Boras, said no, the Rangers would have to come back to him with an answer from A-Rod before discussions could continue. Texas owner Tom Hicks swore Boras to secrecy on the idea, and they took the question to A-Rod. He was hesitant at first to give up playing baseball's glamour position, but within a few days he decided it was worth it for the chance to win the championship he had decided wouldn't be possible with the Rangers.

By the second week of February, two weeks had passed since Cashman approached Hart with the idea, and the Yankees' GM still hadn't told another soul. As a result, no one in the media picked up the scent, a feat Cashman considered remarkable in New York. As he said months later, only half kiddingly, "I was more proud of that than pulling off the deal. I was determined to keep it quiet. My word to John on that was important."

When Cashman felt the deal was close to being done, he told Levine what was happening, and together they presented it to George Steinbrenner, who, as usual, was 1,000 miles away from New York in his Tampa office. Even then Cashman was ultra-cautious in asking for approval to make the deal. He had learned over the years not to allow Steinbrenner to get excited over such a possibility, knowing that he would feel the full force of the Boss' wrath if the deal fell apart. So he made the A-Rod trade sound like little more than a shot in the dark.

"I told him it was 99-to-1 against it actually happening," Cashman would recall, "but just in case, did we have his approval? He said ok, but agreed it probably wouldn't happen. That was on Wednesday [February 11]. A couple of days later word finally started to get out. When [Steinbrenner] saw it in the papers, then it was like, 'You *better* make this happen.' "

By Saturday, February 14, the trade was official, pending approval by baseball commissioner Bud Selig. Cashman had pulled off the deal of a GM's lifetime, and he'd done it without tripping any alarms. His one fear had been that Hart might revisit the Red Sox with the news the Yankees were pursuing A-Rod, and that might change everything. But he knew that Hart was upset about the way the Red Sox handled the A-Rod talks, and he was correct in taking the chance Hart wouldn't go back to them. The Sox made a last-ditch effort when the story hit the papers in New York, but by then Cashman had his man.

As he would say happily: "It came as a shock to the Red Sox."

A-Rod was coming to New York.

In a city that turns stars into legends—Ruth, DiMaggio, Mantle, Gifford, Namath, L. T.—New Yorkers like to think of themselves and their city, above all, as sophisticated, especially in the matter of sports. You want to send a drink over to Broadway Joe's table? That's cool; just give the man his space. This is New York. Every place else is Hicksville, and New Yorkers look down on the kind of small-town euphoria that seems to define the sports culture in other cities.

Like Boston. The locals there use expressions that personify a sense of community: Red Sox Nation. Old Towne Team. New Yorkers cringe: how quaint.

But then Alex Rodriguez came to town, and suddenly New York was just some burgh somewhere, overcome by the magnitude of A-Rod. Or maybe it's just the media that's different now. It's hard to tell. Everything is bigger. Everything is covered more comprehensively, for immediate consumption, on Web sites, cable news channels, and, of course, the Yankees' own TV outlet, the YES Network.

Whatever the cause and effect, New York couldn't escape the celebrity mania that grips American society these days and not only makes *Survivor* participants quasi famous, but transforms the likes of A-Rod from baseball star to pop culture icon. So it was that when Rodriguez became a Yankee, the New York tabloids covered him in a manner usually reserved for Madonna or Michael Jackson at the height of their fame. Where was he going to live? What restaurants would he frequent? What designer does his wife favor? This was more than a sports story. A-Rod's arrival was a happening, and as he flew to New York on a private plane with Derek Jeter the day before his Yankee Stadium press conference, sports editors weren't just assigning a third straight day of A-Rod stories since the news broke; they were browbeating reporters to find out where he was staying in the city that night so that photographers could stake out the spot and get a picture of him for the front page. If the *Post* got the shot and the *Daily News* didn't, or vice versa, there would be hell to pay in news meetings that day. As it turned out, A-Rod stayed at the Ritz-Carlton in midtown, and word got out in time for both papers to get the shot of a smiling superstar arriving in town.

Baseball, more than any other sport, sells newspapers in New York, and A-Rod was not only considered the best player in the game, but one of the most photogenic people in the world. Furthermore, he was a New Yorker at birth, born in the Washington Heights section of the Bronx, home to the largest Dominican Republic population in the United States, before his family moved to the Dominican Republic and then Miami. He spoke Spanish as fluently as he did English, and the huge Latin community rejoiced at his arrival.

At the El Nuevo Caridad restaurant in Washington Heights, a place where many of the visiting Latin players in the major leagues came for lunch when in New York, Dominicans used the trade as an excuse to party, pouring in to celebrate.

"It's like New Year's Eve around here," owner Miguel Montas said that day, waving his arm toward all of the people in his restaurant. "All day, it's all people want to talk about. You're talking about the Latin Babe Ruth."

The press conference at Yankee Stadium for the official unveiling was unlike anything anyone had seen, simply because of the sheer number of reporters. All in all, over 300 of them crammed their way into the Legends Club, a cozy room designed to hold perhaps a third of that number. The press parking lot was full some 45 minutes before the 1 P.M. press conference time, forcing dozens of media types to park their cars on sidewalks and access roads off the Major Deegan Expressway in the Bronx, leaving them to wonder if their cars would be there upon return. Inside, reporters and photographers climbed over one another to find a position from where they could see A-Rod be introduced.

Wearing a gray-and-white striped tie that looked as if he picked it out to go with the pinstriped jersey he tried on for the cameras, A-Rod was predictably awed by the setting. When he stepped to the microphone he looked around theatrically and said, "Wow." But already the story was a couple of days old, so reporters focused more on Derek Jeter. For two days Jeter had fueled speculation that he was less than thrilled about the deal by refusing to so much as comment to reporters after he worked out at the Yankees' minor league complex in Tampa. According to a Yankees official, Jeter only accompanied A-Rod to the press conference in New York because Steinbrenner insisted, and though he smiled for the cameras as he helped A-Rod into his No. 13 Yankee jersey, Jeter otherwise sat through the proceedings without expression, looking like a kid forced to stay after school in detention.

At the very most, he was less than magnanimous in publicly welcoming A-Rod. He made a point that day of saying that he was still the shortstop, and sneered at reporters who brought up the subject of a once-close friendship that had soured over the years.

"The worst thing for the media is for me and Alex to get along," Jeter said.

Reporters rolled their eyes, tired of Jeter's contempt for the media that is never far from the surface when he answers questions in any setting. The Yankees shortstop has been the golden boy since he arrived in 1996, swooned over by fans for his movie-star looks, canonized by the press for his clutch play in big games, especially in the postseason. Yet Jeter was never an easy interview, never willing to play along with the media. He had a condescending edge to him as a young player, and while he smartly learned to smooth over that edge as more and more attention came his way, Jeter's distrust and dislike for the media only seemed to grow over the years. People who know him think his outlook was shaped partly by his experience as a regular on the gossip pages, when he reacted angrily as relationships with the likes of pop singer Mariah Carey became entirely too public for his liking. Jeter doesn't seem to differentiate between the gossip page and the sports page, lumping all reporters into the same category.

Whatever his reservations, Jeter has never seemed comfortable sharing his thoughts publicly, and as a result tries to be as bland as possible. He offers no insights on the events of individual ballgames, or his own at-bats, never mind substantial thoughts on the various issues that forever surround the Yankees. What annoys reporters is that he has plenty more to offer, because they have seen him be funny and personable enough to host *Saturday Night Live*. They saw him do his wink-wink Visa commercial with Steinbrenner in 2003, parodying the controversy that erupted weeks earlier when the Yankee owner accused Jeter of partying too much. And reporters see what a presence Jeter is around the ballclub, laughing with teammates, forever needling someone about something. In short, Jeter has an infectious personality that, together with his unwavering confidence, makes him a natural leader. But with the press he's duller than Bud Selig. As captain of the team since 2003 he knows he is obligated to answer for the team and always makes himself available after games, but he rarely says anything even vaguely interesting, never mind quote-worthy. Reporters have long admired Jeter for the way he plays the game, the way he puts winning ahead of individual stats, and yet many resent him because he keeps them at arm's length, refusing to reveal anything of himself.

All of which made A-Rod's arrival more intriguing. A-Rod loves the spotlight as much as Jeter prefers to avoid it. He enjoys breaking down the game for reporters, offering his thinking on certain at-bats or plays in the field, and from the start was far more approachable in the hours before games if a reporter wanted to talk about issues involving the team or perhaps just make small talk. Of course, he had come to New York with a reputation for using his charisma to influence not only the media in Texas but the Rangers' organization in personnel decisions, which led to clashes with manager Buck Showalter. On the other hand, the Yankees had manipulated the media in their own way for years as most players followed Jeter's lead in making themselves as uninteresting, and in some cases unavailable, to the press as possible. As a result, reporters were hungry for a star who actually seemed to enjoy talking to them.

Indeed, A-Rod had a flair for dealing with the media. On his first day in Tampa, three days before the team's first full-squad workout, he worked out at the Yankees' minor-league complex with a couple of minor-league players. Aware that his every move was being watched by a couple of dozen reporters, he set up to take ground balls from a coach at his new position, third base, for the first time, spread his arms as if looking for advice on where to play, and called to reporters: "About right here?" It was a small gesture but it showed that he was willing to let outsiders into his world. After the workout Yankee PR people said A-Rod wouldn't be available to talk, since he had held a formal press conference, his second in four days, earlier that morning to mark his Tampa arrival. When reporters called to him from outside a fence as he walked off the field, however, A-Rod waved off the PR guys running interference and stopped to answer questions for five minutes. It was a big deal only because it is practically Yankee policy to avoid complying with such simple requests, and reporters were grateful.

A couple of weeks later A-Rod played his first game in Legends Field as the Yankees opened their home exhibition season. It was quite a production, as always, as a host of Yankee legends, including Yogi Berra, Whitey Ford, Ron Guidry, and Reggie Jackson, were introduced before the game. The place was packed with fans, and A-Rod got his first taste of the kind of atmosphere he had longed for during his three years of losing with the Rangers. During the game he walked to load the bases and then trotted home on Jason Giambi's grand slam as the Yankees defeated the Phillies, and afterward he was asked about that moment.

A-Rod smiled and answered quickly. "As I was rounding third, I asked myself, 'Where am I?' It felt like Disneyworld."

Reporters smiled and scribbled. Maybe the quote was contrived, but who cared? It was more interesting than anything Jeter had said to them in years. So sportswriters couldn't get enough of A-Rod, and apparently neither could readers. Weeks after A-Rod had signed, the *Daily News* was still looking for excuses to put A-Rod on the back page because it meant a significant spike in newsstand sales.

But how would such a presence play in the Yankee locker room? By now it was clearly Jeter's locker room, a responsibility bequeathed to him by the likes of David Cone, Paul O'Neill, Joe Girardi, and Tino Martinez, departed leaders of the club that won four world championships in Joe Torre's first five seasons as manager, from 1996 to 2000. And Jeter could huff at the media all he wanted, but his relationship with A-Rod was an issue that couldn't be ignored. It was Jeter who cut off virtually all contact after A-Rod made his cutting remarks in an *Esquire* magazine story that came out during Spring Training 2001.

By then Jeter had won four world championship rings, and though A-Rod had just signed his record $252 million contract with the Texas Rangers, the story made him seem envious of Jeter's status as an icon in New York.

"He has been blessed with great talent around him," A-Rod said of Jeter in the story. "He never had to lead. He can just go out and play and have fun. He hits second. That's totally different than third or fourth in the lineup. You go into New York and you want to stop Bernie [Williams] or [Paul] O'Neill. You never say, 'don't let Derek beat you.'"

On his second day in Yankee camp, A-Rod told a small group of reporters that when he saw the *Esquire* story in print that spring, he realized how it sounded. Rodriguez immediately drove the 90 minutes from the Texas Rangers' camp in Port Charlotte to Jeter's house in Tampa, and explained himself to Jeter. He wanted to remain friends, but implied that Jeter wasn't quick to forgive and forget.

"At that time, I thought it was behind us," A-Rod said. "But we haven't been as tight the last few years."

In fact, a person close to Jeter said the Yankee shortstop wasn't interested in A-Rod's explanation.

"He doesn't let many people get close to him as it is," the person said. "If you betray him, he crosses you off forever. He doesn't like the media, so to him there's no greater betrayal than what Alex did, insulting him in the media. He doesn't like confrontations, so I doubt whether he got into it with Alex. He just moved on. Derek can be cold as ice."

Jeter, of course, wasn't talking about any of this as spring training opened. He dismissed questions about his relationship with A-Rod, saying "we're fine," but refused to go any further on the subject. No doubt he hated that A-Rod was talking about it, but Jeter didn't want controversy. As workouts began he made a point to play catch with A-Rod when players warmed up, beginning a ritual that would last all season, and made small talk with him in the infield, knowing the cameras were trained on the two of them at all times.

Both knew the scrutiny wouldn't go away. How they handled it likely would go a long way toward dictating success or failure for the Yankees.

SIMMERING ISSUES AND A STRONG START—RED SOX

As THE SUCCESSOR TO WILLIAM GRADY LITTLE, TERRY FRANCONA inherited what was, on paper, perhaps the best Red Sox team in a generation.

And, for that matter, potentially one of the most combustible, too.

Consequently, when Francona arrived at the Red Sox' spring training facility in Fort Myers, Florida, during the middle of February, the then 44-year-old skipper of the Red Sox understood he would need to tread lightly. The Red Sox was a talented team capable of great things, but there were also an array of issues still unsettled when the players reported to camp. The Sox had just lost out on Alex Rodriguez. Over the winter, Manny Ramirez had been placed on waivers and Nomar Garciaparra had been all but officially traded. And then there was the disconcerting matter of impending free agency for Garciaparra, Pedro Martinez, Derek Lowe, and Jason Varitek, four players who effectively had served as the nucleus of the Sox franchise over a six-year period from 1998 to 2003, during which the Red Sox had thrice qualified for the postseason but nonetheless failed to win an elusive world championship.

There were lots of new people to meet.

And lots of egos to massage.

Francona had managed a team before the Red Sox almost instantly hired him—"He's an impressive guy," the Sox general manager told reporters after Francona knocked over Red Sox officials during a very abbreviated interview process—but still there was absolutely no telling what the Red Sox were getting when they brought him to Boston. Francona's only previous managerial experience came during a four-year stint with a wretched Philadelphia Phillies team that was 285–363 during his tenure, a record that was hardly Francona's fault. Francona was largely a stopgap measure for a young Phillies team that had neither the talent nor the experience to contend, and there wasn't a manager in baseball that could have won with the hand Francona was dealt in Philadelphia.

Managing, in fact, was not always about having the *best* team, but rather the *right* team at the right place and right time. Many people had long forgotten that New York Yankees manager Joe Torre had posted a losing career record when the Yankees hired him prior to the 1996 season, but Torre nonetheless built himself into a certain Hall of Famer during his time in New York because he finally had the luxury of a talented team at his disposal. Torre also had the right temperament to deal with the nonsense that went along with playing and managing in New York, and it was that asset that proved his greatest tool entering his ninth year with the Yankees.

Entering the 2004 season, in fact, Torre's uninterrupted tenure placed him behind only Joe McCarthy (15 seasons), Casey Stengel (12), and Miller Huggins (11) in the considerable history of the Yankees. Including Torre, those skippers had won an astonishing 21 of New York's 26 world championships.

"It's been pretty incredible," Torre told a *Boston Herald* reporter when the Yankees visited the Red Sox in March for an overhyped exhibition game at City of Palms Park. "It says something to the guy who's 55 or 56 years old and who thinks he's winding down. It's been the most intense experience of my baseball career.

"People looked at me cross-eyed," Torre said when asked why he chose to manage the Yankees in the first place. "My brother Frank didn't think it was the right decision for me to make at that time and everybody was worried about George Steinbrenner's history with managers. But I wasn't really looking long-term at that point."

Torre went on to win four world titles in his first five years with the Yankees and never once missed the postseason during his first eight years with the team, entering 2004. He became so popular among fans in New York that he became untouchable even to the trigger-happy and obsessive owner of the Yankees.

In many ways Joe Torre had more power than George Steinbrenner himself.

The contrast, then, was striking as Francona entered his first camp with a team that was expected to win. Francona was the son of a former major-league outfielder and first baseman, Tito, who batted .272 during a 15-year major-league career with nine organizations. ("Tito" consequently became—and remains—Terry Francona's nickname as a player, coach, and manager.) Terry Francona himself went on to play 10 seasons for five organizations, playing outfield, first base, and designated hitter en route to a .274 career average that was eerily similar to his father's. He was what Red Sox officials wanted as the heir to Little—an engaging, likeable personality whose career in the game earned him instant respect among players and who was more in touch with modern managing techniques that included the use of statistical and empirical data, otherwise known as sabermetrics.

In short, Terry Francona was a baseball blend of the old and the new, and Red Sox officials hoped he could effectively manage the personalities in his clubhouse without getting in the way of the game on the field.

For Francona, being able to communicate with his players was of the utmost importance. Weeks after the conclusion of the 2004 season, he would still talk about the importance of building "relationships," of gaining his players' "loyalty" and "trust." He later acknowledged that the best way to do so with a veteran Red Sox club in Boston was to ease off, so that is precisely what he did.

"I wanted to establish relationships as quickly as possible," Francona said. "I guess I was at a little bit of a disadvantage at the beginning because we were coming off a winter where we put Manny on waivers and a trade with Nomar fell through. If I just tried to jump in . . . loyalty takes time."

Added the manager: "Part of the reason you try to build relationships is because there comes a time when you're going to have to tell someone something they don't want to hear."

Those challenges presented themselves for any manager during the course of a baseball season, though Francona understood that in his case, especially, the simplest way for him to keep the 2004 Red Sox focused and pointed in the right direction was to win. For all of the bickering that could take place in a baseball clubhouse—players griping about playing time, contracts, the media—each of them became infinitely more bearable when the team was winning. In many cases, players were disarmed entirely because to complain about anything would be to reveal a measure of selfishness, something no team player was supposed to do at any time. So Francona occasionally drifted around the clubhouse and talked to players, tried to understand them, joked with them, and, in effect, became their friend, even though managers, ultimately, were a part of management.

The other elements of the job? Francona believed he could deal with them, though he would admit later, too, that there was nothing quite like managing the Red Sox. Similarities were often drawn between the media in Philadelphia, New York, and Boston, and Francona generally had good relationships with the Phillies writers who regularly covered his clubs despite the team's woeful play. The obvious difference was that, in a place like Boston, there was *expectation*, which was something Francona did not have to deal with in Philadelphia. Had the Phillies been contenders, in fact, Francona probably would not have been hired at all, but Philadelphia officials wanted someone at the time who had both the patience to deal with the media and the positive attitude necessary to withstand losing.

As for the media, specifically, Francona treated them with respect—particularly the veteran baseball writers—which only helped the relationship. Whether you managed or covered a bad team, after all, there were sometimes only a limited number of ways to deal with the monotony of the baseball season. And in those instances, writers and managers often had a great deal in common.

Just the same, Francona seemed to keep a distance from the Boston media early in his tenure, though it was not unusual for managers to sift through the throng of reporters until they found ones they could trust. In fact, one of Francona's first experiences with the Boston media was somewhat unpleasant, coming at a time when he had been assured that he would be named the successor to Little, but also at a time when he had not yet been officially named. Francona tried to be as open and candid as possible with Boston reporters who called wanting to know where the interview process stood, and he told reporters from both the *Boston Globe* and *Boston Herald* that he believed he was on the verge of being hired. But when Francona's quotes appeared in the *Globe* despite Francona's belief that the conversation was off the record, the then prospective manager called the *Herald* to apologize for what might have been perceived as a slight and also thanked the reporter for keeping his word.

He apologized to the Red Sox, too, an early sign that the manager was not afraid to take blame, even if he was not necessarily at fault.

Brushing off the minor incident, the Red Sox officially announced the hiring of Francona as the 44th manager in club history. And even while Rodriguez was wearing pinstripes at the Yankees' spring training site in Tampa Bay—Francona and Rodriguez had been together at Texas when Francona served as the Rangers' bench coach in 2002—Francona was entrusted with a club that had championship aspirations, that Sox officials believed would win in excess of 100 games based on computer models they ran before the year. (The Yankees, too, finished in excess of 100 wins based on the same programs.) It was Terry Francona's job to enable those victories, to ensure that everything generally went smoothly given the expectations that came along with being manager of the Red Sox.

Clearly, he was not in Philadelphia anymore.

"I really think I had a pretty good feeling of what I was getting into," Francona said. "The four years in Philly for me were a great learning experience—and I don't pretend that Philly is Boston because it's not. But it's an East Coast city with an edge and we got beat up (by the media and fans)—a lot."

As for the specific problems and contractual issues that faced the 2004 Red Sox?

"What I said in spring training—and I said it the whole year—is that as long as we won, it wasn't going to be [viewed as] a distraction," Francona said. "If we lost, it *was* going to be a distraction. We all knew that."

By the time a relatively uninspiring spring training ended in Fort Myers, the Red Sox had posted a solid 17–12–1 record that was fourth best among teams training in Florida.

Nonetheless, as usual, there were a few blips along the way.

More than anything else, what dominated discussion in Spring Training 2004 were the contracts.

Or, more specifically, the absence of them.

Just as important, however, was the manner in which that void was dealt, particularly among central figures Martinez, Lowe, Varitek, and Garciaparra. Designated hitter David Ortiz also was unsigned beyond the 2004 season. And then there was Ramirez, who breezed into camp without an apparent worry in the world despite having been placed on waivers by Red Sox officials with the hope that someone would claim both him and his contract.

In that way, Manny Ramirez seemed as blissfully oblivious as ever.

What, him worry?

On the whole, the atmosphere at camp generally remained loose and easy-going, just as it had a year earlier, when newcomer Kevin Millar pulled into camp in a pickup truck after driving through the night from his Texas home. Millar was understandably excited about the prospect of playing for the Red Sox after slithering out of an agreement to play in Japan—the player and his agents reneged on the Japan deal by concocting a cockamamie story about how Millar feared going overseas with America having launched the war on Iraq—and it became clear early on that he would bring some much-needed personality to a club that finished the 2002 campaign by going a remarkably boring 53–52 over its final 105 games.

At the time, the Red Sox were rather dull in the clubhouse, too.

"I think this team's developing a makeup," Millar said in February 2002 before even putting on a Red Sox uniform for the first time. "Hopefully we can bring back the mullets and grow the hair out."

A year later, that was still the case, particularly with center fielder Johnny Damon having arrived in camp with long hair and a beard, looking very much like the central figure in Mel Gibson's hot new film of the spring, *The Passion of the Christ.* Damon eagerly played along with the role, often taking a water bottle from his pocket, removing the top and shaking the bottle in the direction of anyone who cared to notice, as if to sprinkle holy water in the name of the baseball gods. Ramirez and Martinez, too, showed up with long hair, giving the entire club a relatively ragged, renegade, and carefree look.

In fact, while Ramirez was remarkably good-natured throughout the spring and worked under the tutelage of Millar and the colorful Ortiz to repair his image and build a relationship with the Boston media, many of the Sox still had things on their minds. Martinez, for one, arrived in camp insisting he was comfortable without a deal—"It's not up to me to get a new contract," he said—though he subsequently spent much of the spring talking about it, albeit in off-the-record discussions with reporters. Cleverly, Martinez actually had introduced the idea of going to the New York Yankees a year *earlier*, in the spring of 2003, even though he was signed for that season with the Red Sox holding a club option for 2004. So Martinez strong-armed the Red Sox into prematurely and unnecessarily picking up his $17.5 million option for 2004, a decision that left the Sox with little bargaining power when it came time to talk about an extension for 2005 and beyond.

And with Schilling now on board, Martinez acted at the outset as if he felt threatened.

"I can't help that they wanted to sign Schilling," Martinez said. "If it doesn't belong to me, it doesn't belong to me. If I don't belong to Boston, it's up to Boston. They run the team. They know what they're doing."

Just the same, Martinez often seemed to obsess about his future, struggling through a spring in which he finished with a 6.75 ERA in just 16 innings. To equate Martinez' spring performance solely with his stagnant contract negotiations was unfair, particularly when he often seemed quite bored with the entire process that was spring training, anyway. Entering 2004, Pedro Martinez had 166 career victories, three Cy Young Awards and five ERA titles during a 12-year career, and there was no possible way he could find anything inspiring about exhibition games against minor leaguers. So Martinez came in and did his work, hit his pitch limits, and walked out of press conferences—"You know what? I'm bored right now," he said before abruptly getting up from a makeshift podium at one point—largely because he did not seem the least bit interested in making spring training out to be more than it was:

A glorified waste of time.

Still, just before the start of the regular season, Martinez was sitting alone in the visitor's clubhouse at Turner Field, where the Red Sox were playing the Atlanta Braves in their final exhibition tune-ups of the spring. He did not appear frustrated by his contract talks as much as he seemed hurt, as if the Red Sox were rejecting him in favor of Schilling.

"If they want him, why don't they just say that?" said the exasperated pitcher.

In fact, the Red Sox wanted *both* Martinez and Schilling for the next few seasons, but the entire negotiations between Martinez and the Red Sox accentuated one of the pitcher's human flaws: he was extremely sensitive and took things personally. That same quality, of course, is what drove Martinez to become one of the greatest pitchers of all time after former Los Angeles Dodgers manager Tommy Lasorda suggested that the 5-foot-11, 180-pound Martinez was too fragile to succeed as a starting pitcher, but the downside was that Martinez regarded almost everything as a slight when he did not get his way.

In some ways, Martinez' greatest human flaw was his greatest athletic asset. When he felt deprived of something, he went out and earned it out of spite. Nobody loved to prove people wrong more than Pedro Martinez.

Garciaparra, meanwhile, was similarly tweaked at the events of the offseason, and he, too, was having trouble moving on. Following the A-Rod fiasco, in hopes of discrediting the popular Garciaparra with an enormous fan base, Red Sox officials leaked the information that Garciaparra had turned down a four-year, $60 million offer during the spring of 2003, well before the club had pursued Rodriguez. Things got so messy between the Red Sox and the player's camp (headed by respected agent Arn Tellem) that the sides effectively agreed to a cease-fire, allowing Garciaparra to enter camp without a contract and with the knowledge that he was likely playing his last season in Boston.

Nonetheless—and like Martinez—Garciaparra arrived at spring training still harboring resentment from the events of the winter. There might as well have been a sign over his locker that said *Unsigned and Unwanted.*

"I think everyone saw their actions," Garciaparra said of Sox officials. "You know what their priorities are and what they were trying to do. . . . I was definitely hurt by it. I probably felt like anyone else who played their whole career in one organization."

While Garciaparra was not nearly the political beast that Martinez was, the entire series of events inspired him, too, to get his message out. Shortly after arriving at spring training, Garciaparra privately sat at his locker with one *Herald* reporter who had taken his side on the matter—"I just want to thank you for always being fair to me," he said—and the player later requested a small gathering with all beat reporters, many of whom with he had somewhat contentious relationships. The simple truth was that Garciaparra generally saw the media as a nuisance that disrupted his routines and invaded his space, but in the early stages of the 2004 season, Nomar Garciaparra seemed to recognize, finally, that he needed to make some effort to deal with the press if he were to remain in Boston.

Or, quite simply, if he were to play in any other town like it.

In some ways, Boston actually was the worst place for someone like Garciaparra, who preferred to focus on the business of playing baseball. Places like Boston and New York came with a varying number of distractions, so players inevitably had to deal with them. In Garciaparra's case, he frequently chose *not* to deal at all, which created a wall between the franchise player of the Red Sox and the reporters who covered the team, a marketing roadblock that frustrated Red Sox management. So, early in the spring, Garciaparra collected a group of reporters in hope of finding a solution that would allow them access to him while affording him the comfort of his routines, a plan that never really materialized for an assortment of reasons, the most significant of which was an injury to Garciaparra's right Achilles tendon that kept him out of games for the large majority of spring training.

At the time, at least, Garciaparra and the Red Sox suggested that Garciaparra suffered the injury when the player was hit on the right heel by a ball during batting practice, though there was some doubt. Three years earlier, Garciaparra aggravated an old injury in his right wrist during the early stages of spring training, but team doctor Arthur Pappas was among those who believed Garciaparra may have suffered the injury lifting weights before camp. The latter struck a nerve with Garciaparra, who was very sensitive about his workout routines, largely because the same work he did at the gym is what gave him the strength and power necessary to truly distinguish himself as a shortstop. (Garciaparra never was a sensational fielder, but he was truly a great hitter.) The problem was that Garciaparra seemed susceptible to nagging injuries, which kept him off the field for short stints throughout the bulk of his career. And so, when it came to his workout routine, Nomar Garciaparra felt damned if he did and damned if he didn't.

As it was, Garciaparra joined outfielder Trot Nixon, who similarly missed much of camp with a back problem that was causing team officials concern. A former first-round pick out of high school in June 1993, Nixon had chronic back problems during the early part of his career, but he had long since learned to manage them en route to becoming a solid and productive major-league player. Still, Nixon's back began bothering him again during the drive from his North Carolina home to spring training in Florida, and the ailment prevented him even from beginning workouts, which was never a good sign.

Meanwhile, Varitek and Lowe were going about their business in contrasting styles, though that was not unusual for the two players, acquired together from the Seattle Mariners in a July 1997 trade. While Varitek was expending the bulk of his energy familiarizing himself with the new pitchers on the staff, Lowe was going 3–1 with a 2.17 ERA during a positively brilliant spring. Both players were represented by superagent Scott Boras, who had lured away Lowe from his previous agent, Mike Nicotera, as Lowe approached free agency. Yet while Varitek and Lowe were linked to the Red Sox in a number of ways, their personalities were extremely different—Varitek the strong, silent type to Lowe's blond hair, goofiness, and carefree gait. During camp, in fact, Lowe often would come and go from the training complex in oversized gym shorts, looking like a high schooler breezing through the hall on his way to gym class.

Lowe had experienced an up-and-down career during his time in Boston, and it was for that reason many feared he might struggle in a free-agent year. But while continuing a stellar spring, the tall right-hander also was able to block out distractions, some of which came from within. Lowe was in the clubhouse preparing for a start midway through spring training when confronted by Sox president Lucchino, who was growing frustrated in the team's inability to sign any of its key players. Lucchino became loud and confrontational—as was his wont—and some Sox players were all too eager to leak the information to the media to further enhance Lucchino's reputation as a bit of a tyrant, though many of the same Sox players had cheered wildly only two years earlier when Lucchino announced Grady Little as the successor to Joe Kerrigan.

In the end, whatever frustration felt by the players, the team felt its share, too. And at the end of camp, even the stoic Varitek acknowledged, to some degree, that negotiations were not progressing as he would have liked, though he also made it clear that he had no intention of letting the absence of a contract affect him in the only place that mattered:

On the field.

"They've made it pretty apparent this is probably the last time the four of us will be together," Varitek said, referring to the group that also included Martinez, Lowe, and Garciaparra. "We've got to hold onto that and win. . . . I'm just getting ready to play the season. I'm getting ready to go out there and keep this [team] together. We'll try win a championship."

On the whole, the Red Sox *were* able to stay together throughout the spring and beyond, though there were dynamics to be watched. Schilling, in particular, often seemed to be trying *too hard* to ingratiate himself with teammates, sometimes lecturing them on, for instance, the benefits of negotiating without an agent. (Some Sox players believed Schilling was serving as an aide to management in the negotiations with Garciaparra, Martinez, Lowe, and Varitek.) And amid baseball's exploding steroid scandal in the wake of a federal investigation into the Bay Area Laboratory Co-operative (BALCO) Schilling placed his foot squarely in his mouth when he told a *Hartford Courant* reporter that baseball players only would agree to a new steroid policy if it involved independent, third-party testing because the players did not trust the owners to conduct the tests.

In fact, baseball already *had* independent third-party testing, which prompted officials from Major League Baseball to publicly (and privately) challenge Schilling, a development that was embarrassing to the player, team, and union.

"The reason I'm doing this is the comments were so completely misinformed with regards to efforts to address [steroid testing]," said MLB executive vice president Rob Manfred in explaining Baseball's decision to publicly address Schilling's remarks. "As is often the case, this instance is caused by an ignorance of the facts."

On the field, however, there was no disputing Schilling's knowledge or ability. In 25⅔ innings covering five spring games, Schilling struck out 25, walked three and posted a 2.10 ERA. He worked hard and tirelessly, making it clear to teammates early on that he meant business on the pitcher's mound. Unlike Martinez, whose approach was entirely different—and not necessarily wrong—Schilling treated every spring training game with the same intensity he took to regular season games. He tried to treat them all the same, he would say later, because that was what worked for him, and there was no disputing Schilling's durability during the course of his career.

In some way, in fact, he was getting *better* with age.

"Once the season starts, pitch count is much less an issue for me than it is for other people," Schilling said. "Honest to God, I could count on one hand the number of times in my career where I've said, 'I'm done, I'm spent.' And most of the time it's been when the weather has been hot and I'm pitching on [artificial] turf—or something like that."

In the end, as spring training drew to a close, the Red Sox still were very much unsettled. Martinez, Garciaparra, Varitek, and Lowe—even Ortiz—remained unsigned. Garciaparra and Nixon began the season on the disabled list, though the Sox were hopeful that both players could return within the first month of the season. And after the team packed up its Florida headquarters and moved north to Atlanta for a pair of exhibition games against the Atlanta

Braves—with cardboard boxes and tape on the floor, the clubhouse had the feel of a college dormitory at the end of the school year—the Sox were confronting the reality that 2004, in some ways, would be more difficult than the magical 2003 season, during which they remained remarkably healthy, focused, and undeterred.

In 2003, after all, there were no real contract issues to deal with. There were no major injuries. General manager Theo Epstein was able to augment the team's roster with early- and midseason trades, and the only challenges that ultimately confronted the Sox were *baseball* issues.

As the Red Sox broke camp in 2004, there was so much more to worry about.

And after the events of October 2003 and the ensuing winter, so much more at stake.

"I think everyone—all the players, the coaching staff and the manager—we're all proud of this team and we all want to see what we can do," said the young general manager. "And when you envision that, you envision it at 100 percent (health). But the reality—and it's the reality for all clubs—is that the season doesn't work that way. Guys get hurt and that's when you find out how good you really are."

And so the Red Sox embarked on the 2004 regular season in search of answers.

From the outset, Terry Francona made it apparent that the Red Sox were going to do things differently. And offering as sure a sign as any that the Red Sox had entered the modern era, Francona wrote out his lineup card by typing his batting order into his laptop computer, then running the card through a portable printer he had stationed at his desk. Where baseball managers from the old school wrote out their lineups in magic marker—managers often selected coaches with the best handwriting to fill out the actual card—Terry Francona opted for Times New Roman or Courier New or Book Antiqua. That was the direction in which the game had turned.

In other ways, too, Francona opted for a more modern approach. While fans gravitated toward managers with fiery personalities who sold themselves as disciplinarians, those types of managers tended to work well with younger teams and frequently wore out their welcome in a year or two. The game had changed some in that way. Players now made exorbitant sums of money, which gave them more power than they had to begin with. Managers always were deemed expendable because talent is what ultimately won games, so clubs were more apt to change managers than to give up on a 26-year-old pitching ace who was grappling with maturity issues. But when you added money into the equation—multimillion-dollar investments over a period of years—managers had less power than ever before and players got away with more and more.

Francona recognized that, so he chose not to fight it. During spring training, on occasions when the Sox faced a long bus trip, Francona allowed some players to lease a small jet and fly to the games, a somewhat curious decision because it created a class system within the team. The players paid for the jet themselves, but something like that, too, seemed dangerous because it could segregate the more accomplished, higher-salaried players from what was, in effect, the middle and lower classes. Still, nobody in the clubhouse seemed to mind too much. And when the regular season began, between series with the New York Yankees in April, some Sox players were allowed to skip the team charter so that they could attend a Boston Bruins playoff game against the Montreal Canadiens, another decision that seemed to fly in the face of conventionalism, particularly in a baseball world steeped with traditional methods.

There were just certain accepted ways of doing things that Terry Francona didn't necessarily subscribe to.

"It's funny. I think if my dad had heard that, he'd probably look at me funny," said Francona, whose decisions nonetheless opened him up for criticism if and when the Sox failed. "This isn't 30 years ago. Guys have private jets and if they can spend a night with their families, great."

On the field, Francona made it known early that he was not often going to bunt, that he would leave the game to be decided by the players, which is precisely what his Red Sox bosses wanted. And while the Red Sox split a season-opening four-game series in Baltimore despite losing by a 7–2 score on Opening Day—Martinez pitched reasonably well in the opener, leaving after six innings with a 3–1 deficit—the club lost the series finale in 13 innings when veteran left-hander Bobby Jones walked five batters in one and one-third innings, including the final Orioles hitter of the game with the bases loaded.

Right out of the gate, Terry Francona was second-guessed for how he handled his pitching staff, for why he didn't bunt, for just about everything.

"Everybody's an expert," Francona would muse later. "But the writers—everybody has a job to do—and what that means is there's so much interest. But with that comes second-guessing and a lot of opinions, and if I'm not smart enough to understand that, then they hired the wrong guy."

As it turned out, the next few days were not much better. Following the 4-hour, 37-minute finale in Baltimore, the Sox had travel difficulties that prevented them from arriving in Boston until 7:24 A.M. on the morning of their home opener, April 9. The club subsequently dropped a 10–5 decision to the Toronto Blue Jays in which Francona was forced to use a positional player, David McCarty, to record the final two outs of the game. And while Epstein called the entire series of events "an unusual set of circumstances" as his team dropped to 2–3 against two opponents that were believed to be inferior, Sox players already recognized that their first challenge of the season was upon them.

"We're paid to perform under these types of conditions," said outfielder Gabe Kapler, who was earning the bulk of playing time in right field during the injured Nixon's absence. "You're not going to get eight hours of sleep everyday and eat four or five meals a day and have everything be perfect.

"I feel like this team is no stranger to adversity," Kapler concluded. "Obviously, we weren't afraid of it last year. In fact, we thrived on it, and I expect the same [in 2004]."

After the Sox subsequently responded by winning the next two against Toronto, rain postponed two games of a scheduled three-game series against the Orioles at Fenway. In the only game of the series that was played, the Orioles blistered Martinez for eight hits, seven runs, and four walks in five innings of an eventual 12–7 loss, sending the Sox into their first meaningful meeting with the New York Yankees since Game 7 of the 2003 American League Championship Series.

Yes, indeed, the Yankees were coming to town.

And the only solace for a Red Sox team that was not playing especially well was that the Yankees were not on the top of their game, either, having gone just 5–4 against the Tampa Bay Devil Rays and Chicago White Sox.

"The first series at home against 'em, I was nervous," said Francona, recalling a four-game series drawing so much attention that media outlets throughout the country assigned reporters to the games.

"I remember thinking, 'This is a headache. I can't wait until the game starts and we go to the next series,'" Francona recounted. "But after looking back, it's pretty fun to play those games and you just can't match that anywhere else. It just doesn't happen. It's different."

Along with Curt Schilling, Keith Foulke and the other new members of the 2004 Red Sox, Terry Francona was about to find out firsthand.

And the lessons were just beginning.

SAINT JOE AND THE BOSS: 'TIL DEATH DO US PART?—YANKEES

IN EARLY FEBRUARY OF 2004, GEORGE STEINBRENNER WAS STOMPING around his Tampa office one afternoon, doing what he does best, second-guessing his baseball executives. Spring training was a couple of weeks away and the Yankees' owner was already in a panic. It was his feeling that the Yankees had lost the off-season battle for reinforcements to the Red Sox, and, as always, he blamed it on GM Brian Cashman and the club's other talent evaluators, largely because they had wanted Javier Vazquez over Curt Schilling.

"We should have traded for Schilling," Steinbrenner barked that day on a conference call. "He's a warrior. Do we have enough warriors? We need more warriors to win the thing again."

To hear this story told months later by a Yankee employee is to instantly conjure a vision of one of those *Seinfeld* episodes parodying the Boss, with creator Larry David doing a hilarious Steinbrenner, firing off commands in staccato voice. Apparently Steinbrenner himself does a pretty good Steinbrenner: Yankee execs are accustomed to hearing him use his favorite expression, but when he drops three "warriors" in a row on them, it's all they can do to keep from laughing out loud.

The Boss, on the other hand, was deadly serious. His obsession with the Red Sox had become a personal crusade since Sox owner Larry Lucchino, already a Steinbrenner foe going back to his days as an executive with the Baltimore Orioles, lightheartedly labeled the Yankees the "Evil Empire" in January of 2003 after losing to them in the bidding for Cuban free agent pitcher Jose Contreras. With that in mind, Steinbrenner was angry for allowing Cashman and his baseball people to talk him into sitting tight in talks for Schilling back in November when the Arizona Diamondbacks were asking for Nick Johnson and Alfonso Soriano. He was angrier because the Sox surprised the Yanks by moving quickly to make a deal for Schilling by Thanksgiving. In addition, the Boss had spent most of December and January waiting for what he felt was the inevitable news that the Sox had found a way to complete the trade for Alex Rodriguez.

In short, Steinbrenner spent much of the off-season in a foul mood after what he considered a humiliating loss to the altogether unglamorous Florida Marlins in the World Series. He was mad as hell that the newspapers were savaging him for letting Andy Pettitte, the classiest of Yankees, leave for the Houston Astros. He was personally wounded when Roger Clemens, who had moved to the top of the owner's "warrior" list during his five years as a Yankee, then unretired to join Pettitte in playing for their hometown team. Finally, he was annoyed, though hardly surprised, when David Wells backed out of a verbal agreement with the Yankees to accept a better deal with the San Diego Padres, much as Wells had done two years earlier in reneging on a handshake deal with Arizona Diamondbacks owner Jerry Colangelo to sign with the Yankees.

It was Wells, lamenting his once-chummy relationship with the Boss, who may have best summed up Steinbrenner's off-season mood: "They lost a lot of guys at once," Wells said after signing with the Padres, "and I think they're in shock."

As usual, Steinbrenner used his checkbook to strike back. Against the advice of his baseball people in New York, he personally pursued Tampa native Gary Sheffield, the nephew of Dwight Gooden, the former Mets' star who works for the Yankees as a minor-league instructor. Cashman and superscout Gene Michael preferred to either sign free agent Vladimir Guerrero to play right field or move Alfonso Soriano to the outfield and sign Japanese free agent Kaz Matsui to play second base, at least partly because they feared Sheffield's reputation for being outspoken, even controversial. But Steinbrenner wouldn't be swayed, and Sheffield became part of the wave of new Yankees. In addition to trading with the Expos for Vazquez, a potentially dominant starter, Cashman rebuilt the bullpen with the signings of Tom Gordon and Paul Quantrill. And when it became clear the Yankees lacked starpower in their starting rotation, Steinbrenner made a desperate grab for Kevin Brown, trading disappointing starter Jeff Weaver to the Dodgers for a 39-year-old right-hander who had a history of injuries in recent years and was owed $30 million over the final two years of baseball's first $100 million contract.

As a result, the Yankees' payroll continued to skyrocket to new heights, and with baseball's new luxury tax and revenue-sharing plan, a payroll pushing $200 million for 2004 actually would cost Steinbrenner millions more. Still, the Yankee owner was more determined than ever to win again. He is famous for his win-or-else mentality, of course, but people in the organization believed that he was now motivated partly by his own sense of mortality. He would turn 74 in 2004, and was worrying about the effects of age even before a couple of episodes during the winter made him feel more vulnerable.

In November, Billy Connors, the organization's pitching coordinator and pal of Steinbrenner, suffered a heart attack while attending a Tampa Bay Lightning hockey game with the Yankee owner and a couple of other colleagues. Connors, who has fought a weight problem for years, survived, but it scared Steinbrenner enough for him to increase his near-daily regimen of exercise on the treadmill and stationary bike. Then Steinbrenner himself fainted at a memorial service for football great Otto Graham two days after Christmas in Sarasota, Fla. He fell so heavily, hitting his head on the floor, that some people at the ceremony were sure he had suffered a heart attack and feared he was dying. Steinbrenner came to quickly, however, and seemed most embarrassed as he assured everyone he was all right. Nevertheless, he let emergency service workers take him in an ambulance to a nearby hospital, where he underwent a battery of tests during an overnight stay. When doctors could find no signs of illness, the Yankees' owner departed quickly, and three days later he was back to work, immediately focused on making the Yankees better, soon growling about the need for more warriors.

Nevertheless, the health scare surely weighed on Steinbrenner's mind. People who know him say he has had trouble coping with the idea of getting old. He is notorious for wearing turtlenecks to hide the folds of drooping skin around his neck, but there has been no hiding the effect of age on his emotions. Never one to cry in victory in the past, Steinbrenner began choking up at championship celebrations in 1999 and 2000, but more recently he has taken to crying during routine interviews—on camera at the 2004 home opener, for example, when he broke down while speaking about how much Yankee fans mean to him. And people who work at the Yankees' Tampa complex say that in recent years he has become very frustrated by his tendency to forget names and places and routine information, and lashes out even more than usual at underlings when he realizes he can't remember something.

With all of this as a backdrop to the Yankees off-season, club executives were apprehensive as usual about the start of spring training, knowing that Steinbrenner could be at his most irrational, demanding answers even after exhibition game losses. But then Cashman pulled off the trade for A-Rod, and the deal seemed to transform the Boss into the happiest man in baseball. Why not? Going back to the first days of free agency, in the 1970s, he always lusted after the biggest stars, from Catfish Hunter to Reggie Jackson to Dave Winfield, and now he had the player widely acknowledged as the best in baseball. Better yet, he'd stuck it to the Red Sox again. So who needed Schilling? Steinbrenner was in such a good mood in the days following the A-Rod deal that one Yankee official likened the change to "[Ebenezer] Scrooge after he was visited by the ghosts of Christmas Past, Present, and Future." Predictably, then, Steinbrenner was a more visible presence at Legends Field in Tampa than he had been the last couple of years, or since the Yankees had stopped winning the World Series. He was unusually happy to chat with reporters, stopping rather than blowing past them in the golf cart he used to cruise the spring training complex. Suddenly he even seemed to like Joe Torre again.

During the turbulent 2003 season, Torre, for the first time in eight years as Yankee manager, had not been able to ignore Boss George's criticisms. For seven years Torre had done the unthinkable, not by winning four World Series but by putting Steinbrenner in his hip pocket. Blessed with an unwavering sense of security about himself as a manager, perhaps because he had been an All-Star as a player, Torre was the first manager that Steinbrenner couldn't faze even a little with criticism, public or private, and the owner hated him for that. He always wanted to feel like he was in control of the people who worked for him, but with Torre it was quite the opposite. Publicly he couldn't get a rise out of the guy, and privately Torre had a subtle way of humiliating The Boss in conversation with dismissive reminders that he didn't understand the nuances of baseball. Over the years Torre's half-kidding yet self-assured guarantee to Steinbrenner that the Yankees would come back to beat the Atlanta Braves in the 1996 World Series after falling behind 0–2 has become the quintessential illustration of the Torre-Steinbrenner relationship, but the manager let the owner know who was boss much earlier in that first season. Steinbrenner was in a panic in June when injuries to the pitching staff seemed to put the Yankees in an impossible position, facing the then-powerful Cleveland Indians in a doubleheader with none of their regular starters on turn or available to pitch.

As is his habit, Steinbrenner called an urgent meeting to discuss the situation, deciding the Yankees would need some special strategy in order to avoid disaster since they were forced to start two rookies, Brian Boehringer and Ramiro Mendoza. Steinbrenner always wanted to treat baseball like football, the sport he coached briefly as an assistant at Purdue nearly 50 years ago. In addition to thinking you should win all 162 games, he wanted to draw up a trick play, perhaps some baseball version of a flea-flicker to fool the other dugout. He drove his past managers mad with this silliness. Not Torre. Steinbrenner gathered his executives in the boardroom at Yankee Stadium that day, the day before the doubleheader in Cleveland, and as he began strategizing, he decided he wanted Torre to be part of the meeting, via telephone.

The Yankees were off that day, and Torre was playing golf in Cleveland at the time. A secretary reached him on his cell phone, and patched him into the conference room via speaker phone.

"Where are you?" Steinbrenner bellowed.

"I'm playing golf," Torre answered.

"Well," said Steinbrenner, "while you're out in the fucking woods having fun, we're trying to figure this damn thing out for tomorrow."

"How the fuck did you know my ball is in the woods?" Torre said, with mock indignation.

The conference room erupted in laughter. Even Steinbrenner couldn't help himself.

And that was that. Torre went on to say he was confident his Yankees would be fine, but his one-liner had sent the message: relax, George, it's baseball; you can't call the plays.

"Joe has a way of putting everything into perspective," Cashman would say, recalling the meeting years later. "He drops those calm bombs, that's what I call them: the one quick, witty line that makes all the tension and stress of a situation evaporate."

Sure enough, the Yankees, remarkably, swept that doubleheader against Cleveland the next day, with rookies Boehringer and Mendoza doing the pitching, on what turned out to be a memorable day in a championship season. And the tone was set between Torre and Steinbrenner.

Nothing really changed, despite various crises, until the 2003 season when Steinbrenner embarrassed Torre publicly, ordering the slumping Jose Contreras to Tampa for personal tutelage from Billy Connors after Torre had told Contreras and the press that the pitcher would be going to Triple-A Columbus to work out his problems for a couple of weeks—a decision the Boss had signed off on a day earlier. Torre could shrug off criticism from Steinbrenner as the owner's right to have his say, but he wouldn't allow him to come between him and his players, and he said so in the newspapers. There would be more public bickering throughout the season, to the point where Torre was sure that somehow the jousting had become personal, at least on the owner's end. He had been told by more than a few people during his tenure as manager that Steinbrenner was jealous of Torre's popularity with players, media, and fans, believing the manager received too much of the credit for the Yankees return to glory since 1996.

Whatever amount of credit he deserved, there was no doubt that Torre had become as big a star as any of his players. His roots as a New Yorker, combined with a personable style that charmed the media and a knack for making the right lineup and strategy decisions over the years, had elevated the manager to a status approaching sainthood in New York. As a result, he knew that Steinbrenner wouldn't dare fire him, for fear of a vicious public backlash, yet Torre wasn't sure he wanted the aggravation any longer of dealing with the Yankee owner, and let it be known publicly that he wouldn't seek an extension as he entered the final year of his contract. The implication was obvious: if the climate didn't change, he'd walk away after the season.

Torre didn't really want to leave. He loved being the manager of the Yankees, perhaps as much for the stature and financial wherewithal it afforded him as for the love of being in the dugout at age 63. Remarried, with a young daughter, Torre enjoyed the chance to be a family man relatively late in life after two divorces during his playing career, but he also enjoyed living the good life. He was treated like a movie star in Manhattan, seated at the best tables in the best restaurants in New York, ordering the most expensive bottle of wine on the menu. Torre knew how to live, all right. He had a house built in Hawaii, where he spent a month or so every winter, playing golf, going to dinner. He'd cashed some nice paychecks during an All-Star career as a player in the pre-free agent era of the 1960s and '70s, and then as a manager for the Mets, Braves, and Cardinals, but nothing like the $5 million a year he was making as Yankee manager. Always dressed impeccably in custom-made suits, Torre was good at spending money, and more than once during his tenure with the Yankees he had said he'd always be grateful to Steinbrenner for making him a wealthy man.

On the other hand, Torre had come to realize he could maintain a similar lifestyle without the headaches of dealing with George. He had established such a reputation during his time with the Yankees that he knew, if the timing was right, either the Red Sox or the Mets would leap at an opportunity to make him their manager. He also knew that even a hint of such a possibility might send the Yankee owner into spasms, so Torre was comfortable with the idea of managing the 2004 season as a potential free agent. Only a few years earlier, when he underwent surgery as treatment for prostate cancer, Torre never thought he'd want to continue managing into his mid-60s, and the private warfare with Steinbrenner again had him thinking maybe it was just time to walk away. But in January he and his wife, Ali, spent a day on a boat with golf legend Arnold Palmer off the island of Maui during his annual retreat to Hawaii, and that changed his outlook. During the course of the day, Palmer, a prostate cancer survivor himself, invited Torre to come play golf with him sometime at his Bay Hill Club in Orlando, Fla. Palmer was talking about making a date during the baseball off-season, but Torre said he might have plenty of time for golf in another year, as he was thinking of retiring.

"Retire?" Palmer shot back sharply. "How old are you?"

Torre told him he was 63, and Palmer, still active on the PGA Champions Tour for senior golfers, scoffed.

"I'm 74," he said. "What does that have to do with anything?"

Palmer's passion, as much as his words, had a powerful effect on Torre and made him rethink the idea of retiring. Still, he'd made up his mind he wouldn't stay with the Yankees if he continued to feel he wasn't wanted, because it was wearing on him to the point where it was affecting his family life.

As he would say weeks later, "The stress last year wasn't because of baseball. That's what bothered Ali. She could see I wasn't having any fun."

So no one was more shocked than Torre when a giddy Steinbrenner came bouncing into the manager's spring training office on February 18, the day pitchers and catchers reported for camp, made some small talk for a while, and then asked "So what do you want to do next year?" The Boss then invited Torre to dinner at Malio's, the Tampa steak house on Dale Mabry Boulevard where the Yankees owner has his own private dining area, and at dinner Torre noticed that the tension between them from the previous year seemed to be gone. People who know Steinbrenner believe his joy over the A-Rod deal did play a role in his thinking on his manager, but they also say that at some point he became petrified by the reality that Torre indeed could move on to manage the Red Sox or Mets after another season, and decided he better make sure it couldn't happen. Finally, Steinbrenner's well-publicized feud with Yankee bench coach Don Zimmer clearly had added strain to the Steinbrenner-Torre relationship, and with Zimmer a Tampa Bay Devil Rays' coach now after a bitter departure from the Yankees, Steinbrenner seemed more comfortable around his manager again.

Whatever the owner's motivation, Torre told him he needed time to rethink his decision not to extend his contract, but within two weeks he was convinced his relationship with Steinbrenner was truly healthier, and agreed to begin negotiations. The timing of his decision to begin talks coincided with the only real controversy of the Yankees' spring training, which meant it wasn't all that coincidental. The steroids cloud that was hovering over baseball suddenly invaded the Yankee clubhouse when the *San Francisco Chronicle* reported that Greg Anderson, Barry Bonds' personal trainer, had told federal authorities in private testimony that he'd supplied Bonds, Jason Giambi, and Gary Sheffield, as well as a few other less famous players, with steroids. As a result, on the day the story broke the clubhouse in Tampa was jammed with reporters from newspapers and TV stations around the country, all of them wanting a confession of some sort from Giambi or Sheffield. Neither player would discuss the subject beyond cursory denials, but in each case their reaction to the storm of media in their face reflected their personality. Giambi, who in two years with the Yankees had disappointed club officials by what they perceived as a lack of mental toughness, was so jumpy that he seemed to fear the feds might be waiting in the dugout to slap handcuffs on him. He cut off questions quickly by saying he wouldn't comment, and then tried to shoo reporters away as nicely as possible.

"Thanks, guys," Giambi said pointedly, as his eyes darted in every direction, nervously avoiding the faces in front of him.

In another corner of the room, Sheffield didn't look nervous at all. He seemed to thrive on controversy, and admitted he'd played much of his career with a chip on his shoulder, partly because he felt people had judged him from his first days in the major leagues as guilty by association with his uncle, Dwight Gooden, the once-great New York Met pitcher whose career was tainted and perhaps damaged by drug abuse.

"I'm tired of talking about this stuff," he said, fixing his eyes on reporters with a hard stare of intimidation.

It made for a tense day at Legends Field. The Yankees being the Yankees, players and team officials were accustomed to media scrutiny, and were practiced in handling the various crises that arose every year. But this was different, with the potential real-life ramifications the steroids scandal presented. No one knew where it was all leading, but at the time it felt like serious trouble for the Yankees and for baseball. That sense was heightened by the response to the *Chronicle* story by baseball commissioner Bud Selig, who issued a gag order for all major-league personnel. No one was to comment on the steroids issue. Even Torre, who always found a way to satisfy the media horde by putting an issue in some perspective, stiff-armed reporters on this day with what amounted to a blanket no-comment. "I can't talk about something I don't know anything about," he said by way of explanation.

Hours later, after Torre had gone from the Yankees' workout to his rented condominium, he made the phone call to Steve Swindall, Steinbrenner's son-in-law, who would handle the contract negotiations, to say he was ready to talk. Torre never admitted to any link between his decision and the steroids issue, but months later a person close to him said the manager was indeed influenced by it. Specifically Torre began to think that he owed it to his players to get the extension and eliminate any distractions a "lame duck" status for the manager, even one as established and firmly in control as he, might create. Even if nothing came of the steroids scandal, the clubhouse figured to be a more volatile place, with more superstar egos than Torre had ever managed. Without a contract extension, the perception that Torre was on the way out surely would gather steam as the season rolled along, and even for him it might make it difficult to maintain the harmony that had helped make the Yankees so successful.

So the next day Torre let it be known that he essentially had made his decision to stay on beyond the 2004 season, and perhaps as he hoped, that news dominated all talk and reporting about the Yankees for a couple of days, and the steroids issue faded at least for the moment. From there spring training moved along smoothly for the most part, though a theme that would dominate the summer surfaced early when pitcher Jon Lieber was sidelined with a groin injury, exposing the rare lack of depth in starting pitching for the Yankees. Even so, it seemed practically trivial at the time, considering the wealth of talent up and down the roster, and all of New York was far more preoccupied with A-Rod than any concerns about pitching as the season opened, first in Japan, and then back in Tampa. It was a disjointed start to the season but by the time the Yankees returned to New York for their home opener against the Chicago White Sox, all was well as the club announced that Torre had signed a three-year, $19.2 million contract extension, with a clause that called for Torre to serve as an adviser to the club for six years after he retired as manager. It all but assured that Steinbrenner would never have to worry about Torre managing the Red Sox, and the manager's mood was light as he spoke about his deal.

Speaking of his relationship with Steinbrenner, Torre said, "I have an agreement that he won't say anything bad about me, and he has one from me that I won't lose a game."

Joking aside, Torre admitted he felt comfortable again in his relationship with Steinbrenner, convinced that whatever was causing the owner's personal animosity toward him had passed.

"This agreement changed my perception," Torre said. "There was a time when I didn't know if the Yankees wanted me. Now I know it's George being George, as opposed to trying to get me out of here."

At the time of the Torre announcement, the Yankees were off to a sluggish start, their lineup of All-Stars hitting .205 collectively after six games, but the last thing anyone was worried about was whether this team would hit. A week later the Yankees were still struggling offensively, but with newcomers Vazquez and Brown pitching well early, and Torre's future settled, the Yankees went to Boston for the overhyped first Red Sox series feeling as if the pieces were quickly falling into place for another championship.

APRIL HEAD-TO-HEAD—WHY THE YANKEES WILL LOSE

Deep down, in their heart of hearts, the New York Yankees must have known early. They must have known the way you know a good melon, by that most reliable of all things, *feel*.

They must have known what it was like to learn that someone else was better than them.

Boston and New York met seven times in 10 days during the early stages of the 2004 baseball season, the Red Sox winning six times and the Yankees winning once. The final contests in that set came in a three-game series at Yankee Stadium, where Boston swept New York while allowing just four runs to an overhyped Yankees lineup that was supposed to methodically bash its way through the American League on the way to another World Series title.

Instead, the Red Sox stuffed the bats down the throat of the mighty New York batting order, leaving the Yankees and their gasping followers to deal with the reality that the 2004 Red Sox had a significant edge over them in the area that mattered most:

Pitching.

Hilarious, eh? The way New Yorkers often spoke, the way they made themselves the authorities on all things—especially baseball—you would think that they would have understood by now. *Pitching wins*. But New York is a place where the residents often saw things from an entirely warped perspective, a place where their home stadium is referred to as the *House That Ruth Built* and where victory celebrations are held in the *Canyon of Heroes*, names that sounded like landmarks on a treasure map in the latest Indiana Jones crusade. New Yorkers often put nice names on things, presumably to disguise the dirt and grime, but the reality is that even the great Yankees and their historic home had significant, major flaws.

That was never truer than in April 2004.

Yankee Stadium, for all of its glorious history, frequently may have provided the best atmosphere in baseball for spectators, but it was one of the worst—and indulge us here—for the visiting media. The press box was small and cramped. There were not enough telephones. And those unfortunate members of the Fourth Estate who were not afforded a pressbox seat had the privilege of working in a dungeonesque workroom equipped with no natural light, a handful of televisions, and a bank of small lockers that made one feel as if trapped in the deepest, darkest corners of Grand Central Station.

If those come off as petty criticisms—and they are—they are nonetheless subtle digs compared to the incessant complaints that members of the New York media had *everywhere* they visited. (Of course, there was no place as good as New York.) And so when a telephone line was inoperative or a clubhouse door failed to open on time or, during a press conference, someone was not pressed on a matter to the liking of the perpetually dissatisfied New York media, someone was going to hear about it.

Where is the caw-fee?

What, no haht dawgs?

And the ever popular: *do you know who I am?*

At a place like Yankee Stadium, in particular, it sometimes seemed as if people did not even recognize real failure because they had become so spoiled with success; instead of focusing on what they had, they dwelled on what you did not. Year to year, the reality was that the New York Yankees entered the season as just another baseball team, no matter what had happened in the past. Each year, for everyone, there was a need to prove oneself again. But in baseball, especially, New Yorkers somehow came to believe that it was all connected, that 1927 and 1949 and 1978 and 1999 were part of one continuous story line instead of what they were: epics unto themselves. Many Red Sox followers similarly succumbed to the same preposterous belief that somehow it was all preordained, that they had no control over the outcome because the script was written long ago. And if by the end of the year it happened as New York expected—if the Yankees indeed had won again—New Yorkers could then go to those special and faraway places that they talked about ad nauseam—the *Canyon of Heroes*?—and that often succeeded in making the rest of the baseball world throw up.

Please.

What a crock.

Fortunately, even in pinstripes, there were always well-grounded exceptions like respected New York Yankees shortstop and captain Derek Jeter, who truly understood the unending challenge that came with any competition, no matter the participants or the history. But too many others—especially in New York—felt they had all the answers or, more specifically, that they somehow had earned a pardon because of what happened decades earlier.

Ultimately, it was like so much else in New York:

A load of bull.

"They've made some good additions," Jeter said of the Red Sox shortly before the 2004 regular season began. "They've added some quality guys and the big one is Schilling. Obviously, you win with pitching and defense and they've added a quality guy."

So, then, the question persisted:

Why did the Yankees go out prior to the 2004 season and amass a lineup of club-wielding cavemen intent on bludgeoning the baseball world to death?

Because they thought they could get away with it, that's why.

Because they genuinely *believed* they would.

And that, dear friends, is the purest definition of arrogance.

All of this tentatively brings us to the landmark sitcom *All in the Family*, a television program created by Norman Lear and situated, coincidentally, in New York. (What a shock.) It was during one unforgettable episode that Edith Bunker became particularly unnerved during a discussion with her pigheaded husband, Archie, after which the couple's daughter, Gloria, was forced to remind her mother—and we're paraphrasing here—of Archie's most annoying personality quirk.

"Ma, you know there are three things you can't talk to Daddy about," Gloria Bunker said matter-of-factly.

And the three things in question?

"Religion, politics or anything else."

So it was with most New Yorkers, who not only believed that they knew more than you did, but that they knew more about *you* than you did.

Especially when it came to baseball.

Couldn't you see?

It was all decided by fate.

So, after the Yankees scored only 23 runs in the seven games with the Red Sox, some members of the New York media and fan base inexplicably shook their heads as if they could not believe what they were seeing. In the first seven meetings of the season against the revamped Red Sox, the Yankees batted .199; in the six losses, they scored just 12 runs and batted a pathetic .186. While newcomer Alex Rodriguez went 1-for-17 in the first series of the year between the clubs—did he *really* know what he was getting himself into?—New York somehow managed to finish the seven games with more strikeouts (49) than hits (47), meaning the Yankees were more likely to walk back to the dugout, bat in hands (and throats), than they were to end up on the bases as the result of a hit.

In the end, it was an ass-kicking.

Plain and simple.

Of course, it was only *April*, something the Yankees and their fans were all too willing to point out. Championships were won in *October*, the know-it-all New Yorkers (redundant?) emphasized, and on that point it was actually quite difficult to argue with them. But after failing so tragically in October 2003 at Yankee Stadium—oops, the *House That Ruth Built*—the Red Sox *needed* to get off to a strong start against the Yankees in 2004. They *needed* assurance that the improvements and changes to their team would translate on the field and have a profound effect on the competition between the teams. They *needed* to beat up on the Yankees, to vent, to take out their frustrations from an off-season that most New Englanders felt began roughly 10 days too early.

In short, they got what they needed.

"Of course we're happy to sweep," center fielder Johnny Damon said after the final game of the three-game series in New York, a 2–0 victory backboned by the inimitable Pedro Martinez. "I just wish we could go back to last year and make these games count."

Said Red Sox first baseman Kevin Millar: "We all remember Game 7, but this is a new year. We went out and played a good series and that tells you about the character of this team. We haven't clicked all the way through offensively, but we will. For now, we're just getting Ws and that's what it's all about."

Indeed, beyond the lopsided 6–1 edge in games, the Red Sox had demonstrated significant improvements in an array of areas since the last time the teams had met in a game of any consequence. While newcomer Schilling pitched just *one* of the seven contests, New York's only victory came against Sox right-hander Derek Lowe in a game also started by Cuban defector and right-hander Jose Contreras, for whom the Sox and Yankees had engaged in a bidding war prior to the 2003 season. During a recruiting visit to Nicaragua, Red Sox officials seemed blindsided upon learning that Contreras had elected to sign with the Yankees—on the night prior to the Contreras decision, Sox general manager Theo Epstein and then-director of international scouting, Louie Eljaua, had been smoking cigars with the Cuban—and subsequent rumors following the event had Epstein tearing up his hotel room in frustration.

Naturally, most of those rumors were traced back to the Yankees.

As things turned out, Contreras was nothing short of a colossal bust after signing a four-year, $32 million contract. And even though the Yankees won his April 18 start against Lowe and the Red Sox, Contreras pitched poorly, failing to endure the third inning.

On top of it all, there was the presence of closer Keith Foulke, who gave the Red Sox something they had never before possessed in recent years against the Yankees: a stable and reliable closer. And while Foulke was not nearly as overpowering as the great Mariano Rivera, his save percentage during the four-year period from 2000–2003 actually placed him *ahead* of Rivera among American League closers during that time, a significant detail given that former major league pitcher David Cone, who pitched for both the Sox and Yanks, once referred to Rivera as the "X-factor" in New York's run of world championships at the end of the millennium.

Against the Red Sox, in particular, Rivera proved valuable because he was someone with whom the Red Sox could not match up. In Game 7 of the 2003 AL Championship Series, for example, Yankees manager Joe Torre relied on Rivera to pitch the 9th, 10th, *and* 11th innings, an unusual request from someone who frequently tried to limit his closer to just one inning of work. And while the Red Sox had enjoyed some measure of success against Rivera in recent years—particularly after Manny Ramirez came to the Red Sox in 2001—Rivera was nonetheless an invaluable weapon in the late innings of close games because the Yankees were all but assured of holding opponents scoreless while he was in the game. That was never truer than in Game 7, when, after Rivera silenced the Red Sox for a third inning under the most intense of circumstances, Boone led off the bottom of the 11th inning with a home run against Tim Wakefield, who had been summoned to pitch in relief because then-manager Grady Little was holding out closer Scott Williamson for a save situation.

In short, New York's formula in close games went something like this:

Bring in Rivera to hold down the fort, then rally against the other team's inferior bullpen to win the game.

And when you got right down to it, *everyone* was inferior when compared with Mariano Rivera.

In the early stages of the 2004 season, however, even that advantage seemed to have been stripped from the Yankees. And while the edge did not necessarily swing to Boston's favor, the presence of Foulke allowed the Sox to neutralize Rivera, something that became crystal clear on the afternoon of Saturday, April 24. With the game tied at 2 after nine innings, Torre summoned Rivera, who pitched a scoreless 10th and 11th. The difference this time was that Sox skipper Terry Francona aggressively and similarly called upon Foulke—managers typically held out their closer for save situations on the road—who endured a 10th inning error and similarly gritted his way through the 11th, after which both managers were forced to go to another level of their bullpen.

In the 12th, with Rivera now out of the game and his impact negated, the Red Sox rallied against Paul Quantrill for a 3–2 victory.

The winning pitcher was Foulke.

"Last year, we didn't have that guy that could go out there and throw a scoreless [10th] and a scoreless [11th]," noted reliever Mike Timlin, who ended up with the save. "As strong as [Foulke] is, he probably could have thrown another inning. The extra dimension we have—we have a three-inning closer, basically."

Said Foulke: "I've said it since the day I started closing: I'm not your typical closer. I'm a pitcher and I pitch out of the bullpen. . . . The only time I've seen Rivera is when I'm sitting across from him. He's a great pitcher, and great pitchers go out and pitch."

Still, for all of the good feeling that existed in Boston after the Red Sox swept the Yankees on April 25 to improve to 12–6—New York by contrast, was a miserable 8–11—just as gratifying was the manner in which New Yorkers appeared positively dumbfounded. Following the four-game series at Fenway Park in early April during which Rodriguez finished 1-for-17—he got a single *in his final at-bat*—some members of the rush-to-judgment New York media already were suggesting that Rodriguez was "soft" and "not mentally tough." While Rodriguez played significantly better during the three-week series in New York a week later—he went 6-for-11 with a home run in that series—the Yankees overall did not, leading to more New York explanations, excuses, and theories as to what troubled the mighty Yankees.

Among the more popular and amusing suggestions was that the Yankees were still reeling from a season-opening trip to Japan, during which they split a pair of games with the laughingstock Tampa Bay Devil Rays. The Yankees had been back in the United States for more than three weeks by the time the Red Sox left Yankee Stadium on April 25 with a 6–1 record in the head-to-head meetings between the clubs, but there were still those suggesting that the journey had left the Yankees log-legged and jet-lagged. Few focused on the fact that the Yankees simply were not hitting, something that was not unusual for any team or April or May, when the weather was colder and pitchers had the advantage. And what happened in the spring often happened in the fall, when temperatures dropped and the games grew exponentially in magnitude.

In April, at least, the more unnerving truth for New Yorkers (if they bothered to recognize it) was that the Red Sox did not hit, either. Boston finished April batting .260 for the month and scoring only 103 runs, an average of just 4.9 runs per game that was only slightly higher than the 4.5 runs per game scored by the Yankees. But where Yankees pitchers were largely mediocre at the start of the season, Red Sox pitchers were positively brilliant, finishing the first full month of the season with a sterling 2.95 ERA that led the major leagues. In the end, given virtually the same offensive circumstances, the Red Sox were winning where the Yankees were losing, an amusing development given that the teams had so frequently been in the reversed positions under similar circumstances.

But in the early stages of 2004, at least, two things seemed to be different.

First, the Red Sox had better pitching.

And second—on the field, at least—there seemed to be absolutely no connection between 2003 and 2004, the kind of link that the Yankees and their fans had so often relied upon.

"I don't think about last year. I don't think, 'What if we did this or that, things would be different,'" Williamson said during the weekend trip to New York. "These are totally different circumstances. The only thing that's the same is our uniforms. What happened is over, and hopefully things will be different now and this team will go on to win a World Series. I don't see why we can't."

Game 7 of the 2003 American League Championship Series, it seemed, was indeed history.

APRIL HEAD-TO-HEAD—HATING PEDRO

If it weren't for Pedro Martinez, New Yorkers might actually feel an occasional twinge of sympathy for Red Sox fans. Oh, sorry. That's right, they're not fans. They're a nation. Red Sox Nation.

Everyone south of Hartford rolls their eyes at such pretension. Anything to call attention to the fans' plight as the victims of the Curse of the Bambino; isn't that what's behind all the cutesy catchphrases?

The Sox have long been the favorite team of every poet in America, it seems, but enough already with the odes to romanticism, fatalism, or whatever other euphemisms for losing that literate New Englanders want to use to explain a century of finishing second to the Yankees. Losing is losing, not a sociology thesis or a metaphor for puritanical suffering.

On second thought, then, maybe nothing could make New Yorkers sympathetic toward their rivals. How does anyone feel sorry for people who secretly revel in their own misery—who would lose their identity as a deprived Nation should they ever win a championship?

So maybe Pedro just makes it easier for Yankee fans to hate the Sox. He's not just a headhunter from the Roger Clemens school of intimidation. Yankee fans once despised Clemens when he wore the Sox uniform, but at least he had some respect for the game and an unmatched work ethic that gave him a redeeming quality. As far as New Yorkers can tell, Pedro flaunts his superstar status by coming and going as he pleases, answering to no one, least of all his teammates, for the privilege of arriving to work late and leaving early when he feels like it, and often acting like a clown in the dugout during games when he's not pitching.

For many of those same reasons, the Yankees themselves have built up a genuine rage toward Pedro over the years. They feel he has made it personal, not only by plunking so many Yankees, but by singling out catcher Jorge Posada for some reason and constantly mocking him from the Red Sox dugout when he wasn't pitching. Thanks to the designated hitter rule, the Yankees couldn't make Pedro pay with a retaliation pitch, but when the opportunity presented itself last October, it was their collective hatred toward Pedro that prompted Don Zimmer, their then 72-year-old bench coach, to charge the Sox pitcher as dugouts emptied during the brawl in Game 3 of the ALCS. Zimmer was out of line, and wound up looking like a fool, as Pedro pushed him to the ground. The old coach made a tearful apology for embarrassing his sport the next day, but the apology wasn't meant for Pedro.

"I would never apologize to him," Zimmer said in the days after his famous bullrush. "He's done some of the most unprofessional things I've ever seen on a ballfield."

So nothing delighted the Yankees quite like storming back to beat Pedro in Game 7 of the 2003 ALCS. Now, as the teams met for the first time in 2004, they were curious to see how Martinez would respond and also whether he would change his act at all with a new manager in the dugout.

Not that their curiosity couldn't have waited another month or so. About the only people happy to see the Yankees pull into Boston in mid-April were TV executives and T-shirt vendors. For everyone else it seemed far too early in the season for the hype and hysteria that now surrounds each and every meeting between these teams, especially this one as Alex Rodriguez officially became part of the rivalry. It was far too early for the Yankees, a jet-lagged ballclub still shaking off the cobwebs from the season-opening trip to Japan while just getting to know one another after an off-season of dramatic change.

Yet they were comforted by a belief that, for all the fight their archrivals had put up in 2003, and for all the improvements the Sox had made during the winter, these were the same old Red Sox. April or not, one piece of news had already convinced them: Pedro was up to his old tricks.

The Yankee players, in contrast to the front office, really don't pay much attention to the Red Sox when they're not playing them. Their feeling is the Sox are just another team they beat every year en route to the World Series, and, well, what's the big deal?

The exception is Pedro, the man who has put so many Yankees either flat on their backs or, occasionally, into an ambulance to get X-rays with his knockdown pitches. Not surprisingly, then, word spread quickly among some of the veterans that on the very first night of the season, Pedro, after being knocked out of the game against the Orioles, had left the clubhouse in Baltimore before the game ended—a universal no-no in baseball.

More significantly, as they saw it, new Red Sox manager Terry Francona had excused Pedro's transgression, publicly blaming himself for not spelling out his team rules. Yankee players all but winked at one another, delighted to see that Pedro once again was going to be allowed to play by his own rules, creating a lack of team discipline they were convinced hurt the Red Sox over the course of a season.

"Looks like nothing's changed there," one Yankee veteran said privately. "Pedro is still calling the shots."

Basically the current Yankees take a condescending view of the Red Sox, forever noting the contrast of their nonconformist ways to the professionalism that Joe Torre demands. It's much the way Yankee fans have looked down on Bostonians for decades, amused by their endless obsession with trying to beat the pinstripes when it counts. In any case, the Yankees were sure the reason they always found a way to beat the Red Sox was because they were tougher mentally, bound tighter as a unit than the Sox because of their commitment to one another.

That belief was tested in April when, rather shockingly, the Sox won six of seven games over consecutive weekends to leave the Yankees a bit dazed and confused. Pitching had been the subject of much scrutiny during spring training because, for the first time in Joe Torre's nine-year tenure, the Yankees didn't have a surplus of proven starters. And when a groin injury sidelined Jon Lieber, they were forced to open the season with an untested rookie, Jorge DePaula, as their No. 5 starter. Yet pitching wasn't really the problem in this first test against the Red Sox—except for Jose Contreras, that is.

The Cuban righthander quickly established that nothing had changed from his first year. He still lost his poise at the first sign of trouble, still couldn't get the Red Sox out, and once again left the manager exasperated. Torre always has the big picture in mind, especially in April, but if there is one thing for which he has no patience, it is pitchers who nibble at the corners of the plate, afraid to challenge hitters. It's the reason that over the years, veteran left-hander Kenny Rogers and right-handed reliever Jeff Nelson drove him crazy at times, as they were always falling behind in the count, always trying to throw the unhittable pitch, even with a three-run lead and nobody on base. Contreras just seemed afraid to throw his fastball with runners on base, forever trying to get hitters to chase his off-speed forkball. When he began doing it even with a 7–1 lead in the third inning on Sunday in Boston, the third game of a four-game series, Torre reacted with a quick hook that was out of character for a manager who had won championships with a patient style defined by his faith in the players. In this case, Torre's impatience was a sign that Contreras likely would never earn his trust, as well as an acknowledgment that, after losing the first two games of the series, it was important to get off the schneid against the Red Sox, even in April.

Contreras aside, the issue in April was the lack of offense. Alex Rodriguez went 1-for-17 in Boston, and later in the year admitted the weekend felt "like an out-of-body experience" because he wasn't yet comfortable as a Yankee, trying too hard to do something spectacular in his first taste of the Yankees-Red Sox rivalry. He began to hit the next week in New York, but by then Derek Jeter was in the midst of an 0-for-32 slump, the longest hitless streak of his career. The Yankees scored a total of 12 runs in the six losses to the Sox, and months later Torre would second-guess himself for overemphasizing the importance of playing the Red Sox. The Yankees had opened the season in Japan against the Tampa Bay Devil Rays, splitting a pair of games before returning to Florida to finish up four days of spring training before restarting their season. The idea was to give the Yankees time to recover from jet lag, but Torre believed the disjointed nature of the start of the season hadn't given his team, which featured so many high-profile newcomers, time to get a feel for one another.

"We didn't know who we were yet," was the way Torre put it months later. "I probably over-did it talking about the Red Sox, telling the new guys about how every game with them takes on a life of its own. I think I made them so tight they tried way too hard to make something happen. The good thing about getting our ass kicked was that it forced these guys to pull together and we began to develop a personality."

Their personality would be defined mostly by a defiance built on offensive firepower that would translate to a major-league record number of comeback victories. But there were no comebacks against the Red Sox in April, and Pedro delivered the final indignity in the final game of the seven, the only one in which he pitched. He threw seven shutout innings in a 2–0 victory that showcased a craftier Pedro, one without his old 95 mph fastball. In his first start against the Yankees since the infamous Game 7 of the previous October, he didn't try to intimidate the hitters, rarely came inside at all, but baffled them mostly with off-speed stuff. The Yankees were surprised, caught looking at third strikes five times, but found it comforting in a way that Pedro felt he had to change his style so dramatically against them.

After that game Bernie Williams offered a revealing backhanded compliment:

"I've seen him nastier," Bernie said, "but he's more of a pitcher now. He has to be. He knows he can't blow people away anymore."

The message was as pointed as a knockdown pitch: bring that same weak-ass shit to the mound next time, Pedro, and you better be ready to duck.

Losing six out of seven in April may have been a wake-up call for the Yankees, but they were as sure it was an early-season fluke as they were that Jeter would hit higher than .175—his batting average as the Sox left town. The Red Sox had earned their respect in 2003, especially in that unforgettable playoff series, but the Yankees' feeling of superiority remained.

Their utter disdain for Pedro meanwhile mirrored the feelings New Yorkers have had about the Sox and their fans forever. In some ways Yankee fans didn't mind losing to the Red Sox in April. It merely set the Nation up for bigger disappointment when it counted.

FIRST SIGNS OF TROUBLE—RED SOX

For the Red Sox, in the immediate aftermath of their three-game sweep at Yankee Stadium on April 23–25, the game of baseball became astonishingly easy. Boston returned home for a three-game series against the Tampa Bay Devil Rays and systematically dispatched its opponent, winning the first two games of a three-game series by scores of 6–0 and 4–0. By the time Tampa finally scored two runs in the first inning of the series finale—an eventual 7–3 Red Sox win—Boston pitchers had thrown 32 consecutive scoreless innings going back to the seventh inning of the team's 3–2 victory over New York on April 24.

Things were going so well that the Red Sox even got a major contribution from beleaguered Korean right-hander Byung-Hyun Kim, who came off the disabled list to allow just one hit in five shutout innings of the 4–0 victory, the first game of a doubleheader.

By the time both the Red Sox and Devil Rays left town, in fact, the Red Sox had outscored their opponents, 33–7, over a six-game stretch that left their record at a sparkling 15–6. Even without Nomar Garciaparra and Trot Nixon, each of whom remained on the disabled list, the Sox looked positively dominating, particularly at the front end of their pitching staff. Derek Lowe, Bronson Arroyo, Pedro Martinez, Curt Schilling, and Kim all won games during the stretch, a span during which opponents had to contend with, in order, a sinkerballer, a curveball specialist, the consummate master craftsman, the prototypical big right-hander, and the submarine-style Korean. Only rain prevented a sixth weapon, the dancing knuckleball of Tim Wakefield, from appearing in the Boston arsenal during what was truly an awe-inspiring week.

The Red Sox pitching staff looked so deep and so versatile that most everyone was thinking the same thing.

This team isn't as good as everyone thought it would be.

It's better.

"We couldn't even touch this group," said television analyst and soon-to-be Hall-of-Fame inductee Dennis Eckersley, comparing the 2004 Sox to the 1978 club that won 99 regular season games before losing to the Yankees in an unforgettable one-game playoff. "It's very unique to have what they have. Usually you just have three guys that throw hard. But they're not just throwing, either. It's guys that know how to pitch.

"I hate to get carried away, but they could win 110 games," said the Eck. "That's the kind of thing I'm thinking about."

That's the kind of thing everybody was thinking about.

The Red Sox were on a roll.

Pedro Martinez was coming off his best outing of the year as the Red Sox began the month of May, but his contract extension—or more specifically, the absence of one—was still on his mind. So before an eventual rainout in the scheduled opener of a three-game series against the surprising Texas Rangers, Martinez decided that he'd had enough. After having agreed to negotiate with the Red Sox into the early part of the season, Martinez abruptly decided that he would no longer have discussions with the team, venting to *Boston Herald* reporter Michael Silverman, with whom Martinez shared a strong relationship.

"I'm just really sad for the fans in New England who had high hopes that at this time I could say, truly, that I was going to stay in Boston," Martinez said. "But now [the Red Sox] are going to have to compete with the rest of the league. . . . I gave them every chance I could. That's from the bottom of my heart. The fans in Boston, I know they don't understand what's going on, but I really mean it from my heart. I gave them every opportunity, every discount I could give them to actually stay in Boston and they never took advantage of it. Didn't even give me an offer."

In fact, the fans in Boston *did* know what was going because they had seen this kind of thing before. Contract struggles between the Red Sox and their star players were a common occurrence in Boston—from Roger Clemens to Wade Boggs to Mo Vaughn to, now, Martinez, Garciaparra, Varitek, and Lowe. General manager Theo Epstein indirectly answered Martinez' remarks the following day by issuing a statement that said such disputes were "unfortunate but . . . inevitable," though the young general manager's comments also included an emphasis on the club's "core values: team over individual, a World Series over everything else." The obvious implication was that Martinez was in violation of the latter, particularly at a time when the Red Sox were playing so well.

Whether by coincidence or circumstance, the Red Sox' fortunes promptly changed. Martinez went out on May 2 and was hammered by the Rangers in an 8–5 defeat in the nightcap of a doubleheader and Texas followed with a 4–1 victory over Wakefield on Sunday night, completing a three-game sweep that ultimately turned into a five-game losing streak when the Sox dropped the first two games of a four-game series against the inferior Cleveland Indians. The Red Sox went from winning six straight to losing five in a row—just like that—and the only possible turning point in the eyes of fans, especially, was the moment that Pedro Martinez decided to gripe about his contract, to violate the team's "core values," to put himself before the team.

Naturally, Martinez was skewered in the Boston media and on talk radio, and the entire matter turned comical when Ramirez suggested he would defer part of his salary to keep Martinez in Boston. Nonetheless, for all of the hot air that often came from the lips of players—and there was a lot of it—the good news for the Red Sox was that Pedro Martinez found some measure of closure in the uncertainty of his contract discussions. Whether Martinez and the Red Sox would negotiate again during the season was largely irrelevant; what was important was that Martinez felt he had had control, that he would decide his future, that he was *in charge*. The fruitlessness of contract talks with the Red Sox made Martinez feel helpless, powerless, incapable of determining his own fate. So the cornerstone of the Red Sox did what any fiercely competitive athlete cursed with an enormous chip on his shoulder would do.

He made a preemptive strike, disarming the Red Sox before they could disarm him.

You can't fire me.

I'll quit first.

Yet, as noteworthy as the entire, brief exchange was between player and team, impossible to overlook was this simple fact: Pedro Martinez was uniquely and hopelessly competitive. He could not stand to lose, on the field or off, a trait that often led the pitcher to do foolish things while on the mound. During the 2003 American League Championship Series with the New York Yankees, for instance, it was Martinez' inability to pitch effectively that prompted him to throw a fastball behind the head of Yankees outfielder Karim Garcia. That single pitch triggered a succession of events that ultimately prompted then 72-year-old Yankees bench coach Don Zimmer to charge at Martinez, who instinctively grabbed Zimmer by the head and pushed him to the ground.

In New York—and across the country—the bullfight between Martinez and Zimmer earned a place in infamy. But it was Martinez' initial transgression—the pitch to Garcia—that highlighted the pitcher's real shortcomings:

He did not know how to deal with failure.

And he did not know how to react when deprived of something he wanted.

In fact, while Martinez subsequently shut down the Yankees for the balance of that afternoon—in the process, even in the eyes of teammates, he sacrificed some dignity—his career was dotted with similar events. Once, while pitching in Minnesota, Martinez became annoyed when Twins outfielder Matt Lawton stepped out during the pitcher's windup. Enraged by the tactic—in an attempt to disrupt the pitcher's rhythm, many hitters employed similar methods against Martinez, who was a fast worker—Martinez restationed himself on the mound and fired the next pitch off Lawton's kneecap, once again making it clear that he was the one in charge. An irritated Lawton shouted at the pitcher while Martinez methodically went back to work, the message loud and clear.

His game.

His rules.

Incidents like these were not uncommon with Martinez, so much so that it became a running joke among beat reporters anytime a batter stepped out against Martinez in the middle of the pitcher's windup. Under the code by which Martinez played, for a hitter to step out of the batter's box in the middle of a pitcher's delivery was a sign of disrespect. Pitchers were taught from an early age *never* to truncate their deliveries because of the threat of injury, and so Martinez often would follow through to the plate anyway, even if time-out had been called before the pitch. And then, invariably, he would step back on the mound and fire the next one at the hitter, delivering a reminder that the batters had a higher power than the umpire to answer to.

As a result, Martinez' actions on the mound earned him the reputation as a headhunter, something he truly resented. Much of the reputation was established in the early years of Martinez' career when, as a hard-throwing righthander with the Los Angeles Dodgers, he lacked the control necessary to command the strike zone. But by the middle and later stages of his career, when he had blossomed into one of the most complete pitchers and marksmen in the history of the game, he was still throwing with a purpose. He was not afraid to come inside, to knock batters down, to push them off the plate. He actually seemed to take pride in it. And if there was a situation that called for retribution—if a Red Sox pitcher or batter had been threatened or disrespected in some way—Martinez was not afraid to balance the ledger.

"If you're fresh with me or show me up," Martinez once said after plunking Oakland A's designated hitter Olmedo Saenz, "I'll drill you in the ass and I'm not afraid to do that."

Saenz' crime?

A night earlier, against then Red Sox reliever Jim Corsi, he had made little effort to get out of the way of a pitch. Saenz latter homered in the game, but it was the first act that stuck in the minds of the Red Sox.

So the next night, when Saenz stepped in against Martinez, the righthanded hitter was dealt a 95-mile-per-hour fastball in the back.

Take that.

By that stage of his career, of course, Martinez was almost skilled and talented enough to purposely hit three consecutive batters, then strike out the next three, just to offer himself a challenge. During the 1999 and 2000 seasons, in particular, Martinez was so positively brilliant that he often seemed to be playing a different game than everyone else. In 2000, when he finished the year with a microscopic 1.74 ERA—the overall number in the American League was a relatively gargantuan 4.91—Martinez actually finished the season with more victories (18) than he allowed *hits* with runners in scoring position (17). It was the kind of statistic that demonstrated just how truly gifted he was, how dominating, how downright dictatorial he was when standing on the pitcher's mound.

Generally speaking, Martinez did not often allow runs, hits, or walks, which made opponents all the more suspicious when one of them was hit by a pitch.

By the time the 2004 season had arrived, however, Pedro Martinez was a different pitcher. Martinez missed almost all of the 2001 campaign with a shoulder injury that threatened his career, causing him to dramatically overhaul his off-season conditioning program and approach on the mound. The strength in his arm was still there when he needed it, but he did not throw as consistently hard, particularly early in games. He relied more on precision and command, introducing a fourth pitch, a cut fastball, into a repertoire that already included an above-average fastball, curveball, and change-up. And through it all he continued to win, going a combined 34–8 over the 2002–03 seasons, during which he posted an aggregate 2.24 ERA and won two ERA titles, the fourth and fifth of his career.

Then came 2004, the contract talks, the uncertainty about his future. Throughout the 2004 season, some Sox officials privately questioned whether Martinez' sole objective was to remain healthy so that he would not hurt his value on the free-agent market at the end of the year. Late in the season, when an uninspired Martinez went through the motions in a meaningless game at Tampa Bay, one voice even suggested that the pitcher had approached the entire season with his contract in the forefront of consciousness. And along the way, there were the usual clubhouse criticisms that Martinez operated by his own set of rules, that he required special treatment, that he came and went as he pleased, and that he was not the kind of teammate off the field that he appeared to be on it.

Most of it was true.

But whatever the issues, people tolerated it all for one reason and one reason only: Pedro Martinez could pitch and he was a truly intense competitor. And after blowing up in Texas on May 1, after formally bringing closure (at least in his mind) to his contract saga with the Red Sox, Martinez took the mound in Cleveland five days later, on May 6, and pitched seven strong innings in a 5–2 Red Sox victory. He continued to pitch well right up to the All-Star break and slightly beyond, going 7–1 with a 3.41 ERA over a span covering 13 starts. And excluding one wildly uncharacteristic outing at Anaheim on June 2, Martinez posted a 2.84 ERA over the next two and a half months after getting things off his chest regarding his contract and his future.

Pedro Martinez, it seemed, was focused on pitching again.

Which is what both he and the Red Sox wanted in the first place.

Where others appeared preoccupied, Manny Ramirez seemed entirely at peace. In the 2004 Red Sox season, that may have been the most extraordinary irony of all.

Really, how could anyone explain it? Of all the players who had cause to reassess following the 2003 season, Ramirez had the most. Arguably the most gifted right-handed hitter in the game, Ramirez and the remaining five years of his contract were placed on waivers with the hope that someone else would claim him. And when nobody did—Red Sox officials knew it was "a long shot" Ramirez would be claimed, according to one member of management—Manny Ramirez was forced to confront a cold, harsh reality.

He was there for the taking.

And, thanks to his exorbitant contract, nobody wanted him.

But while Martinez, Garciaparra, and Lowe had to deal with the uncertainty of their future—unsurprisingly, the tough-minded Varitek seemed to have little trouble focusing on baseball—Ramirez had something the others did not: a contract. Under the terms of the deal he signed between the 2000 and 2001 seasons—when Dan Duquette was still the general manager and the Yawkey Trust managed by John Harrington still owned the Red Sox—Ramirez signed through 2008 at the annual salaries of (beginning in 2004) $20.5 million, $20 million, $19 million, $18 million and $20 million. Some of that money was to be received in deferred payments, but the bottom line is that Manny Ramirez was assured of nearly $100 million over the final five years of his contract.

And that was true no matter where he played.

So while Martinez, Garciaparra, and Lowe seemed at times to struggle with the off-field aspects of the game, the events of the winter had precisely the opposite effect on the fascinatingly complex Manuel Aristides Ramirez. From the start of spring training, in fact, Ramirez looked more carefree and happier than ever before, a significant development given how uncomfortable and out of place he frequently appeared during his first three years in Boston. Teammates Kevin Millar and David Ortiz made a noticeable effort to help Ramirez deal with the media, and teammates noticed that Ramirez was making much more of an effort to accommodate the press.

"You know why he's doing this?" Martinez asked rhetorically during spring training. "He knows I'm tired of talking to you guys. He's trying to help me."

Whatever the explanation—and with Ramirez, there was no way to know for sure—the results were impossible to ignore. During one early stage of spring training, when reporters wanted to speak with Ramirez, the talkative Millar stood on a chair near Ramirez' locker and served as a liaison between the player and the media. Reporters would ask the questions to Millar, who would in turn relay them to Ramirez. Ramirez then would direct his answer to Millar—it was almost as if Ramirez were more comfortable speaking to his teammate—and Millar would promptly relay the answer back to smiling reporters, who found the entire scene wonderfully entertaining, particularly during the monotony that spring training often dissolved into.

And when a reporter asked a question that Millar, in particular, did not especially care for, the engaging first baseman deflected the issue in a manner that made even reporters laugh out loud.

"That's a dumb-ass question. Stupid question," Millar said with a warm smile. "No comment. Next question."

Ramirez, too, laughed.

And so the wall that existed between the media and Manny Ramirez slowly began to crumble.

"We talked. We gave him some ideas," Ortiz would say later about the manner in which Ramirez approached the 2004 season and, in particular, dealing with the media. "But he knew pretty much what he wanted to do."

Said Millar: "He's been this way with us. Now the fans are getting to see it. The fans are getting a chance to know him, and that's great, because Manny is phenomenal."

By the time the regular season began, Ramirez seemed poised to have his best season as a member of the Red Sox. While many of the Red Sox hitters struggled to get comfortable in the early stages of the regular season, Ramirez batted a stellar .388 with five home runs and 16 RBI during the month of April. He followed that by batting .317 with nine home runs and 21 RBI in May, a month during which his relationship and popularity with fans also began to blossom.

Still one of the most unknown superstars in Red Sox history to that point in his career, Ramirez officially came out of his shell at Fenway Park in a 5–3 victory over the Cleveland Indians on May 11, one day after the Red Sox excused him from the series opener so that he could take a U.S. citizenship exam in Miami. Ramirez passed the test—"It was 15 questions. They give you a book. It's not hard," he deadpanned—and jogged out to his position in left field on the next night waving a miniature U.S. flag. When he came to bat for the first time, Ramirez received a standing ovation from the sellout crowd at Fenway Park, the members of which were getting to see more of Ramirez' personality for the very first time.

For teammates, the playful side of Ramirez was nothing new. But to most of the media and the fans, the player was showing the side of him that routinely bounced around the clubhouse wearing headphones, joked with teammates, made wisecracks. They saw a smiling Manny, a happy Manny and, most important, a productive Manny. In Boston, the two went hand in hand. Where Ramirez' first three years in Boston were remembered largely for his blunders—failing to run out a ball at Tampa Bay in 2002, sitting out a series against the Yankees in 2003, refusing to pinch-hit during a critical game at Philadelphia later in 2003—the opposite was now true. People were focusing instead on the *good* qualities of a player who was as oblivious as Mister Magoo and as lovable, too.

Example: When asked if he had a special feeling upon taking the oath to become an American citizen, Ramirez shrugged.

"Not really," Ramirez said with a straight face. "I just stood up."

The response was classic Manny.

Teammates, of course, had long since seen this side of the player, but the colorful and engaging Ramirez was an entirely new person to Red Sox fans, in particular. Media members who traveled regularly with the club also saw the man behind the batting average and the home runs, but fans did not. Yet as Ramirez continued his customary assault on opposing pitchers, his personality began to seep out, little by little, endearing him to a Red Sox following that desperately wanted to love and embrace the latest power-hitting, right-handed-hitting superstar to play in the shadow of Fenway Park's fabled left field wall.

By June, in fact, even Ramirez' blunders were becoming an accepted part of the deal with a man who already had staked his place as one of the most prolific run producers in baseball history. In a June 11 interleague game against the Los Angeles Dodgers at Fenway Park, the Red Sox were leading by a 1–0 score in the bottom of the ninth inning when Ramirez dropped a short, routine fly to left field that should have ended the game. The colossal blunder allowed

Dodgers infielder Alex Cora to score the tying run, taking the air out of Fenway Park on what was otherwise a wonderfully festive night.

While Fenway fans hushed and Red Sox followers throughout New England shouted at their television sets, Ramirez returned to the dugout at the end of the inning and dropped an unforgettable one-liner on his teammates.

"Well," said Ramirez, whose defense had long been recognized as one of the weaker points of his game, "there goes my Gold Glove."

The dugout erupted with laughter, naturally, and the Red Sox rallied in the bottom of the ninth for a 2–1 victory.

In the bigger picture, of course, the development was significant: Manny Ramirez was learning to laugh at himself. He was learning to admit his mistakes, particularly to the media, and he was learning to deal with the harder parts of playing in a place like Boston, where every game, every play, every mistake was magnified. As serious a baseball town as Boston had become, one of the most fascinating ironies was that it required a certain carelessness to function there. Players needed to be either immune to criticism or oblivious to it, or they needed to be able to laugh it off. Whatever the solution, they needed to accept the fact that there were certain things that they could not control, no matter what, and the trick was to focus on the things they could.

In the case of Manny Ramirez, he was learning to cope. As a hitter, one of Ramirez' finest traits was that he had the extraordinary ability to separate his at-bats, never linking one to the next, a true indication of his confidence in the batter's box. Ramirez could strike out three straight times and still seem completely at ease in the batter's box, and it was that ability to forget, to focus on the here and now, that left teammates in awe as much as the tape-measure home runs and picturesque, rhythmic swing. Now Ramirez seemed to be applying that same approach to the game in general, to playing in Boston, where one of the keys to succeeding was to forget what had just happened, to ignore the past, to move forward without fear of the consequences.

"Maybe people thought I was going to come here all mad, but I got like five (more) years in Boston, so I decided to go out there and try to do my best—and get the best out of it," Ramirez told *Boston Herald* reporter Karen Guregian during a particularly candid interview after his induction as a U.S. citizen. "I want to make the best out of those years instead of being all mad and not talking at all. . . . I want people to know I'm a nice guy.

"You know something? The days go easier for you than when you're not talking, or when you're mad, or when you're taking everything so personally. I've learned if you stop and talk for five minutes with the media and try the best you can, people may say, 'His English isn't too good, but at least he's trying.' And it's better if they see me trying."

Offered Martinez: "He's good-hearted, I know that for a fact. He's just in his own world. He's very shy. If Manny was able to speak the way he'd like [in English], people would get to know him a lot better."

As it was, as the Red Sox labored through the months of May and June, people were indeed getting to know Manny Ramirez better.

And in Boston, fans finally were starting to accept Ramirez' flaws with his attributes.

They finally understood that it was all just Manny being Manny.

By the time May ended, nobody was talking about a 110-win season. Though the Red Sox won seven of their final 10 games during the month, they went 16–14 overall against a schedule that consisted primarily of American League weaklings Cleveland, Kansas City, Toronto, and Tampa Bay. The Sox had lost three games in the standings to the Yankees—the teams were now tied atop the American League East Division—and the unexpectedly prolonged absences of Garciaparra and Nixon were starting to have an effect. Lowe, meanwhile, went a positively abysmal 1–4 with an 8.19 ERA during a month when the overall pitching was largely mediocre. And the Red Sox proved to be extremely vulnerable on defense, allowing an astonishing 24 unearned runs in 30 games.

Soon, there was even more to worry about.

During a three-game series between the Red Sox and San Diego Padres on June 8–10, right-hander Curt Schilling visited a private Internet chat room on a Web site called sonsofsamhorn.com—the Sox fan site was named for the beefy and former Sox first baseman who now worked as a cable television analyst—and revealed to site members that he had an injury to his right ankle that would require surgery at the end of the season. The news eventually leaked out into the conventional media on June 10, a night Schilling was scheduled to pitch against the Padres. And soon it was common knowledge that Schilling was pitching with an ankle problem that frequently required him to take an injection of Marcaine, a local anesthetic, before nearly every start.

Following the San Diego game—a 9–3 Red Sox win in which he pitched seven strong innings—Schilling acknowledged that he would have had surgery immediately if it were the off-season.

"I would get it taken care of," admitted the pitcher, "[but] I'm not sure this is a situation where you give yourself a lot of other options [than to keep pitching]. Whatever we're doing right now [to treat the ailment], it's working."

While that news was disconcerting to the Sox and their followers, Schilling's apparent need for attention also was coming to light. From the moment he joined the Red Sox, the pitcher seemed intent on challenging the media, addressing fans directly in chat rooms and calling in to talk radio shows. (He became known at all-sports station WEEI as "Curt in a car.") Schilling took the stance from the beginning that those two media allowed him to interact with fans directly—there was no editing in live radio, no reporter to manipulate his quotes on the Internet—and those points were impossible to argue. Yet it often seemed as if Schilling were intent on ticking off writers, using the chat rooms as a forum to comment on the media as well as anything that pertained to him and the Red Sox.

Still, it was Schilling's openness about his injury that caused some teammates to shake their heads in disbelief. Among most athletes, after all, it was frowned upon to discuss injuries publicly. While some players believed that doing so would give a psychological edge to opponents—longtime Red Sox pitcher and future Hall-of-Famer Roger Clemens was a big proponent of this theory—others simply felt that to do so was to call unnecessary attention to oneself. In baseball, especially, the wear and tear of the regular season ultimately required most players to deal with an assortment of injuries, aches and pains. That was understood. And if one member of a team dwelled on his ailments, it was a message to the others that he was hurt worse than they were, that he was making more sacrifices, that he was enduring more pain.

In principle, in the eyes of players, that kind of behavior went against everything they were supposed to stand for.

Many of them dealt with the same things. And they dealt with them *together.*

Was Schilling hurt? Yes. But as one Sox teammate pointed out, "He's not afraid to let you know about it, either."

Even Red Sox officials recognized that quality in Schilling, though by then Schilling's tendency to dramatize was understood in the front office, too. Nonetheless, Schilling continued to take the ball every fifth day and he continued to win. While the Red Sox generally were spinning their wheels through much of May, June, and July, Schilling went 9–3 and, along with Ramirez and Ortiz, kept the team afloat. Though the injury to his ankle compromised Schilling's ability to go deep into games—he began to tire after the sixth inning, or at about 90 pitches—he nonetheless provided the foundation for the entire pitching staff, particularly with Lowe continuing to struggle.

It was at times like that, especially, that the value of a true ace was recognized, that a man like Schilling could prevent a team like the Red Sox from spiraling into a losing streak and out of control because he provided stability.

Said Epstein later in the year when asked about Schilling's performance: "You could probably make more of a case for the MVP than for the Cy Young."

And he was right.

During that month, too, the fun-loving Ortiz proved similarly indispensable. In 25 June games during which the Red Sox went a disappointing 11–14, Ortiz batted a sizzling .365 with 10 home runs and 31 RBI. And as usual, be it as an advisor to Ramirez or a big, easygoing presence for the remainder of the players in the clubhouse, Ortiz kept things loose. In that way, leadership in the Red Sox clubhouse was remarkably well distributed among white players like Millar and Varitek, a Dominican like Ortiz, an African American like Ellis Burks, who similarly contributed a steadying dignified presence despite spending much of the season on the disabled list. No matter who you were in the Red Sox clubhouse, you had someone to confide in, relate to, who understood you. And that was something every team needed.

Ortiz, however, had a way of making everyone feel comfortable, with a gentle-giant type of presence, warm smile, and undying sense of humor. Once, when Grady Little was manager, Ortiz stuck his head into the manager's office during the manager's daily pregame briefing with reporters and offered his playful assessment of what was to take place on the field that night.

"We're going to kick their ass, drink their beer and rape their bitches," a smiling Ortiz said as if imitating a gangster.

The room exploded with laughter.

During the middle of the season, especially, that kind of humor was invaluable. That was particularly true of a Red Sox team that was playing with the burden of enormous expectation, though at times it hardly seemed it. Often, it seemed the Red Sox played through the meat of their schedule as if on cruise control, perhaps recognizing that the baseball season would not begin in earnest until August, after the annual trading deadline and after teams made their final, key acquisitions for the stretch run. In the clubhouse, there was very much a veteran feel to the 2004 Red Sox, as if they had been there before, as if they had recognized what needed to be done, as if they knew they could flip a switch and begin winning games anytime they wanted to.

But throughout the bulk of June, given the depth of talent on the club, there was also reason for fans to begin feeling frustrated. One week before Nixon returned from a quadriceps muscle he pulled while rehabilitating from the back problem he suffered on the way to spring training, Garciaparra returned for a June 9 game against the San Diego Padres. Even then, a moment that should have qualified as a celebratory event was darkened by the continued strained relationship between the player and team. As Garciaparra's return neared, some Red Sox officials began whispering that the player's return was taking too long, that he was being deliberate in his rehabilitation so as to assure his health for the balance of the season with free agency looming. There also was speculation that Garciaparra was making the Red Sox wait, that, like Martinez, he was dictating when and where he would return in an attempt—at least in his mind—to regain control of his career.

"I've heard that theory," Epstein said as Garciaparra's absence, originally expected to be for just the first few weeks of the season, stretched into two months. "But I choose not to believe it."

Nonetheless, Garciaparra immediately came under fire upon his return, which was hardly what the shortstop was expecting. Getting dressed in front of his locker before his June 9 debut against the Padres, Garciaparra privately assured a skeptical *Herald* reporter that he "wasn't sticking it to anybody," though it was clear at that moment that the relationship between Garciaparra and the club had deteriorated to an irreparable state. The Red Sox, after all, were making assertions and allegations behind the back of one of their star players, which seemed a clear attempt at undermining the player's credibility.

And so Garciaparra took the field under circumstances that were hardly ideal, though it would benefit both him and the Red Sox for Garciaparra to play well.

Having long served as the prestigious No. 3 hitter in the Boston lineup during his career, Garciaparra returned to the lineup as the No. 5 hitter behind Ortiz (third) and Ramirez (fourth), a decision that was impossible to argue given the success of each player in the first half. And while the Sox lost Garciaparra's debut by an 8–1 score, his presence behind Ramirez paid immediate dividends a night later, the Padres intentionally walking Ramirez in the fifth inning of what was a 4–1 Sox lead. With the bases now loaded, Garciaparra hooked a two-run double off the left field wall that made the score 6–1 and triggered a five-run outburst, sending the Sox on their way to a 9–3 victory. And less than two weeks later, after another intentional walk to Ramirez in what was a 4–1 lead in the seventh inning against Minnesota, Garciaparra ripped a grand slam into the center field seats that propelled the Red Sox to a resounding 9–2 victory.

On the whole, however, Garciaparra's return—or, for that matter, Nixon's—did not have the desired effect that the players, the Red Sox, or their followers would have hoped. By the time the Red Sox were once again due to cross paths with the New York Yankees, Garciaparra was batting just .233 with one home run and nine RBI in 15 games. The Red Sox had slipped five and a half games behind the Yankees in the American League East and were due to confront a New York team that had gone 23–8 over a 31-game stretch and was pulverizing opponents with a frightening display of power.

"I don't think the league's seen the best of either team yet," a diplomatic Brian Cashman, the general manager of the Yankees, told a *Herald* reporter in the days leading up to the series. "I don't think [Boston] had a chance to see the real Yankees team [in April] and I don't think the Yankees had a chance to see the real Boston team. They just played better than we did at that time."

This time, it seemed, the Yankees were the ones playing better.

And the Red Sox were in the familiar position of having to chase their rival New Yorkers.

THE HOTTEST SHOW IN TOWN—YANKEES

On the first day of May, a cool, overcast Saturday afternoon, 54,103 people paid their way into Yankee Stadium to see a game with the Kansas City Royals, the worst team in the American League. Alex Rodriguez wasn't hitting much yet, a month into the season, but the highest-paid player in baseball was already paying off for George Steinbrenner by "putting fannies in the seats," to use the owner's favorite definition of marquee value.

Not that the Yankees necessarily needed an attendance boost, having set a franchise record in 2003 with 3,465,640 customers. In fact, the Yankees already had the whole rock-star aura before they acquired A-Rod: on the road their security staff cleared out hotel lobbies and escorted players to and from team buses, frustrating legions of fans who showed up in various cities looking for autographs. When A-Rod came on board, however, the frenzy factor seemed to quadruple. One columnist wrote that it was "like Elvis joining the Beatles."

Such star power didn't necessarily guarantee championships, as Steinbrenner himself found out in the 1980s, but it sure helped to sell tickets. In 2004 the Yankees would again set a new franchise attendance record—and lead the majors—by totaling 3,775,292 fans at home. It was the sixth straight year they would surpass the three-million mark, another record, but as fans filled up the old ballpark against teams like the Royals, it was clear the Yankees had become something bigger than just the hometown team. Indeed, there were indications that their star-driven success had turned them into an international tourist attraction, as much a part of the New York experience for out-of-towners as a

Broadway play, the Empire State Building, Fifth Avenue, and Ground Zero where the World Trade Center once stood.

As GM Brian Cashman would say, rather unabashedly, one day as another near-capacity crowd filed into the stadium: "We are the thing to see if you're in town. In the past we competed with all the other sports, the Broadway shows and the beaches and everything. Now they're all chasing us."

The signing of Hideki Matsui alone had a significant impact on attendance, especially when Matsui agreed to serve as an ambassador to New York City Tourism in 2004, doing Japanese radio ads and promotional videos. According to Cristyne Nicholas, president and CEO of NYC & Company, the marketing agency for New York City Tourism, tour operators reported a 66 percent increase in packages that included tickets to Yankee games, and the overall number of Japanese tourists increased from 292,000 in 2003 to 336,000 in 2004. The Yankees even made a point of having the league schedule the Seattle Mariners in New York in May during Golden Week, a Japanese holiday week, so tourists could see Ichiro Suzuki as well as Matsui. That may help explain how a series with the last-place Mariners drew 158,916 fans over three days.

Said Nicholas: "The Hideki factor, as we call it, has been off the charts. He has boosted [NYC tourism] to a level we never imagined."

Whatever Matsui's international impact, it was surely matched by the additions of A-Rod and Gary Sheffield on the home front. Some 38 million domestic tourists visited New York in 2004, and, according to Nicholas, there was more interest in baseball, particularly the Yankees, than ever. The Yankees' road attendance was further proof of their national appeal, as they broke the American League record, drawing 3,308,666 fans in other cities; the next highest total in the majors was the 2,895,206 drawn by Barry Bonds and the San Francisco Giants. Of course, Yankee glamour has always been a draw on the road, but the home numbers are something of a recent phenomenon, after years of public debate about the safety and convenience of Yankee Stadium. Apparently four championships have done wonders for the image of the Bronx.

It was only a decade ago that Steinbrenner was campaigning hard for a new stadium, preferably in a more desirable location. If the city wouldn't build him a gleaming new palace like the spectacular Camden Yards in Baltimore, which opened in 1992, the Boss said he'd find someone who wanted his team, while making veiled threats about going to New Jersey. He insisted he needed a place with more luxury boxes to compete, and he implied that the minority neighborhoods surrounding Yankee Stadium created a safety issue in the minds of fans driving in from Westchester and North Jersey. Security issues and traffic headaches were keeping people from going to Yankee games, he said, and the numbers gave him cause for concern. As recently as 1995, the year after major-league players went on strike, forcing the cancellation of the World Series, the Yankees drew only 1,705,257 fans, despite making the playoffs for the first time since 1981. In '96, the year they won their first championship under Joe Torre, they drew 2,250,839 fans. But then, even as ticket prices increased with each championship, and traffic and parking remained problematic, the Yankees became a must-see attraction. In addition to the attendance boom, Steinbrenner reaped huge profits when he created the YES Network, and for all of his faults, the owner became a hero to a new generation of Yankee fans by continuing to plow his profits back into his ballclub.

As a result, with All-Stars at every position except second base, the 2004 Yankees would prove to be more entertaining than anything Broadway had to offer. They weren't as efficient as the pitching-rich teams Torre had managed to championships, but, man, could they hit. No sooner had the Red Sox left them reeling, with those six wins in seven games in April, than the Yankees began to establish themselves as a relentless offensive force against which no lead could be considered safe.

Trailing 8–4 in the eighth inning against the Oakland A's in the first game after getting swept at home by the Red Sox, the Yankees struck for six runs and a 10–8 victory that launched an eight-game winning streak and avoided any early-season eruptions from Steinbrenner. It was the first of 61 comeback victories, the most in major league history. Such a statistic can be misleading, of course, since coming back from a 1–0 deficit in the second inning is quite different from trailing by four in the late innings. In the case of the Yankees, however, it told you everything about their season: their starting pitching put them in too many early holes, yet their offense refused to surrender, bludgeoning opponents en route to the best record in the American League. The Yankees, together with the Chicago White Sox, would lead the majors with 242 home runs, a total that broke the franchise record set in the famous 1961 season, when Roger Maris hit 61 home runs to break Babe Ruth's single-season record.

Here's the truly revealing stat about the comeback ability of the 2004 Yankees: nine times, including this night against the A's, they would come back to win games in which they trailed by four or more runs—that too was a major-league record.

"Never seen anything like it," Gary Sheffield would say late in the season. "We got guys with a ton of heart."

Sheffield, as it turned out, had as much as anyone, delivering an MVP-caliber season, full of clutch hits, while playing with a left shoulder so sore that he tried to catch fly balls at his waist whenever possible, just so he wouldn't have to lift his arm. That he turned out to be an inspiration to teammates, as well as a feared slugger, came as a pleasant surprise to the faction in the organization that was leery about signing him as a free agent. In that way, Gary Sheffield was to the Yankees what Manny Ramirez was to the Red Sox.

Most prominently, GM Brian Cashman and superscout Gene Michael were opposed to the idea of signing Sheffield, largely because of his reputation for being outspoken over the years. Never afraid to spark a controversy, Sheffield had publicly blasted team executives with the Dodgers and Brewers over contract disputes and what he considered lousy personnel decisions while playing with those teams. Over the years he'd also made vague allegations of racism toward Major League Baseball in regard to recognition for black players—most notably Sheffield himself.

As a result, Sheffield had been portrayed as disruptive at times, more than once demanding a trade from the Dodgers, to the point where even some players thought of him as trouble. When the Mets were trying to trade with the Dodgers for Sheffield in the spring of 1999, Robin Ventura and Todd Zeile made a point of telling then-GM Steve Phillips they were against the idea, believing Sheffield would harm the clubhouse chemistry they felt was important.

But most people who played with or managed him came to realize that, strong opinions aside, Sheffield cared about all of the right things. Old-school managers such as Jim Leyland, who won a world championship in 1997 with Sheffield as part of the Florida Marlins, and the Atlanta Braves' Bobby Cox, raved about Sheffield's toughness and professionalism. Cliff Floyd, a teammate on that '97 Marlins team, once said of Sheffield, "He's the kind of guy every team needs, because he's a great player and, when it's needed he's not afraid to tell other guys to get their shit together. He's a guy nobody wants to mess with."

He's also Dwight Gooden's nephew, the son of Gooden's older sister, and that was no small factor in Sheffield becoming a Yankee. A reclamation project of Steinbrenner's since his drug problems with the Mets, Gooden has worked for the Yankees in their baseball operations department in Tampa since retiring four years ago. He'd been bending the Boss' ear about Sheffield, and how much he wanted to play in New York, throughout the 2003 season, updating him regularly on Sheffield's stats—he wound up hitting .330 with 39 home runs and 132 RBIs for the Braves. And when the Yankees couldn't solve the Marlins' power pitching in the World Series, Steinbrenner decided he had to have Sheffield. The Yankee owner even conducted negotiations personally with Sheffield, which led to much confusion. When the three-year, $39 million deal nearly broke down after an apparent agreement, Yankee people leaked word that Sheffield had made additional last-minute demands. Months later, however, sources on both sides said the problems resulted because Steinbrenner, whose memory has become fuzzy in recent years, couldn't remember the details of the deal he'd agreed on verbally with Sheffield, and had to be convinced that Sheffield wasn't trying to pull a fast one on him.

In spring training Steinbrenner may have been wondering if he'd made a mistake. Along with Jason Giambi, Sheffield was linked to the BALCO scandal, having testified before a federal grand jury in 2003. Later in the year he would tell *Sports Illustrated* that in 2002 he'd unknowingly used a steroid cream supplied by Barry Bonds' personal trainers while working out during the off-season with Bonds, and MLB officials basically responded with a shrug, saying they wouldn't follow up, at least partly because MLB had no policy against steroids until 2003. But in February, when the story was fresh, the uncertainty of the situation seemed to cast a darker cloud over Sheffield. Then, two weeks into spring training he showed the Yankees how defiant he could be, publicly taking on Cashman over the GM's handling of an injury to Sheffield's right thumb.

After playing at least part of the 2003 season with sprained ligaments in the thumb, Sheffield aggravated the injury in early March. And though Sheffield insisted he could play through it again, the Yankees were concerned he might need surgery, and sent him from Tampa to see a hand specialist in New York. Sheffield didn't know that Cashman had told reporters of the club's concern, and when he arrived in New York he was stunned to find that his injury was back-page news, complete with speculation that he might need surgery.

When he returned to Tampa, after the doctor agreed that he didn't need surgery, Sheffield lashed out at Cashman, telling reporters that the GM had no business "talking [to the press] about the extent of my injury without telling me."

In the Bronx Zoo days of the Yankees, when there was a good chance of Billy Martin or Reggie Jackson or Steinbrenner saying something fairly outrageous every day, Sheffield's mini outburst wouldn't have raised an eyebrow. But this was rather shocking in a clubhouse that had been defined by harmony and good vibes during the Joe Torre era. For that matter, you don't see players speak their mind anywhere much anymore. Image is everything in sports these days, when any hint of discord can turn into hours of debate and discussion on local sports talk radio, and even nationally on ESPN shows such as *Pardon the Interruption* and *Around the Horn* that desperately need nuggets of controversy to justify their existence. So now players take part in media training seminars, learning how to answer reporters' questions without really saying anything. Meanwhile, the club's public relations people are trained essentially to be firefighters, grabbing their hoses at the sound of an alarm and rushing to the scene to put out the flames. In this case, Yankees PR director Rick Cerrone, noticing the crowd of reporters interviewing Sheffield at 9 A.M., before the club's morning workout, ascertained the nature of the comments and immediately used his cell phone to call Cashman, who was in nearby Clearwater, taking part in an MLB meeting regarding arbitration hearings.

Cashman, no doubt envisioning screaming headlines the next day, immediately excused himself from the meeting and made the 20-minute drive back to Tampa, where he found Sheffield in the trainer's room and did some damage control. Sheffield was upset because he had wanted the Yankees to hide his injury from the public—and pitchers who might want to pound him inside—the way he said the Braves had done a year earlier. Cashman, in turn, told him the Braves could get away with that in a one-newspaper town like Atlanta. But he knew better than to think it can work that way in New York. The media scrutiny is too intense. Lying can make you look foolish.

"We operate in a fishbowl," Cashman said that day. "Gary's preference is not to deal with the questions about his thumb, but I told him that's part of playing in New York. You can't hide anything here."

Cashman is a sharp GM at least partly because he has excellent communication skills. It was unlike him to leave himself open for criticism, and he obviously should have had a similar conversation with Sheffield before the right fielder went to New York to see the doctor. He just didn't think it would be such an issue, and maybe it wouldn't have been had Sheffield not already been holding a grudge against Cashman, knowing the GM had been against signing him as a free agent.

"That's what it was really all about," a friend of Sheffield's said months later. "He wanted Cashman to know that he knew."

Apparently that's why Sheffield took the issue to reporters rather than directly to Cashman. That's why he stood at his locker, saying he was "pissed off" at Cashman for making news of his torn ligament public.

"Talk to me before you talk to anyone else," Sheffield lectured, speaking indirectly to the Yankees' GM.

When Cashman hustled back to Tampa, the two of them wound up hashing everything out. By late morning Cashman was relieved, knowing he'd defused the issue before it could reach the back page of the tabloids the next day.

"In Yankee-land, you don't want anything to fester," Cashman said. "You want to stay ahead of the curve. On this one I was little behind but I closed the gap quickly."

His awareness of such matters is part of what makes Cashman good at his job, particularly as it applies to New York. Sheffield appreciated getting the chance to have his say with the GM.

"I respect that a lot," he said of Cashman's quick response. "A lot of people wouldn't do that."

But even after he had been defanged, Sheffield had to let people know he wouldn't be some house pet, not even in the Yankees locker room.

"When something doesn't run smooth, I'm going to let you know," he said. "Not that I need special treatment. I don't. It's just like, 'move out of my way, let me go play baseball.' When people interfere with that, I'm going to let them know. I need to create my space to do what I do. A lot of people take that as, 'he's pampered.' And that couldn't be further from the truth. If anything, it's just the opposite. I've had to go out and fight for everything I've gotten."

That's the root of Sheffield's defiance, a feeling that he had to overcome an image of him he believes was formed because of the drug problems that tarnished the career of his uncle, Gooden, the one-time phenom with the Mets who won a Cy Young Award in 1985 at the age of 20.

Sheffield himself was 18 years old, in his second year in the minors, when Gooden first tested positive for cocaine in 1987, and he says the guilt by association with his uncle has followed him since then.

"From that first time people talked about me like I was doing the same thing," Sheffield says. "You get to the point where you resent people for cheering you when you get a big hit or something, because you know they're talking bad about you. That's how I played the game for years. I resented the cheers. When people booed me, it fueled me."

Such candid militancy sounded out of place in a Yankee locker room that had been carefully stocked in recent years mostly with quiet conformists—David Wells being one obvious exception—who were more than happy to let Torre do most of the talking to the media. Even Giambi, who, as the long-haired leader of the Oakland A's, was famous for saying "I want to party like a rock star and play like a superstar," instantly turned into something of a cliché-speaking bobblehead as a Yankee. It was as if he'd been neutered the day he signed that $120 million contract to wear pinstripes.

Yet while Giambi struggled to find his niche in the Yankee locker room, Sheffield fit in immediately in his new ballclub. The veterans respected the intensity he brought to the ballfield; Derek Jeter, who longed for the return of all-out gamers like Tino Martinez and Paul O'Neill, in particular seemed to like Sheffield's no-nonsense style. Funny, but nobody worked harder at his game than A-Rod, who was showing up at 7:30 in the morning during spring training, at least an hour ahead of other players, to take ground balls at third base as he learned a new position. Yet teammates were not as quick to embrace him as they were Sheffield. Surely his famous fallout with Jeter over quotes in an *Esquire* magazine article was a factor. But not the only factor. In general, players tend to resent teammates they think spend too much time talking to the media, and Sheffield and A-Rod were both magnets for quote-starved reporters. Yet where A-Rod struck teammates as someone who played up to the media mainly to improve his Q rating, Sheffield was accepted as someone who just felt compelled to speak his mind, and simply didn't know how to be dull.

Of course, Sheffield was easy to like when he started hitting those whistling line drives that made third basemen check to make sure their protective cup was in place. Like A-Rod, Sheffield got off to a slow start, but where A-Rod struggled noticeably in clutch situations all season, Sheffield got locked in by late May and became the centerpiece in the Yankees' relentless offense that not only began to dominate the American League as the weather warmed up in May and June, but made astonishing comebacks seem normal.

Indeed, some of the comebacks played out as if scripted for a Disney movie. The hardest to believe, at least in the first half of the season, was on Sunday afternoon, June 13, when the Yankees denied Wells, their old teammate, a win on a day when he made a memorable return to New York. Taken out with his San Diego Padres leading 2–0 after seven innings, Wells watched, flabbergasted, on the TV in the visitors' clubhouse as Hideki Matsui and Kenny Lofton hit back-to-back, two-out home runs in the ninth inning off of one of the game's best closers, Trevor Hoffman, to tie the game.

As if that weren't enough to send Wells running to his favorite haunts in Manhattan for the night, the Yankees came back again in the 12th inning—against Rod Beck this time—after the Padres had scored three in the top half of the inning to take a 5–2 lead. Ruben Sierra delivered the final blow, a sacrifice fly to center to give the Yankees a 6–5 win.

Afterward Wells looked as if he'd seen one of those ghosts the Yankees like to believe help them out at the stadium from time to time.

"When you're here, it's great," Wells said. "When you're on the other side and it happens to you, you just shake your head and say, 'it's still happening.'"

Nevertheless, the irony was that it may have hurt the Yankees more to watch Wells dazzle them for seven innings than it did for Wells to watch them steal his win. Wells' brilliance was a painful reminder of how much the Yankees could have used the left-hander, no matter if he was now 41 years old and rounder in the belly than ever. In fact, concerns about pitching continued to nag the Yankee decision makers, as Kevin Brown had gone on the disabled list only a few days earlier with back problems that would bother him the rest of the season, while Jon Lieber, Jose Contreras, and even Mike Mussina had all been alarmingly inconsistent. To this point, in fact, Javier Vazquez had been the only bright spot, and so the search was on already in the front office for pitching help.

You couldn't blame the Yankees for being cavalier about Wells after his back injury forced him out of Game 5 of the 2003 World Series in the first inning. It was particularly galling to the Yankees, not only because it may have cost them a world championship, but because only a day earlier Wells had bragged at a press conference about his effectiveness at age 40 despite the fact that in terms of conditioning, he was the anti-Clemens. "If you're blessed with a great arm," he'd said, "you can be fat and out of shape." Wells thought it was funny, but by then he'd once again worn out his welcome with Joe Torre and Mel Stottlemyre, much as he did in his first tour of duty with the Yankees. This time his poor work habits prompted the understated Stottlemyre to publicly criticize one of his pitchers for the first time in 20 years as a pitching coach.

So the Yankees offered Wells, who had back surgery in early December, only a nonguaranteed contract for 2004, which they say Wells accepted verbally, then reneged on a month later when the Padres offered him a guaranteed one-year deal worth $1.25 million and incentives that wound up being worth $6 million. It didn't seem like much of a blow at the time, even if Wells was a proven big-game performer. By June, however, as Wells came to town, the Yankees would have been all too happy to forgive him his transgressions for the chance to put him back in pinstripes, but the Padres were in a pennant race themselves, and they weren't dealing their best pitcher.

Still, the Yankees weren't in a panic, by any means. In a matter of just a few weeks after losing six of seven to the Red Sox in April, they'd reclaimed first place in the AL East. And by the time they pulled off their astounding comeback to deny Wells a victory, they were leading the Sox by three and a half games. So as the crowds continued to pour into the Bronx, night after night after night, the George Steinbrenner All-Stars were giving folks their money's worth. Their late-inning bullpen of Paul Quantrill, Tom Gordon, and Mariano Rivera looked bulletproof, and their Sheffield-led comebacks were already making it seem as if this team were destined to win it all. Especially since there wasn't an owner, a GM, a scout, or even a PR intern anywhere in baseball who didn't think the Yankees would find a way to add a front-line pitcher to their rather wobbly starting rotation by the July 31 trading deadline.

But for now, at least, the Yankees had to take care of some business with the Red Sox.

JUNE HEAD-TO-HEAD—O, WOE IS US

Throughout Red Sox history, especially as it pertained to the New York Yankees, there invariably were those moments where everything went wrong, where the Red Sox did more than just lose, where they embarrassed themselves and nearly choked the life from the six-state New England region that so loyally and faithfully supported them.

This was one of those times.

So while the easy thing to do now would be to poke fun at the Yankees, their fans, and the I-told-you-so New York media, the truth is that during a three-game series from June 29 through July 1, everything the Yankees and their followers ever said about the Red Sox was true. Against the Yankees, the Red Sox found ways to lose. One way or another, they unfailingly reminded you that they were the Red Sox and the Yankees were the Yankees, and there was a very good reason for all of it. And they reminded you that no matter how much things changed, no much how much the Red Sox and their fans wanted to believe that things would be different this time, there was always that seed of doubt planted deep in the soul of every New Englander, waiting to grow into a familiar pit in your stomach.

At times like this, there was no point in mocking the Yankees.

Beating up on the Red Sox was far more therapeutic.

When the Red Sox arrived at Yankee Stadium on Friday, June 29, nobody needed to be told of the significance: the games meant more to Boston than to New York. The Red Sox trailed the Yankees by five and a half games in the American League East, and the division was at risk of slipping away. Deep and talented teams like the Red Sox and Yankees were capable of just about anything, but to ask either one to overcome a significant deficit against the other was a bit unrealistic. The Red Sox and Yankees were just too good. Boston and New York were scheduled to have 19 head-to-head meetings during the regular season, and more than likely the teams would effectively beat up one another during those games, whether the final series tally was 10–9, 11–8 or 12–7. And to expect one of them to stumble against the balance of the American League—New York and Boston had the two highest payrolls in baseball—was unrealistic. For both teams, the way to win was to keep the competition close and steal it at the end.

Of course, during the previous two months, the Red Sox had done exactly what many believed would not happen. After leaving New York with a 15–6 record on April 25, the Red Sox already had a two-and-a-half-game lead in the American League East. But in between meetings with New York, the Red Sox went 27–26 over a 53-game stretch during which their two-and-a-half-game advantage turned into a five-and-half-game deficit, meaning the Yankees were eight games better during the same span. For the Red Sox, that was ultimately where the problem rested, though the damage was done. Now the Red Sox had to find a way to play themselves back into striking distance in the most difficult of all places, Yankee Stadium.

The House That Ruth Built.

From the very beginning, the signs were mixed. Derek Lowe was scheduled to start the series opener and had been pitching better of late, going 2–1 with a 2.08 ERA over his previous four starts, three of them Red Sox victories. Yet one of the most frustrating things about Lowe is that he had been entirely unpredictable to that point in the season, and games against the Yankees were unlike any other, no matter what kind of momentum a player carried into the game.

Lowe had made two starts against the Yankees in April—one good, one bad—and there was just no way to predict what he was going to give the Red Sox this time.

"He scares the shit out of me right now," Francona privately acknowledged while playing catch in front of the Red Sox dugout prior to the first game.

Meanwhile, sensing a Yankees kill, the bloodthirsty New York media was circling. Prior to the game, a reporter from *Newsday* witnessed an exchange between pitcher Curt Schilling and catcher Jason Varitek that he interpreted as a sign of inner turmoil. The report appeared in the paper a day later—following a lopsided 11–3 Yankees victory that substantiated Francona's fears about his starting pitcher—and caused a minor stir among Boston reporters, in particular, largely because it involved two of the most dominating personalities on the team. In the exchange between the players, as it was reported, Varitek confronted Schilling for missing a standard scouting meeting between pitchers and catchers before the series opener. The incident allegedly took place in the dugout as the Sox were preparing to stretch before batting practice, though the encounter was not the focus of the column in which it appeared.

Nonetheless, it was difficult to assess who was more irked—the Red Sox or the reporters who covered the team. Asked about the encounter by a reporter he trusted, the upstanding Varitek shook his head, chuckled, and revealed, "I said it as a joke." Francona dismissed the report entirely. Schilling did, too. And while players, managers, and coaches all were known to lie in order to cover up something they did not want dispensed to the public, the manner in which Francona, Varitek, and Schilling all addressed the matter suggested that the report was more fiction than fact or, perhaps, a misinterpretation by someone who did not know the principals involved as well as the reporters who dealt with Varitek, in particular, on a daily basis.

In the Red Sox clubhouse, after all, there was nobody more discreet than Jason Varitek, who never criticized teammates—at least in public—and never aired his dirty laundry. *Never*. While there were a handful of reporters who shared a good relationship with the catcher, the reasons had nothing to do with Varitek's willingness to share clubhouse gossip or provide insight into team politics. In fact, it was quite the opposite. Teammates, fans, and media respected Varitek precisely because he did *not* allow himself to be dragged into such things, because he did not allow himself to be baited by the countless distractions that could destroy a team. Jason Varitek focused on the *important* things. He was a stickler for game preparation, a tireless worker, an intense competitor. And while it was well within the possibility that he would confront a teammate who was shirking his responsibility, the idea of him doing it anywhere within eyeshot of a reporter was extremely hard to believe.

Jason Varitek, quite simply, was smarter than that.

Still, the entire incident only highlighted the tug-of-war that existed between the Boston media and their New York brethren. The idea of being scooped by a Yankees reporter was infuriating to Boston writers, many of whom resented the know-it-all attitude of the New York media. (OK, we admit it.) Rightly or wrongly, there was the perception—in any industry—that the best of the best worked in New York, though the reality was that New York was no different than anyplace else. There were good reporters and there were bad reporters, and the only difference was that there were more of each. That fact meant that there were more stories written—accurate and inaccurate—explaining why the New York media had long since developed a reputation for being cutthroat, ruthless, and, in some cases, reckless.

Naturally, the Boston media was not much different. Those were the side effects of competition, and no cities in America had fiercer competition among the sports media than Boston and New York. Ultimately, reporters all were out to scoop one another, to get the story first, particularly in an information age where cable television and the Internet were becoming prominent players. The race for the exclusive was moving faster than ever, and the resulting pressure inevitably led to sloppiness and inaccurate—or, at least, *incomplete*—information. So when one member of the media was wrong, the others took all too much joy in beating the credibility out of another reporter who neglected to follow the rules.

And from the Bostonian's perspective, if that renegade media member happened to be from New York, that was all the sweeter.

As it was, the members of the Boston media had plenty to write about the Red Sox, whose series-opening defeat dropped them six and half games behind the Yankees. Unlike the series opener, the second game was far more competitive, the Red Sox holding a 2–0 lead into the seventh inning, when, with one out, the Yankees put runners on first and third against knuckleballer Tim Wakefield. With the key members of his bullpen having had the first game off, Francona replaced Wakefield with setup man Scott Williamson, who struck out Bernie Williams for the second out. After walking Jorge Posada to load the bases, Williamson effectively lifted himself from the game complaining of discomfort in his right elbow, which had been surgically repaired earlier in his career.

So, with two outs and the bases now loaded, Francona called upon reliever Mike Timlin, who got Tony Clark to whistle a hard grounder toward David Ortiz, whom Francona had started at first base so that Kevin Millar (in right field) and Trot Nixon (the designated hitter) also could be in the lineup against the Yankees' right-handed starter, Jon Lieber. Clark's grounder broke through Ortiz' glove for an error that produced a pair of runs, tying the game at 2. An inning later, Timlin and Embree allowed RBI hits to Gary Sheffield and Hideki Matsui, respectively, and impenetrable Yankees closer Mariano Rivera struck out all three Red Sox batters he faced in the top of the ninth to preserve the 4–2 Yankees win.

In the aftermath of this defeat, Bostonians did not need the New York media to tell them that the Red Sox appeared to be unraveling. While Ortiz' error further highlighted the defensive deficiencies of the club, the team's frustration was beginning to show. Following the final out, Francona left the dugout and walked up the runway to the Red Sox clubhouse, where a cluster of reporters already had gathered to descend upon the Red Sox following another tough loss. From a reporter's perspective, this was one of the only true benefits of covering a game at Yankee Stadium, where the holding place for the media allowed a clear view of the clubhouse door. Francona clearly was aware of that fact as he scurried by, so it was uncertain whether his actions were truly genuine or simply theatrical in nature.

In any case, it made for great copy.

"Fuck!" screamed the frustrated manager as he zipped into the clubhouse.

Within the next 18 hours, before the Sox and Yankees played the unforgettable series finale that permanently altered the course of the Red Sox season, there were more signs that the Red Sox were reaching their breaking point. During Francona's pregame session with the media, a television reporter from New York asked the manager about another alleged confrontation between teammates, this one involving Schilling and Williamson. Francona claimed to have no knowledge of the incident, but he did not deny it, either. Neither did Schilling, for that matter, a notable contrast to the response of the pitcher—and the team—following the perceived incident between Schilling and Varitek.

This time, it turned out, the confrontation was real.

And the reaction of the Red Sox proved it.

Up to that point, in fact, there had been a growing feeling among Sox players and officials that Williamson was unwilling to pitch through pain, that he was unwilling to make the sacrifices that many players deemed necessary in order to win. It was all part of the code that players lived by, and the fact that Schilling was the messenger was fitting, if only for the reason that he was continuing to deal with his problematic right ankle. For all of Schilling's bluster, even teammates felt he had a right to speak up on this one, to confront Williamson at a time the Red Sox were struggling to stay within arm's length of the Yankees in the American League East. Even after the Red Sox left New York and traveled to Atlanta for the Fourth of July weekend—and even after it became clear that Williamson's injury was legitimate and would require surgery—one club official defended Schilling's actions, suggesting that the message to Williamson "needed to be said."

Schilling did not admit confronting Williamson, but he did not deny it, either.

"I'm not going to comment on that. Anything that happens within this clubhouse is going to stay within this clubhouse," Schilling said.

Pressed further on the matter, Schilling said: "To come in and scream and yell doesn't do any good. We're grown men. There are going to be times when tension increases in this clubhouse when we're not doing well. This isn't about anybody coming in here and chewing anybody's ass out. This is about making sure the name on the front of the jersey is more important than the name of the back."

Enough said.

Yet for all that happened on the field and in the Red Sox clubhouse over the first two days of the Yankees series, the third and final game was about to trump it all. (Or is that Trump?) On July 1, with the Yankees holding a seven-and-a-half-game lead, the Red Sox and Yankees met in a contest of obvious importance. With a Red Sox victory, despite all that had gone wrong in the first two games, the Red Sox could leave New York only six and a half games out of first place, having sacrificed just one game in the standings. With a Yankees victory, New York could open a whopping eight-and-a-half-game lead nearly halfway through the season, and the Yankees were not the kind of team to blow an eight-and-a-half-game lead against anybody, let alone the Red Sox.

In some ways, it seemed as if both teams recognized that the 2004 American League East might very well be decided on July 1.

And, consequently, they played like it.

Though the game seemed to be a mismatch on paper—the Sox sent Pedro Martinez to the mound against unknown left-hander Brad Halsey—the Yankees took a 3–0 lead into the sixth, when Boston rallied for a pair of runs. The Red Sox added another run in the seventh, tying the score at 3 and further setting the stage for what many would later describe as one of the greatest regular season games in baseball history. Both Francona and Yankees skipper Joe Torre managed the game aggressively—Francona called upon closer Keith Foulke to start the eighth inning with the game *tied*—and both the Sox and Yanks repeatedly dodged bullets—the Yankees stranding 11 baserunners from the sixth inning through the 12th, the Red Sox leaving two on in the sixth, two in the seventh, and a combined four in the 11th, 12th, and climactic 13th.

Along the way, what initially appeared to be a subplot exploded into a full-blown controversy surrounding arguably the two most identifiable players on the respective teams, the shortstops, Nomar Garciaparra and Derek Jeter. Given the magnitude of the game, many media members were stunned to learn that Garciaparra was not in the starting lineup, Francona instead going with a squad that had Varitek batting fifth and defensive wizard Pokey Reese at shortstop, batting ninth. Both the Red Sox and Garciaparra had indicated that there would be occasions when the player needed to rest his right Achilles in the wake of the injury that had sidelined him for roughly three months, but the timing seemed odd given the opponent and the circumstances.

Prior to the game, Francona was somewhat vague about why Garciaparra was absent from the lineup, leading to speculation that the player had asked for the night off. That theory gained considerable steam when, during the game, respected Yankees television analyst Jim Kaat spoke of a pregame conversation he had with Francona in which the Red Sox manager said he gave Garciaparra "every opportunity" to play, putting the onus squarely on the shortstop. And when the Red Sox went on to lose by a 5–4 score in 13 extraordinary innings, when the Sox scored once in the top of the 13th only to allow two runs in the bottom of the inning, when the fearless Jeter squelched a Red Sox rally in the 12th by recklessly diving headfirst into the box seats to catch a popup, everyone wanted to know the same thing:

Where was Nomar?

Why didn't he play?

Why wasn't he as committed as Jeter, who emerged from the box seats, ball in glove, bloodied and bruised, and had such little regard for his personal well-being that the play knocked him out of the game?

Television cameras only heightened the contrast, particularly when Garciaparra was shown sitting on the bench, alone, while the rest of teammates had gathered on the top of the dugout steps, as captivated by the events on the field as any paying spectator. All of it only pounded home the belief that Nomar Garciaparra frequently operated in a cocoon, that he was not the same kind of leader as the far more charismatic Jeter—who was?—that he was still struggling with the events of the offseason and that he was making decisions for *him* first.

And to the public, at least, the explanations were not satisfactory.

"About the ninth [inning], he was trying so hard to be available," Francona said in a vague explanation after the game. "The more the game progressed, he was trying to get loose so that he could go in."

Said Garciaparra: "I tried to get loose, but there were also points we thought I may go in. If there was an opportunity, we would have."

Of course, in a 13-inning game, there were countless opportunities. And while the matter would continue to escalate in subsequent days to the point where Sox general manager Epstein actually went on record as saying that Sox medical personnel deemed Garciaparra incapable of playing that night—the remark reeked of damage control—the lasting effect was that Garciaparra lost the respect of some of his teammates. Rightly or wrongly, the contrast between Jeter and Garciaparra was striking to them, too, and even Red Sox players were marveling at Jeter following the defeat, which bumped the Sox eight and half games behind the division leaders.

"That's why he's got four of those big fucking rings right here," said Schilling, pointing to the knuckles on his left hand and referring to the four championships the Yankees had won during Jeter's career.

Indeed, while the relationship between Nomar Garciaparra and the Red Sox was continuing to crumble, Jeter's place in the eyes of New Yorkers and Bostonians alike was becoming more exclusive. Shortly after Jeter barreled into the box seats and walked off the field, Yankees general manager Brian Cashman blew through the Yankee Stadium workroom at a frantic pace, on his way to the clubhouse with a concerned look on his face. He was going to check on his shortstop and captain, whom almost everyone recognized was the key to the success of the Yankees, along with indomitable closer Rivera.

In New York, of course, they often needed to be reminded of that because, as usual, they took greatness for granted. This was primarily the case with the members of the media, who found Jeter to be uncooperative in some of the same ways that the Boston media found Garciaparra difficult. Jeter was available to speak with reporters after every game, but his quotes were bland. He gave them nothing beyond clichés and the obvious rhetoric. Derek Jeter was a winner, one of the great clutch performers in baseball history, and he played the game with genuine, indisputable enthusiasm that was always apparent. He cheered on his teammates. He blamed no one. He did whatever it took to win a game—from putting down a sacrifice bunt to hitting a home run—and he did it all because that was *the right thing to do*.

But, naturally, the New York media wanted more.

They wanted him to be quotable and entertaining off the field, too.

At least that's how we Bostonians saw it.

Nonetheless, at dramatic times like this, even New York celebrated the uniqueness of Derek Jeter the baseball player, the competitor, the winner. And so as the Red Sox and Yankees once again parted ways roughly halfway through the baseball season, New York had an eight-and-a-half-game lead in the American League East and the Red

Sox had some serious soul-searching to do, and nobody in New England wanted to think about the possibility that things could get worse before they got better.

Publicly, at least, the Red Sox were putting on a happy face. Following the epic 5–4 loss in 13 innings, Francona waited at the clubhouse door—again, the media was watching—and greeted his players with very visible handshakes and pats on the back. ("Way to go! You guys are playing fucking great!" the skipper shouted loud enough for everyone to hear.) Inside the room, the players similarly and defiantly dug in their heels, as sure a sign as any that they, too, knew they were slipping.

"We're a good ballclub and we believe in that," Millar said after the sweep at the hands of the Yankees. "These are good times, these are good times to go through, this is what builds you, this is when you are judged and when you are tested because it's easy to come off the field when everything is going right and hunky-dory. These are good times for this team to go through now because this will make us stronger in October.

"These are minor disappointments, not major catastrophes," Millar continued. "Losing five games in a row, playing .500 ball for a month—it's a minor disappointment because we're a better club. It's not a major catastrophe, making an error in a game. These are good times to go through now because this makes our team stronger. And I promise you this team will be stronger will all this stuff."

Red Sox fans could only hope that was the case.

Deep down, after all, their traumatized souls were losing hope and faith.

JUNE HEAD-TO-HEAD—
REVELING IN RED SOX MISERY

For baseball reporters, writing on deadline during and after games—usually as midnight either approaches or passes—is a stressful process that sometimes makes you wonder why anybody would want to do it for a living. With practice, however, you learn to lock in and focus whether the crowd is roaring for a strikeout in the bottom of the ninth, Sinatra is blaring from the loudspeakers as the game ends, or the clean-up crew's gasoline-powered blowers are howling in the stands after the crowd has gone home. It's the nature of the beast. When deadline is approaching, the guy next to me better not have a heart attack, because I may not even notice.

Yet when the Red Sox are in town, there are exceptions to the rule. When the Sox lose, New York reporters take secret delight in sneaking peeks, deadline or no deadline, at their esteemed colleagues on the other side of the press box. The boys—and girls—from Boston will deny it until Ted Williams returns from his frozen state, but you can't convince us they don't take these things personally. After a tough loss you can see them working themselves into such a frenzy that smoke is all but rising from their laptops, they're pounding the keyboard so hard.

Damn Sox. Damn Pedro. Damn Nomar.

It's a different mentality for those guys. Ninety-nine percent of the Boston press corps grew up in New England practicing the religion that is Red Sox fandom. It's not that it keeps them from doing a professional job. They don't cheer openly for the Sox or anything. Quite the contrary, they're like the high school coach whose son is on the team; he's harder on his own kid than anyone else. For that matter, when the Sox lose, the local scribes lash out at times like parents compelled to deliver a spanking.

We like to believe we can be tough in New York, as well, but even the harshest rip jobs never seem quite as personal as some of the stuff you read in the Boston papers.

Before Massarotti howls in protest about my typical New York haughtiness, I offer objective testimony: Yankees' backup catcher John Flaherty is one of only a few players who have played for both the Red Sox, in 1992–93, and the Yankees, in 2003–04, and he nods his head when presented with the take-it-personally observation.

"I'd have to agree with that," Flaherty said. "When I first came up as a rookie with the Red Sox, a few of the veterans pulled me aside to warn me about certain writers who would really go after guys. I haven't experienced anything like that in New York. The media can be tough in New York, but I haven't seen where it's unfair. I do think it's a little different in Boston."

Maybe it's just that the attachment for New York reporters to either the Yankees or Mets isn't nearly as emotional, because we haven't experienced decades of longing for a championship—or perhaps because, in the case of the Yankees, George Steinbrenner runs the club with an arrogance and disregard for the media that makes it impossible to root for them.

In any case, in New York we get a chuckle out of watching the Sox press corps agonize every year over the club's inevitable failure to beat the Yankees when it counts. But as the Red Sox arrived in late June for a midweek three-game series, we were hoping not to see their usual exasperation. The Sox were already five and a half games out, playing uninspired baseball, and in New York we wanted a pennant race. If Boston couldn't put some heat on the Yankees, it would make for a long, boring summer of covering meaningless games against nondescript teams like the Tampa Bay Devil Rays and Toronto Blue Jays while waiting for October to arrive.

The Yankees had gone 40–15 since losing 6-out-of-7 to the Red Sox in April putting them comfortably in front, but questions about their pitching created a sense that they were still vulnerable. However, the Sox looked helpless in losing the first game 11–3, as they made three costly errors, and again their shaky defense cost them in the second game, as David Ortiz made a crucial error at first base late in the Yankees' 4–2 victory. At this point even we on the Yankee side of the press box were starting to sympathize with the Sox writers; watching this team add annually to its legacy of failure was as predictable as it was infuriating.

Yet even as the Yankees were pushing their lead to seven and a half games and heaping pressure on Pedro Martinez to rescue the Red Sox in the Thursday finale, they were confronted with a mysterious problem that stole at least some of the satisfaction of knowing they'd already won the series. Of all things, they were being attacked by a parasite.

On the day the series began, Jason Giambi was diagnosed as having an intestinal parasite in his system, which the Yankees thought explained the chronic fatigue he'd been experiencing. Of course, it also raised eyebrows, since Giambi was known for his love of the nightlife, and, well, surely you had to do something out of the ordinary to wind up with a parasite in your system. Giambi said that blood tests hadn't been able to determine the cause of his parasite, and the medical definition left it open to speculation: common causes include sexual activity; contact with contaminated water, undercooked food, poorly washed fruits and vegetables; or passage through the nose and skin.

Whatever the cause, Giambi was relieved to at least have an answer for his complete lack of energy in recent weeks that had rendered him ineffective at the plate, and was just plain making him feel old. "I'm 33, not 50," he complained.

Still, the news also made teammates wonder about Giambi, the one-time rebel leader of the A's who had tried but didn't fit comfortably in the Yankee environment since coming over as a free agent after the 2001 season. Ballplayers could relate to a hamstring pull or even the flu, but not a parasite. They had only a vague idea about what it was, but they knew it didn't belong in a locker room.

"Is it contagious?" one player quietly asked a reporter upon hearing the news. "What's he into, anyway?"

On the whole, however, players weren't concerned, assuming that Giambi somehow had only himself to blame for contracting a parasite. That changed the next day, however, when they learned Kevin Brown had been diagnosed with a parasite as well. He, too, had been at a loss for weeks to explain a constant feeling of fatigue that he was sure had nothing to do with the back problem that forced him onto the disabled list on June 9. Teammates may have thought Brown, a first-year Yankee, was a little crazy, having witnessed his extremely intense pursuit of perfection, but they were pretty sure they knew what he was into: he dedicated himself to pitching, on and off the field, and took exceptional care of his body. If he, too, had a parasite, maybe they were all at risk. Players began asking questions, to the point where GM Brian Cashman asked team physician Dr. Stuart Hershon to address the team an hour before the final game against the Red Sox and assure them the parasite wasn't contagious. Obviously it wasn't the ideal way to prepare for a game against Pedro and the Red Sox.

"The intensity wasn't really there when we took the field," Gary Sheffield recalled months later. "But Pedro took care of that."

You could see it coming from the press box. Sheffield, not quite ready as Pedro went into his windup against him in the first inning, asked for time and stepped out of the batter's box—not once, but twice in the same at-bat. Uh-oh. Sheffield may as well have given Pedro the finger, at least as far as Martinez was concerned. Sure enough, Martinez nailed Sheffield in the left shoulder with the next pitch, as unmistakable a purpose pitch as you'll ever see. Sheffield barely flinched, but as he moved a couple of steps toward first he glared at Pedro and growled, "Don't mess with me. You're messing with the wrong guy." Jason Varitek, who would intervene rather famously when Alex Rodriguez had similar words for Bronson Arroyo a few weeks later, said nothing to Sheffield, probably because he knew Pedro had hit him intentionally. Pedro himself didn't jaw with Sheffield, who had a reputation among fellow players as a true tough guy, perhaps at least partly because he took the most vicious swing in baseball and hit the ball so hard that Luis Sojo moved way out of the third base coaching box when Sheffield was at the plate. Sheffield, meanwhile, wasn't looking for a fight, at least not this time.

But later in the season, before the playoffs began, Sheffield issued a warning to Pedro, telling Tom Verducci in a *Sports Illustrated* story: "If he says one word to me, he's done. Pedro, your buddy pass is over. If he tries anything again, I won't hurt my team, but I'm telling you, I will take care of him."

On this night, Sheffield made his point and continued on to first base. No fireworks, but, as he said later, "I think that got everybody's juices flowing."

One way or another, it set the stage for one of the great regular-season games ever played between these teams. The Sox' desperate need to avoid a sweep added drama as the game went into extra innings, and for a while it looked as if it would be remembered for a spectacular play by Alex Rodriguez in the 11th inning to preserve a tie game. With the bases loaded, A-Rod made a diving stab of a hot shot, tagged third base with his glove for a force-out, then from his knees looped a throw perfectly over the runner, Manny Ramirez, to Jorge Posada, who applied the tag to complete a double play that seemed all the more remarkable considering A-Rod was still a relative newcomer to third base.

"To see that play," Joe Torre said, "you'd think he'd been playing there all his life, not three months."

Even so, A-Rod's game-saver became little more than a footnote an inning later when Derek Jeter made perhaps the play of the year. With runners at second and third and two outs, Trot Nixon flared a blooper into shallow left field, near the foul line. Because Jeter was shading the left-handed hitting Nixon toward second, he had a long run to get to the ball, at an angle almost perpendicular to the foul line. Racing at full speed, Jeter made the catch just inside the foul line and, because there is so little room between the line and the stands, had no chance to stop on the field. Instead he launched himself headfirst into the box seats, which were separated by metal railings. By itself the catch was a great play, a testament to both Jeter's quickness and acceleration. But what made it the talk of New York was the courage it took to make the catch at such speed, for Jeter knew a crash landing was unavoidable. In fact, as he caught the ball he made a conscious decision to dive over the photographers' pit, because he'd fallen in there making a less perilous catch in the playoffs in 2001, and discovered the hard way that it had a cement floor.

"So I tried to jump over that," he recalled weeks later. "Unfortunately, I ran into a chair."

Face-first, that is. Jeter went in so hard that he practically disappeared amid the fans, most of whom tried to grab him and help break his fall. He hit his face and shoulder so hard that he was left dazed, and it took him several seconds to gather himself and push himself to his feet. A-Rod, trailing the play, saw blood streaming from Jeter's face and signaled frantically to the Yankee dugout for medical help. "It looked like he'd been hit by Mike Tyson," A-Rod would say later. Jeter had a gash on his chin and a bruise under his right eye that left his face discolored. He was groggy as the Yankee trainers examined him, and Torre knew Jeter was hurting when, for once, he didn't put up a fight to stay in the game. Instead he was taken to nearby Columbia Presbyterian Hospital for X-rays on his cheek, which were negative, and medical people there told him how lucky he'd been, judging by his bruise, that he hadn't broken any orbital bones around his right eye.

"You don't think about that when you're making the play," Jeter would say later. "But after seeing (the tape of the play), I know I was lucky."

Back at the ballpark, meanwhile, the drama continued. The Red Sox pulled off their own Great Escape, preventing the Yankees from scoring after Miguel Cairo led off the bottom of the 12th with a triple. With Jeter out of the game, and the Yankee bench nearly depleted, Torre had to move A-Rod to short and Sheffield to third, a position he hadn't played since 1993, as the game went to the 13th inning. When Manny Ramirez blasted a home run off Tanyon Sturtze, it seemed the Sox would overcome all of the Jeter karma in the stadium. But then, with two outs and nobody on in the bottom of the 13th, Ruben Sierra singled off reliever Curtis Leskanic, and Cairo doubled to the wall in right-center, once again tying the game 4–4. By now the Yankees had substituted for their DH, and with Sturtze due to hit, Torre sent his last available position player, backup catcher John Flaherty, to pinch-hit. Flaherty pulled a Leskanic pitch down the left field line, over Ramirez' head, scoring Cairo without a play to give the Yankees a 5–4 win and stamp this game as an instant classic—as well as still another example of the one-sided history between these teams.

In the press box that night, there was precious little time to put such an extraordinary night into perspective. The game took four and a half hours to play, so the rush to make deadline was even more frantic than usual. Reporters scrambled to get down to the clubhouse, to get a reaction to the Pedro-Schilling staredown, the A-Rod play, the Jeter play, the late-inning madness on both sides. The game was practically a book in itself, and yet you couldn't forget the big picture. The Yankees' sweep now buried the Red Sox eight and a half games back in the standings—a full nine games in the loss column. As the exhilaration of the final innings gave way to the reality of the result, everyone seemed to understand what it meant: the race was over. The Sox were done, at least in the AL East. The Yankees weren't blowing this kind of lead, not unless the parasites in their locker room began multiplying.

The proof was in the keyboard-pounding on the other side of the press box. The Sox writers were pummeling Nomar Garciaparra, taking out their frustration on the star shortstop for not only choosing this night to rest his sore Achilles, but for sitting stone-faced on the bench, seemingly uncaring, even while teammates were on the top step of the dugout in the late innings. Late as it was, I couldn't resist a dig:

"Careful, Massarotti," I called out. "The vein in your forehead looks like it's about to pop."

I'm sure he heard me, but my distinguished coauthor never looked up from his laptop. He was in lockdown mode with deadline fast approaching. Apparently another Red Sox obituary took precedence over a New York wisecrack.

TROUBLED SOULS—RED SOX

IN THE END, NOMAR GARCIAPARRA NEVER ESCAPED FROM NEW YORK.

But for a time, at least, the original wonder boy of the Red Sox found refuge in Atlanta, where the Red Sox touched down following their forgettable three-day trip to Yankee Stadium. Atlanta was home to Georgia Tech University, where Garciaparra starred in college, and so it was a particularly familiar and comfortable place. That was especially important for a man who relied heavily on his routines, who nervously tugged at his batting gloves and obsessively tapped his toes during every at-bat, who went to painstaking lengths to merely put on his uniform, who would methodically place both feet on each stair while going up and down the dugout steps as if he were a toddler still uncertain of his ability to walk.

Yet for all of Garciaparra's quirks, tics, and neuroses, he remained a terrifying figure to opponents in the place that mattered most: the batter's box.

And by the conclusion of Fourth of July weekend in Atlanta, most everyone would be reminded of that.

Nonetheless, in the immediate aftermath of New York, Garciaparra remained under fire. Given the heroics of Yankees shortstop Derek Jeter in the final innings of the series finale, Garciaparra's absence from the game was striking to Red Sox officials and fans alike. Garciaparra was vilified on talk radio in Boston and questioned within the walls of Fenway Park, and, in retrospect, it was at the moment Jeter went headfirst into the box seats at Yankee Stadium, emerging bruised and bloodied, that Garciaparra's fate and future with the Red Sox were effectively and eternally sealed.

Derek Jeter was a winner.

As for Nomar Garciaparra—as preposterous as it seemed and was—there were those who now had their doubts.

"If this is his final chapter in Boston," Red Sox general manager Theo Epstein said in defense of his shortstop before the Sox opened the weekend series in Atlanta, "it's not how I want it to end."

Garciaparra, for his part, did his best to remain unaffected, shrouding himself in the cocoon of his game-day routines shortly after the team's arrival at Turner Field. Garciaparra won two batting championships during his Red Sox career and entered the 2004 season with identical regular- and postseason career averages of .323, and, prior to the disappointing 2003 postseason, he had batted .383 with seven home runs and 20 RBI in 20 career playoff games. He believed all of that counted for something. But Boston was a town where only one question mattered—what have you done for me *lately*?—and most all of Garciaparra's greatest achievements in a Red Sox uniform came before John Henry and his partners bought the team, before Larry Lucchino became club president, before Epstein became the youngest general manager in major league history.

Once at Turner Field, Garciaparra was getting dressed at his locker when approached by *Boston Globe* columnist Dan Shaughnessy, who informed Garciaparra that the player would be Shaughnessy's subject for his next column, to appear on the following day, Saturday, July 3. It was Shaughnessy's belief that the Red Sox should trade Garciaparra, an opinion the writer relayed to the player. And so before Garciaparra even took the field for batting practice on the night of Friday, July 2, he was aware that one of the most prominent sports columnists from the biggest newspaper in New England would be urging the Red Sox to trade him.

In retrospect, Shaughnessy's column should have raised a red flag. As a young reporter for the *Baltimore Sun*, Shaughnessy covered the Baltimore Orioles when Lucchino and Sox executive vice president of public affairs Charles Steinberg were employees for that team. And so years later, rightly or wrongly, there was a developing belief among some in Boston that Shaughnessy's opinions were being shaped by Lucchino and Steinberg, with whom he had maintained a relationship. Such occurrences were not uncommon in the media because certain writers had certain people they talked to, and those discussions frequently generated ideas. That was how the business worked. And if you were Larry Lucchino or Charles Steinberg, it made perfect sense to float the idea of trading Garciaparra by a writer like Shaughnessy, who could put it up for public debate while protecting the team's allegiance, at least publicly, to the player.

In regard to his relationship with Garciaparra, Shaughnessy tried to do the noble thing. Whether players liked it or not—and they didn't—reporters spent an extraordinary amount of time in the clubhouse, too. Unlike the other major sports, which restricted media access to players and coaches alike, Major League Baseball allowed reporters in the locker room three and a half hours before every game up until 45 minutes before the first pitch, then again 10 minutes after the final out. The clubhouse always could be closed at select times for team meetings and the like, but reporters otherwise had as much right to be in the room as the players themselves, which frequently created conflict, particularly in a place like Boston, where an enormous media contingent could often overrun the cramped space at antiquated Fenway Park.

In the clubhouse, players and writers would often acknowledge one another as if they were all workers in a large office building. Players and writers sometimes would engage in playful banter—"You're a no-style mother-fucker," former Red Sox first baseman Mo Vaughn once shot back at a *Herald* reporter who teased him about a rather bold outfit Vaughn once wore to the ballpark—but there was always an indisputable line never to be crossed. Ultimately, at the end of the day, most players and writers operated with an *Us versus Them* mentality, and the clubhouse belonged to the players. Shaughnessy thought it disingenuous to smile and laugh with a player like Garciaparra one moment, then sit down at his laptop and write a column bashing the guy's brains in. So Shaughnessy showed his cards, something certain writers sometimes did, so as not to be accused of an ambush when the paper hit the streets.

Does that mean everyone agreed with that practice? No. Some reporters, in particular, felt it was presumptuous to think that any player would care the least bit about what they wrote. Others felt no obligation whatsoever, fearing that any disclosure would be tantamount to relinquishing control. Others simply did not care enough to even think about it.

By the time Shaughnessy left the clubhouse, Garciaparra was annoyed. Garciaparra believed all reporters had an obligation to be fair, though he was among the many players who failed to understand that columnists were not only allowed to express their opinions, they were *encouraged*. That was their job. Still, in Garciaparra's mind, Shaughnessy had deprived him of the right to defend himself. He believed that Shaughnessy formed an opinion and had no intention of changing it, so what good did it do to talk to him about it? The entire Red Sox clubhouse was virtually empty by the time Garciaparra drifted into a hidden corner, where he relayed his version of accounts to a reporter from the *Herald*.

"Shaughnessy comes over and says, 'I'm going to write that they should trade you,'" Garciaparra said. "What does he want me to say? If I say something [convincing], is he going to change his mind? No."

At moments like this, and in the wake of the Yankees series, Garciaparra's insecurities were terribly apparent. He cared deeply about what people thought of him and he believed he was a good person, yet he simply could not control the perceptions and opinions of everyone, something he often grappled with during his career. Garciaparra loved being a superstar and role model and husband to the internationally recognized Mia Hamm, but he hated being criticized by people who did not know him and he allowed few people in his cocoon. He played hard. He played well. He gave back to the community and he did nothing to disgrace the Red Sox or himself. He expected to do everything right—and more often than not, he did—but he often felt as if he could not meet the unrealistic expectations of his critics.

Frequently, of course, his expectations for himself—and, often, of others—were far less reasonable.

More than any other event during Garciaparra's distinguished eight-year career in Boston, the controversy surrounding him following his final series at Yankee Stadium highlighted one of his greatest weaknesses: an inability to effectively communicate. Garciaparra was vague and circumspect about his absence from Game 7, and that only fueled the fire that was burning at his feet. But anyone who had examined or paid attention to Garciaparra's career in Boston would have noted that he almost *never* answered a question directly, which spoke primarily to the player's insecurity about being able to convey his message.

Example: in February 2003, following an off-season during which he and Hamm were engaged, Garciaparra reported to spring training and gave an inaugural spring address, as he did each year and as was expected of the star players on the Red Sox. Whether it was Vaughn or Roger Clemens, Garciaparra or Pedro Martinez, the player would sit at a chalky red picnic table just outside the team's spring training complex and bring reporters up to speed on the events of the off-season. *Was he healthy? Was he encouraged by the team's off-season maneuvers? Did he think this could be The Year?* Season after season, superstar after superstar, the drill was the same. It was one of the rites of a Red Sox spring.

That particular spring training, someone asked Garciaparra if he indeed had been engaged to Hamm, a question to which everyone already knew the answer. But the reporters wanted to hear it straight from Nomar's lips. At a moment where a succinct, simple *yes* would have sufficed, Garciaparra awkwardly spit out words and toyed with a bottle of spring water, often looking, to borrow a phrase from Michael J. Fox in *The Secret of My Success*, "like a long-tailed cat in a room full of rocking chairs."

So was it true that he and Hamm were getting married?

"Am I getting married? I don't know," Garciaparra answered. "Every time I read about it, you know what I mean, it's 'Am I getting married?' or 'Am I doing this or other things?' But yes, I am getting married, eventually. When that time comes, when our schedules permit, I'm sure we'll get married. So yeah."

Later that morning, away from the media horde, Garciaparra leaned against a wall in the Red Sox clubhouse and bared his soul for one of the few times in his Red Sox career. Most reporters came to believe that Garciaparra detested the media during his time with the Sox, but what he truly detested was *the process*. Like any player, Garciaparra liked some members of the media better than others, but he was painfully uncomfortable answering questions, particularly in larger settings, where he had little control over the interpretation of his remarks. To a large extent, Garciaparra *feared* the media, which is something most reporters never understood about him. Nomar Garciaparra often was *terrified* that he would say the wrong thing or, worse yet, *tell the truth*, revealing that, yes, he sometimes had selfish and petty thoughts, just like everyone else. That he was, of all things, human.

So it when it came to dealing with reporters, Garciaparra locked up and did the worst thing he could do: he gave the media nothing. He came off as uncooperative and standoffish. He seemed to focus on the bad things about playing for the Red Sox more than the good things.

If only people could have understood him better.

"I definitely expect myself to be a certain way, but at the same time you're in an environment where you're walking on eggshells and [that] can ruin you," Garciaparra said during the spring of 2003, giving a peek into the pressure he placed on himself every day as a member of the Red Sox. "Let's face it: There are things that still get brought up about some guys from six, seven or eight years ago so you have to watch everything. You're constantly stressed. And so if you're not careful, everything gets destroyed that you've worked so hard for. . . . My rapport is with the fans. I've got a job to do. This is who I am. Everybody knows I have a regimen. I'm meticulous. That's why I'm successful. I want people to respect that."

More than a year later, from the moment the New York series came to a close, Garciaparra was on the hot seat. During the final days of Garciaparra's two-month absence from the team to start the 2004 season, some Sox officials began whispering that maybe Garciaparra was sticking it to team officials by coming back on his terms and his terms alone. Asked about such a possibility, Epstein, for one, resisted the urge—"I choose not to believe that," he said—but the young general manager seemed to be in the minority. And when such theorizing began appearing in the media through unnamed sources—Shaughnessy was among the first to offer a hint of speculation—Garciaparra pinned his resentment almost squarely on club president Lucchino, who had an abrasive personality that, over the years, had ruffled more than a few feathers in baseball. Whether Lucchino was the actual leak was irrelevant, of course, because in the structure that was the front office of the new Red Sox ownership, Lucchino was indisputably the "bad cop" to Epstein's "good cop."

And in the eyes of Nomar Garciaparra, especially, Larry Lucchino was the guy to blame.

So, by the time Garciaparra returned to the Red Sox following his injury, he was carrying enough baggage to fill a cargo jet. Garciaparra was still bitter about the team's efforts to trade him and, just as importantly, the team's pursuit of Rodriguez, whom owner John Henry literally had wined and dined.

Emotionally and physically, he was hurt. It was a contract year. And now people were questioning both his work ethic and his integrity, all of which helped explain why he arrived at Yankee Stadium in late June with a .233 batting average, albeit in just 14 games after being activated from the disabled list.

Looking distracted and disinterested, Garciaparra made two errors in the New York series opener, an 11–3 loss. He played better the next night but finished 0-for-4 in another defeat—this one was 4–2—and, with the Red Sox facing a sweep, was absent from manager Terry Francona's starting lineup before the series finale. That fact did not sit well with either Sox fans or officials, who had long since developed a chronic inferiority complex when it came to the Yankees. As a result, an absurd and unreasonable amount of emphasis was placed on the games with New York, whether they were played at the beginning of a season, the end, or in this case, the middle. That type of mentality only would have caused someone like Garciaparra to dig in his heels further, which is precisely what he did.

If Nomar Garciaparra wanted or needed a day off, he was going to take one.

No matter who, what, when, or where.

Said Garciaparra prior to the Yankees finale while joining his teammates in pregame batting practice: "Why does it matter if it's here or anywhere else?"

Whether Garciaparra was unavailable or unwilling to play remains forever uncertain, and over the next several weeks the player, manager, and team engaged in a game of verbal tennis. Had the Red Sox won the epic against the Yankees—a 5–4 loss in 13 positively scintillating innings after overcoming a 3–0 deficit entering the top of the sixth—there is no telling how insignificant the matter may have been. There is no telling, too, if things might have been different without the heroics of shortstop Jeter, Garciaparra's counterpart and measuring stick, who played the role of Joe DiMaggio to Garciaparra's character of Ted Williams in the greatest rivalry in professional sports.

Instead, Garciaparra was roundly criticized for failing to appear in the game, for failing to *force* his way in, for failing to sacrifice himself like Jeter did. He was criticized even for failing to join his teammates on the top step of the dugout during the game's tensest moments, choosing instead to remain on the bench, where television cameras made him look even more isolated. Garciaparra would say later that he *always* remained on the bench because it was one of his superstitions—"Everywhere we go, I have a place where I sit," he said—even suggesting that teammates probably would have sent him back to his seat if he did anything out of the ordinary. In short, Garciaparra felt that he would have been criticized no matter what he did, a statement that contained more than a measure of truth.

But where many people would have shrugged and moved on, Nomar Garciaparra felt paralyzed.

"So you tell me," Garciaparra said. "How should I act?"

Alas, the controversy carried into Atlanta, where Shaughnessy approached Garciaparra before a pitch was thrown. Garciaparra subsequently went out and collected three hits in a 6–3 loss on Friday, three more (including a home run) in a 6–1 victory on Saturday. In the Sunday series finale, he went 1-for-4 with an intentional walk, the latter coming when accomplished Atlanta manager Bobby Cox chose to bypass Garciaparra and load the bases *in the third inning*, bringing to the plate the estimable Manny Ramirez, one of the most productive hitters of the 2004 season and annually one of the most feared sluggers in the game. At that moment, having pounded pitch after pitch at spacious Turner Field, Nomar Garciaparra had at least the respect of one of the most esteemed managers in baseball history.

When Ramirez followed by scorching a two-run double in what would become a three-run Red Sox rally, the Red Sox had a 4–0 advantage. The lead was 4–1 entering the fifth inning, when Sox starter Derek Lowe completely unraveled in a nine-run Atlanta rally that propelled the Braves to a lopsided 10–4 victory. And so just as Garciaparra was beginning to wake up, just as the Red Sox appeared to be righting their ship, Derek Lowe melted in the Atlanta heat and destroyed any momentum the team seemed to be building.

Derek Lowe now became the object of scorn among Red Sox fans and officials.

And Nomar Garciaparra, it seemed, was off the hook.

"I think he has friends on this team that talk to him and I feel comfortable talking to him. Has that happened? I can't confirm or deny," Red Sox catcher Doug Mirabelli said when asked about Garciaparra's awakening. "But I do know we need him if we want to win. We need him. He's an All-Star shortstop and somebody this team counts on, the sooner the better, and it looks like it's coming."

Said Red Sox catcher Jason Varitek, one of Garciaparra's best friends on the team and a former teammate at Georgia Tech University: "I think there was an overall consensus, not just with him, but this team came to a realization going into that last game in New York. Yeah, we lost [to the Yankees], but guys were going about things the right way. I don't think anybody said anything to him [in particular]. It's been more of a team thing. A lot of guys have been doing a lot of talking about how we can turn this thing around."

Added Varitek of his friend and teammate: "He's just starting to find his swing. It's a beautiful thing to see."

Indeed, it was.

At least for a while.

Derek Lowe never showed up at his locker to explain himself following his July 4 implosion at Turner Field, as sure a sign as any that he, like the Red Sox, had hit rock bottom. Now 80 games into the 2004 season, the Red Sox were a mere 43–37 overall and a miserable 28–31 since their 15–6 start. Incredibly, the Sox were just two and one-half games better than the Tampa Bay Devil Rays, who were a surprising 40–39 thanks to a recent hot streak. But where the Red Sox had a payroll approaching $130 million, Tampa Bay entered the season paying its players a combined $29.5 million, not much more than the Red Sox were paying Manny Ramirez alone.

Nobody was more emblematic of the team's struggles than Lowe, who was now 6–8 with a gruesome 6.02 ERA and whose entire career in Boston had been defined by dramatic climbs and falls.

As frustrations in the clubhouse were mounting, Lowe was losing the support of his teammates and, more important, his manager. Even before the Atlanta game, Sox skipper Terry Francona had obvious concerns about his slumping sinkerballer, and that was before Lowe caved in against the Braves. Typically an apologist for his players, Francona met with reporters following the Braves game and said, rather pointedly, that Lowe "didn't come close to stopping the bleeding."

For Francona, that qualified as a cannon shot.

And there was more.

"It can't happen," said the manager. "He's got a pitching coach that has confidence in him, he's got a manager that has confidence in him and he's got teammates that have confidence in him. At some point, he's got to do it."

Said pitcher Curt Schilling when asked of Lowe: "The bottom line is you've got to will yourself to do some things."

In fact, everyone already had lost confidence in Derek Lowe.

Including Lowe himself.

Such a happening was not unusual for Lowe during his career, which is part of the reason why the Red Sox ended up with him in the first place. Blessed with tremendous athletic ability, Lowe was headed to college on a basketball scholarship when the Seattle Mariners drafted him in the eighth round of the 1991 draft. Within several years, after an unpredictable minor-league career with the Mariners, Seattle officials had come to the conclusion that Lowe was what many scouts referred to as a *drifter*, meaning that he lacked the focus necessary to succeed in the major leagues. So the Mariners traded him for veteran relief pitcher Heathcliff Slocumb on July 31, 1997, a trade in which the Mariners also sent the Red Sox another player who had been a disappointment, catcher Jason Varitek.

In Boston, Slocumb for Varitek-and-Lowe would become a baseball Brinks Job, one of the most favorably lopsided trades in Red Sox history.

Once with the Red Sox, Lowe continued to oscillate between good and bad. In 1998, he began the season as a starter, going 0–7 before finally winning a game. Late in the year he was transferred to the bullpen, where he began to blossom as a middle reliever and setup man for closer Tom Gordon. Lowe had a solid 1999 season and became the closer in 2000, posting 42 saves to tie Detroit Tigers closer Todd Jones for the American League lead. A year later, Lowe was a mental mess again, finishing 5–10 with a 3.53 ERA and 24 saves in 30 chances, demonstrating such infuriating inconsistency that the Red Sox acquired a new closer, Ugueth Urbina, from the Montreal Expos. So Lowe went back to the rotation, winning 21 games in a brilliant 2002 campaign, then won 17 more in 2003 season that gave him more victories over that two-year span than any pitcher in baseball but Toronto Blue Jays ace right-hander Roy Halladay.

By 2004, expectations for Derek Lowe were high.

And when he began sinking like a cast-iron coffin, he was dragging the Red Sox down with him.

Lowe was not the only reason for the team's disappointing play, of course, but there were few players in baseball who could wallow in self-pity quite like him. In 2001, when Lowe was struggling through his second season as a closer, the player was sitting at his locker, slouched in a clubhouse chair, following what had become a painful but familiar defeat. Lowe had a beer in his hand as Varitek sat nearby, nervously watching his friend and teammate when a reporter approached. Lowe spoke slowly, slightly slurring his words at times, lamenting his plight as a tragic figure on what was, at the time, a similarly underachieving team.

Where players like Jason Varitek would get angry and *fight*, Derek Lowe would frequently sulk.

It took him a great deal longer to fight back, to get mad.

"Everyone tells me to trust my stuff," said Lowe, who was blessed with a dominating sinker. "But it's not that easy."

And the tougher it got, the harder Derek Lowe made it for himself.

After the Atlanta game on July 4, as if recognizing that they were throwing away their season, the Red Sox finally awakened. The Sox opened a six-game home stand against the Oakland A's, the team they had beaten in the 2003 AL Division Series and a playoff contender again in 2004. The Sox blistered the A's by a combined score of 22–3 in the first two games of a three-game series, then took the finale, in 10 innings, by an 8–7 count. The team then posted consecutive victories against the Texas Rangers by scores of 7–0 and 14–6—Lowe did not pitch especially well in the latter game, but received tremendous run support—before a somewhat disappointing 6–5 loss to Texas in the first-half finale. But after going 1–5 on the road against New York and Atlanta, the Red Sox had returned home to go 5–1 against the A's and Rangers, entering the All-Star break with a 48–38 record and renewed optimism, albeit seven games behind the first-place Yankees.

Still, there were problems. Two days prior to the Texas game—but after having replaced Garciaparra as the punching bag of the month on Boston sports radio—Lowe was approached on July 8 by a reporter asking a rather coarse question: *how's your head?* The query clearly struck a nerve with Lowe, who, in fact, already had been seeing renowned sports psychologist Harvey Dorfman through the suggestion of the pitcher's agent, Scott Boras. Lowe also had heard similar criticism from former Sox pitching coach and manager Joe Kerrigan during Kerrigan's five-year stint in Boston, and there was little doubt that his nerves were fully exposed on the night of July 8.

Derek Lowe was frustrated.

And he needed to vent.

"When Pedro or Curt or anybody pitches a bad game, they pitch bad. I pitch bad and I'm a mental gidget. Obviously it's gotten to the point where I can't take it anymore," Lowe said. "I'm pitching like shit; I'll be the first one to admit it. I've had one of the worst first halves in baseball; I'll be the first one to admit that. Why can't it be that I just pitched like shit? Why is it always the approach of the mental side?"

Concluded the pitcher: "You can talk about the physical stuff all you want. It's when you continue talking about someone's mental approach, when you really don't maybe know somebody . . . there does come a point and time where you actually have to stick up for yourself."

From the perspective of the rest of the Red Sox, this was precisely what they wanted: for Lowe *to fight for himself.* But Lowe went out two days later and allowed six unearned runs in the game against Texas, a performance that nonetheless earned him a win when Red Sox hitters, almost in spite of their pitcher, abused Rangers hurlers (and starter Kenny Rogers, in particular) for 11 runs in the first three innings. And so Derek Lowe went into the All-Star break with a 7–8 record and 5.57 ERA, hardly the type of numbers the Red Sox expected from their No. 3 starter when the team broke camp at the end of April.

A few days later, when the Red Sox opened the second half in California against the Anaheim Angels, Francona made the bold decision to begin anew with Lowe in a remarkable show of faith. The Red Sox subsequently went out and absorbed a lopsided 8–1 loss as Lowe allowed nine hits, four runs, and three walks in just four and two-thirds innings. The Sox responded by winning two of the next three games from the Angels before a disappointing split in Seattle against the woeful Mariners, then returned home to lose twice more to the inferior Baltimore Orioles. And so, after showing so much promise during the days just before the All-Star break, the Red Sox had once again slipped into a funk, possessors of a 52–43 record with a mere 67 games to play in the 2004 campaign.

Along the way, the most symbolic scene of the early second half came in Anaheim, where designated hitter David Ortiz uncharacteristically erupted at home plate umpire Matt Hollowell following a called third strike. Though remarkably good-natured, Ortiz had developed a reputation for complaining about balls and strikes, a flaw that in this case earned him an ejection. An enraged Ortiz, responded, in turn, by heaving bats from the Red Sox dugout in the direction of Hollowell, an unfortunate decision that ultimately would earn the player a four-game suspension from the powers that ran Major League Baseball.

And so, just nine games into a second half during which the Red Sox had won four games and lost five, the final message was clear.

Derek Lowe was not alone in feeling frustration from the 2004 baseball season.

And as luck would have it, the Yankees were coming to town next.

With Lowe struggling, general manager Theo Epstein was doing something he never anticipated in the weeks leading up to the July 31 trading deadline: searching for pitching. After generally keeping intact a 2003 Red Sox lineup that had rewritten history, Epstein believed he had addressed the team's pitching deficiencies with the off-season additions of Foulke and Schilling, the latter of whom was a proven big-game pitcher and had won the 2001 World Series with the Arizona Diamondbacks.

But with Lowe fouling up the plan, Epstein once again initiated discussion with the Diamondbacks, this time about prized left-hander Randy Johnson.

It was following Lowe's meltdown in Atlanta, in fact, that word of the Sox' interest in the left-hander first leaked, though Red Sox officials always remained cautious when speaking about deals for players like Johnson because such trades seldom materialized. If the off-season pursuit of Alex Rodriguez proved anything to the Red Sox, it was that no trade was complete until the final pieces were in place, and even then there were complexities that could thwart the deal. In the case of Johnson, the pitcher would have to approve any trade, and that was not likely to take place without a contract extension. Even then, Johnson would later tell reporters in Arizona that he had no desire to go to a place that *theoretically* had a chance to win, a fact that led most baseball observers to conclude that Johnson was interested in going one place and one place only.

New York.

Nonetheless, the Red Sox were prepared to take on Johnson for the balance of 2004, not to mention 2005, when Johnson was due a salary of $16.5 million. Privately, the pitcher's agents—Alan Nero and Barry Meister—were indicating that Johnson's first choice was to play for the Yankees, though New

York had even greater shortcomings than the Red Sox when it came time to negotiate a deal. Even more so than the Red Sox' farm system, which was in the process of being rebuilt under Epstein, the Yankees' system had been depleted as the result of New York's aggressiveness in signing free agents, which often required the forfeiture of compensatory draft picks. Add to that the trades the Yankees had made in recent years and New York had very little to offer in the way of young, blossoming talent to a team like the Diamondbacks, which was enduring a positively wretched 2004 campaign.

In Boston and New York, predictably, the Johnson talks took on a life of their own, and Epstein more than once expressed frustration at the manner in which the media was covering the story. The Los Angeles Dodgers and Anaheim Angels also were believed to have an interest in Johnson for a time, and there was reason to believe that either of those clubs had a better chance of securing Johnson than either the Red Sox or Yankees. In the end, the idea of Johnson ending up in Boston slowly drifted away, though that did not stop Epstein from discussing a variety of trade scenarios involving Lowe, including one with the San Diego Padres (for Brian Lawrence) and another with the Philadelphia Phillies (for Kevin Millwood).

As the July 31 deadline approached, then, it became increasingly clear that Epstein was not interested in making a trade unless it was a deal of significance. A year earlier, while trying to address a handful of needs, Epstein reluctantly made a deal for Pittsburgh Pirates right-hander Jeff Suppan, who was the best pitcher available on the market. Suppan proved so ineffective in the final two months of the season that the Red Sox removed him from their playoff roster for the American League Division Series against the Oakland A's. And though Suppan was added to the playoff roster in time for the AL Championship Series against the Yankees, the right-hander never appeared in any of the seven games with New York.

In the wake of all of that, Theo Epstein had learned his lesson.

He was not interested in making a trade for the sake of making a trade.

And he was not afraid to think big.

CAPTAIN CLUTCH: GUARDING GREATNESS—YANKEES

More than a decade later it seems unthinkable, but in the summer of 1992 the Yankees were in the middle of their fourth straight losing season. In their first year as a tandem, manager Buck Showalter and general manager Gene Michael were slowly beginning to restore pride to an organization that had become nothing short of a laughingstock, thanks to years of bad free-agent signings, six managerial changes between 1988 and 1992, and, finally, George Steinbrenner's suspension from baseball for paying a huckster named Howie Spira to dig up dirt on one of his stars, Dave Winfield, with whom he'd been feuding for years.

Showalter's attention to detail and demand for hustle, and Michael's commitment to rebuilding a barren farm system rescued the Yankees from disaster and planted the seeds that blossomed during Joe Torre's tenure. History will mark 1996, Torre's first season as manager, as the beginning of another championship era for the most storied franchise in sports, but to find a true starting point you probably have to go back to that 1992 season—and particularly June 4, the day that baseball's annual amateur draft was held.

Derek Jeter was never supposed to wind up a Yankee. He was considered the best high school player in the country that year, a hard-hitting shortstop from Kalamazoo, Michigan, with the kind of long, lean, athletic body that scouts love for purposes of projecting into the future. The Yankees, drafting sixth that year because of their lousy 71–91 record in 1991, didn't think they'd have a shot at Jeter. In baseball, however, the odds of such can't-miss prospects making good on their potential are considerably longer than in sports such as football and basketball, particularly for high school players who are thought to be at least three or four years away from reaching the major leagues. And as bonuses for the highest first-round choices had risen into the $1 million range in the previous few years, teams were becoming more and more cautious about picking high school players.

At the time the Yankees couldn't afford to be wrong, as they desperately needed to restock a farm system that had withered in the '80s when Steinbrenner was signing free agents such as Dave LaPointe, Andy Hawkins, and Steve Kemp—flops that cost the organization No. 1 draft picks. And Jeter was a risk in more ways than one. He had already accepted a scholarship to the University of Michigan, and baseball people knew that signing him wouldn't be easy, at least partly because both of his parents wanted their son to attend college. In addition, drafted high school players have built-in leverage because, unlike basketball, they have the right to go play in college if they don't sign, and then are eligible for the draft again in three years—or just one year if they attend a junior college.

As Yankees' GM Brian Cashman, then a baseball operations assistant, recalled years later, "Word on the street was that Jeter was going to be a tough sign. But our Michigan area scout, Dick Groch, worked hard to assess the situation, and he told us that if Jeter was still on the board, we couldn't pass him up."

What Groch had learned was that Jeter was a Yankee fan because he had spent the bulk of his summers as a young boy visiting his grandmother in Pequannock, New Jersey, and, he would say, "she always had the Yankees on TV." As a result, Jeter came to idolize Winfield as his favorite player and began to dream of playing for the Yankees. Still, as the draft approached, baseball people were telling Jeter there was no way he'd last past the fifth pick.

"I never thought about the Yankees," he said years later. "I was supposed to go either first or fifth. Houston had the first pick, and people were saying they'd take me. If not, I was definitely supposed to go to Cincinnati at No. 5. I think both of them decided they wanted a college player, someone who was closer to being ready for the big leagues."

By all accounts, that was the case with the Astros, who decided they couldn't pass up infielder Phil Nevin, the college player of the year from Cal-State Fullerton who has gone on to become an accomplished major leaguer.

The next three picks were college players as well: the Cleveland Indians took Paul Shuey, a hard-throwing pitcher from North Carolina who has become a decent major-league reliever; the Montreal Expos picked Billy Wallace, an outfielder from Mississippi State who never made it to the majors; and the Baltimore Orioles took Jeffrey Hammonds, an outfielder from Stanford who has had some solid years in the majors.

So Jeter was there for the Cincinnati Reds, but they elected to take Chad Mottola, an outfielder from Central Florida University who had only a marginal major-league career. At the time the Reds said they preferred a college player, but baseball people say the decision was purely a matter of money. The team was owned at the time by Marge Schott, who had a reputation in the industry for being notoriously cheap, especially when it came to scouting and player development, and word around the majors, then and now, was that she overruled the scouting department and refused to let them draft Jeter.

A current National League general manager who was an assistant GM at the time, recalls that "their scouts were livid about it. Their baseball people all wanted Jeter."

Upon being asked about that draft day a decade later, Jeter quickly rattled off the names of the five players drafted ahead of him, then smiled.

"For whatever reason, I'm glad those teams didn't draft me," he said. "Or obviously, I wouldn't be a Yankee."

Such a notion seems unfathomable all these years later. The Yankees grabbed Jeter that day and signed him to a bonus of $800,000. They resisted the temptation to move him to another position, à la Mickey Mantle or Bobby Murcer, when he made 57 errors in his first full minor-league season, believing his defense would improve as he gained professional experience. From the start the Yankees were impressed by his maturity off the field, and his instincts on the field, none more so than Torre, who decided that Jeter would be his starting shortstop practically from the first moment he saw him as a rookie in spring training of 1996. But no one in the organization imagined that Jeter would quickly stamp himself as a Yankee legend, partly because of a selfless style that has defined the Torre era, but more so because of a remarkable ability to deliver with both his glove and bat in the biggest games.

"We knew he had good makeup, that's one of the reasons we wanted him," Michael, now the Yankees' top scout, said, years after drafting him. "But you couldn't know he'd be such a special player. The things he does, he never stops amazing me."

By 2004 the Yankees thought they'd seen Jeter do it all. There were so many memorable moments, most of them in the postseason, that Reggie Jackson, an adviser to the club who traveled with the team from time to time, had begun calling him Mr. October II—no small acknowledgment, considering Reggie went through the U.S. patent office a few years ago to have the nickname patented as his own. And though Jeter had just turned 30 in June, it seemed likely that he already had made the signature play of his career with his famous catch-and-backhand flip of an overthrow from the outfield to nip Jeremy Giambi at the plate in the 2001 playoffs against the Oakland A's. But then came the catch-and-dive into the stands against the Red Sox on July 1, a play that redefined his budding legacy, and, because of the attention it received, probably went a long way toward earning him his first Gold Glove, the defensive award voted by opposing players, coaches, and managers, after the 2004 season.

For years Jeter had been known for his clutch play and his uncanny baseball instincts, not to mention his cover-boy good looks that left females, both young and old, breathless. His toughness, by contrast, was largely unheralded, yet it was the quality his teammates appreciated most about him. Jeter would sooner reveal the identity of his latest girlfriend to the gossip-page editors than admit to being bothered by an injury. He has played through a variety of ailments over the years that likely would have put other players on the bench, refusing to use them as an excuse even when they affected his play. Jeter played through so many injuries that Reggie once said of him, "You'd have to put a gun to his head to get him out of the lineup."

Not even Jeter could tough his way through a dislocated shoulder in 2003, however, the result of a freak play in which Toronto catcher Ken Huckaby, hustling to cover an open base, came crashing down on Jeter's headfirst slide at third base. The injury forced Jeter to miss 36 games, but typically, as he was walking off the field that day, in pain but unaware of the extent of the injury, he told Joe Torre he'd be ready to play the next day.

"I'm sure he believed it, too," Torre recalled months later.

Jeter made no such promises after his dive into the stands against the Red Sox, perhaps because he was too dazed to think straight. But sure enough, he was back at shortstop the next night at Shea Stadium as the Yankees and Mets met for Part II of the annual Subway Series. Doctors had sewn seven stitches into Jeter's chin to close the gash he received, courtesy of the wooden chair and metal box-seat railing, and his right cheek was still puffy and discolored. Surely he could have used a night off, and the timing was right, after the 13-inning victory the night before had opened an eight-and-a-half-game lead over the Red Sox. But Jeter dismissed such suggestions from the Yankees' medical people, insisted he was fine, and couldn't understand why anyone would think otherwise.

Jeter reluctantly met with reporters in the visitors' clubhouse at Shea to answer questions about his condition, and, as usual, left them frustrated. They wanted him to say something poignant, something profound, something funny. Anything that would reveal at least a little bit of the inner Jeter, the computer chip in his brain that accounted for such fearlessness. Instead he talked about the play with his usual detachment, as though describing a routine ground ball, and dismissed suggestions he had done something heroic.

"You've got to play hard," he said. "That's your job, to lead by example. It's a bonus that we won, but I would have done the same thing if you told me we were going to lose."

This was both the beauty and the curse of covering Jeter. His simple approach, unaffected by his rise to superstar status, made him the most admirable of ballplayers. His brief, simplistic answers, on the other hand, made him a maddening subject. He had long since mastered the art of answering questions without revealing much of anything about himself, and especially at a time like this, when the media wanted only to canonize him, it could be exasperating. It was also a subject of constant debate among reporters: was Jeter consciously refusing to play along, or was it merely a reflection of the depth of his personality?

More than the other major sports, baseball is the one, for better or for worse, in which players and reporters can't help getting to know one another. By decree of Major League Baseball, clubhouses are open to the press three and a half hours before game time, giving reporters a couple of hours before and after batting practice to interview players or just strike up casual conversation. For the most part, as long as a team isn't underachieving badly and taking a beating in the papers, it makes for a friendly relationship, at least among the beat reporters who cover the team on a daily basis and generally aren't asked to write critical columns of players. Over the years players and reporters have socialized as well, occasionally winding up in the same bar for a beer after a game. To a degree it still happens, especially in smaller media markets where there are fewer reporters and less aggressive reporting than New York or Boston. But in general, as multi-million dollar salaries have turned players into mini corporations, the gap between players and reporters has widened significantly over the last 10 to 20 years.

Nowhere is that gap wider than it is around the Yankees, where players are ever wary of reporters and have taken to spending most of their time before games in areas of the clubhouse that are off-limits to the press. The size of the media is a also factor in the changing nature of media relations around the Yankees; because they have become by far the biggest story over the last 10 years, New York newspapers send as many as seven or eight reporters and/or columnists to big games at home, and three or four even when the Tampa Bay Devil Rays are in town. Throw in reporters from more than a dozen smaller papers in New Jersey and Connecticut, and the locker room can be bulging with 40 to 50 print reporters, as well as camera crews from a handful of TV stations, at most every home game. Of course, the numbers are often formidable across town for Mets games as well, yet the atmosphere is far less tense and players are far more approachable.

The Steinbrenner-induced paranoia around the Yankees explains some of the tension, but Jeter's reticence has set a new tone over the years as well. He has kept reporters at such arm's length that after nine seasons, not even the beat writers feel like they know him. He almost never acknowledges reporters by name, and some guys who have been on the Yankees' beat for years swear he doesn't know their names. But in truth, Jeter knows more than he likes to admit, and apparently reads the clips provided by the team of even the newspapers he doesn't see, living in Manhattan. In spring training of 2003, for example, he made a point of singling out Bergen (New Jersey) *Record* columnist Bob Klapisch one day. Klapisch had written an item in a Sunday column during the off-season noting that Jeter now owned a private plane, with a pilot on call, and was using it to fly back and forth between his off-season home in Tampa and Michigan for visits with his parents. When the subject of media scrutiny came up as he talked with a few reporters at his locker, Jeter, as is his habit, noted how reporters too often get things wrong.

"Like the private-plane thing," Jeter said, addressing Klapisch. "I don't own that plane, I rent time on it. So get it right."

On weightier issues, Jeter could be calculating if he felt he'd been wronged by a story. He was furious with the *Daily News* in February of 2003, before spring training opened, over a back-page headline that read, "Party On." The story was a follow-up on George Steinbrenner's public criticism of Jeter that off-season, in which he essentially wondered whether the shortstop's production had gone down because Jeter was staying out late too much. Jeter, whose work ethic has always been exemplary, thought the criticism was absurd, so when *Daily News* reporter Roger Rubin asked him about it after a pre-spring training workout in Tampa, he said he had no intention of changing his habits.

"I'm not going to change," Jeter told Rubin. "Not at all."

The implication was that Jeter didn't need to change because he was far from a party animal. However, the quote left just enough wiggle room for the *Daily News* to turn it into something more controversial, a back page that made it seem as if he were David Wells, defiantly defending his right to cruise the bars and clubs in Manhattan until the sun came up. Jeter had a right to be upset, but as usual, he turned it into something bigger, holding a grudge against the entire New York media. When he was ready a couple of weeks later to address Steinbrenner's comments at length for the first time, just before he reported for spring training, Jeter had his agent arrange an interview with the Associated Press, a national wire service, purposefully snubbing the reporters who had covered—and glorified—him for years.

Of course, when Jeter subsequently cashed in by making the TV commercial with Steinbrenner for Visa that lampooned the "Party On" controversy, suddenly the injustice didn't seem so egregious to him. However, it's not as if he handed out cigars to reporters to say that all was forgiven. It's not as if he needed the money to do the commercial either, what with his $18 million a year salary.

In any case, no one was surprised a year later, as the 2004 season unfolded, that Jeter seemed more unapproachable than ever. Reporters again were convinced that he was carrying a grudge toward all of them because a couple of columnists had suggested in February that Jeter should be magnanimous enough to offer to move to second base and allow newcomer A-Rod, the reigning AL Gold Glove shortstop, to take over the glamour position in the infield. It was a thought the Yankees never considered, partly because Torre regarded Jeter so highly, and partly because baseball people agreed that where Jeter has the lean frame and the athleticism that will allow him to retain the necessary quickness and agility to play shortstop for years, A-Rod has a thicker build that, much like Cal Ripken Jr., will slow him down in his 30s and eventually force him to move to third anyway. Nevertheless, all indications were that Jeter was highly offended by any suggestion that he should move to another position. A friend of Jeter's likened it to the *Esquire* magazine story from 2001 in which A-Rod essentially belittled Jeter's status as a star player, opening a wound in their friendship that, in Jeter's eyes, could never be fully healed, even now that they were teammates.

"He takes things to heart," the friend said. "It's his personality. People forget: he's got this unbelievable life now, but it wasn't always so easy for him. He dealt with a lot of racial stuff when he was younger."

Indeed, if Jeter seems overly sensitive at times, maybe it's at least partly the result of growing up as the son of an interracial couple. His mother is white, his father black; they met in Frankfurt, Germany, in 1972 when both were in the Army, and married a year later. It's not a subject Jeter has ever discussed at any length with reporters, but in a book he coauthored with Jack Curry of *The New York Times* in 2000, he acknowledged some hurtful encounters with racism, both subtle and blatant, while growing up in Kalamazoo. He recalled the stares that he could feel when his parents would take Jeter and his younger sister, Sharlee, out to dinner. He recalled how his mother had to go by herself to rent an apartment, after vacant apartments suddenly became unavailable when the Jeters tried to rent them as a couple. Above all, he remembered being called the "N" word in his hometown one night.

Home from his first minor-league season, in 1992, Jeter was driving around in the red Mitsubishi 3000 GT he had purchased with his signing bonus, when he pulled into a Taco Bell. After parking the car he was walking toward the entrance when someone in a car full of teenagers yelled, "Take that car back to your daddy, you n——."

Jeter, who was something of a local celebrity by then in Kalamazoo, recalled watching in stunned disbelief as the car peeled out of the parking lot: "I figured people would be proud of me for making it to the Yankees, and instead I had to listen to that nonsense." He admitted he had a hard time shaking the memory of that incident, and it's only logical to conclude that such incidents have made him both wary of allowing the world to get to know him and sensitive to criticism.

But that's for psychologists to chew on. As the entire city fawned over him after his incomparable play against the Red Sox, sportswriters just wanted a little material for their Jeter-worshiping stories and columns that filled the newspapers for a couple of days. Celebrating Jeter was hardly a new phenomenon in New York, but his dive into the stands seemed to inspire a whole new level of adoration for the Yankee captain. That, in turn prompted a caustic critique from *Daily News* columnist Mike Lupica, the city's best-known sportswriter and notorious Yankee critic.

Referring to a play the Red Sox' Pokey Reese made on a pop-up in the same game, where he also tumbled into the stands, though nowhere near as violently as Jeter, Lupica wrote in his Sunday "Shooting from the Lip" column:

"You think Pokey Reese is wondering why his play in the stands isn't being covered like it was braver than hitting the beach at Normandy?

"No kidding, I can't tell from reading the papers the last few days, did the captain of the Yankees make a superb, fearless play to win a ballgame, or get us out of Iraq?"

This wasn't a shot at Jeter, but what Lupica liked to call "the Yankee media." On all things Yankee, he considered himself a journalistic watchdog of sorts who provided a balance to otherwise overhyped coverage of Steinbrenner's millionaires. Of course, plenty of Yankee fans, and some competing colleagues, knowing Lupica had grown up in New Hampshire and attended Boston College, just considered him a thinly disguised Red Sox fan.

Either way, Lupica was never shy about taking on Steinbrenner or the Yankees—even Jeter, the golden boy. Earlier in the year Lupica had caused a stir by openly wondering whether Jeter's terrible start at the plate was related to A-Rod's arrival and the pressure of needing to prove he was still the best shortstop in town.

By season's end, Lupica was back in Jeter's corner, saying it was A-Rod who suffered in comparison by playing alongside Jeter all season. But that didn't mean he thought Jeter should get the Purple Heart for plays like the one he made against the Red Sox.

In any case, whether the Jeter coverage was over the top or properly appreciative of his dive, it surely rendered the start of the series with the Mets as something of an afterthought. That seemed only fitting since the Mets, always the No. 2 team in town except during their championship run in the '80s, were being covered in 2004 like they'd slipped to No. 3—behind the Red Sox as well as the Yankees.

But the Mets forced the city to pay attention to them over this July Fourth weekend, posting the first sweep of a three-game series against the Yankees since interleague play began in 1997. Surely the Yankees suffered from an emotional hangover after their own sweep of the Red Sox, and in particular the epic 13-inning game on Thursday night, but that excuse had legs for only the first game, an 11–2 rout in which the Yankees all played the way Jeter undoubtedly felt.

For the rest of the weekend it was hard to tell if it was just lousy pitching that cost the Yankees, or the likelihood that they never quite took the Mets seriously enough to regain their intensity. No matter how much the annual Subway Series meant to the New York fans, it was a ho-hum affair to the Yankees by now. Beating the Mets, which they had been doing regularly since '97, didn't do much for their egos, especially in the last few years after the team in Queens again had fallen on hard times. So even after the Mets finished off the sweep by scores of 10–9 and 6–5, completing the three-game set that would be the highlight of their season, the Yankees could afford to shrug. They were still seven and a half games in front of the Sox, after all.

Whatever their nonchalance, however, the Yankees couldn't pretend they weren't concerned about the state of their pitching. Mike Mussina and Jose Contreras were each bombed in the first two games, and Javier Vazquez was starting to show signs of struggling, walking five hitters while lasting only five innings on Sunday. The Contreras start was particularly troubling because of its timing. The Yankees had been holding out hope that the celebrated defection of his family from Cuba the previous week would get him over the hump emotionally. Contreras had been despondent without his wife and two daughters, and had smiled more in the week since they arrived than he had in the year and a half without them. If anything could turn him into the confident dominator he'd once been in Cuba, the pitcher who had prompted the Yankees to outbid the Red Sox and guarantee him $32 million over four years, it was his family's presence. When he went out a few days after the reunion and pitched very effectively to beat the Mets at Yankee Stadium, Yankee executives crossed their fingers. Maybe they had something. But then, six days later, Contreras looked as unsure of himself as ever, allowing seven runs on eight hits, including three home runs. Right then and there, Brian Cashman knew he was going to do everything he could to deal Contreras by the trading deadline at the end of the month.

In the meantime, the Yankees righted themselves after the Mets' sweep, going 10–5 over their next 15 games that led them into Fenway Park for another go-round with the Red Sox. It was good enough to restore the same eight-and-a-half-game lead they'd taken away from their last meeting, but it was hard to judge how well the Yankees were playing, since the 15 games had been with the Tigers, Devil Rays, and Blue Jays—the kind of mediocre ballclubs they could simply wear down with all of their offensive talent. If 19 games a season with the Red Sox seemed like too many at times, considering that each one was treated like Armageddon, they were also a welcome contrast to the assembly line of humdrum games with bad teams that filled stretches of the season. Every game with the Sox was truly a big game, no matter the size of the Yankees' lead, and more than ever, after their last meeting, that meant you never knew when Derek Jeter might do something unforgettable.

JULY HEAD-TO-HEAD—HATING A-ROD

Under the circumstances, Jason Varitek did what any self-respecting Red Sox loyalist would have done.

He found the nearest person in a Yankees jersey and shoved a hand in his face.

That the punching bag turned out to be Alex Rodriguez was purely a bonus, though it was more than a little symbolic, too. Hit by a Bronson Arroyo pitch in the third inning of a July 24 game the Yankees led, 3–0, Rodriguez did what the Yankees and their followers often did: he made it about *him*. Never mind that New York had complete control of the game up to that point. Never mind that the Red Sox had been without even a baserunner against the immortal Tanyon Sturtze. Never mind that the Yankees had won the opener of the series by an 8–7 score, giving them four consecutive wins against the Red Sox and suggesting, once again, that New York was just a little bit better, bigger, stronger.

No sirree.

Alex Rodriguez was more worried about himself, his actions revealing both a personal arrogance and an institutional elitism that inevitably came from being a New Yorker.

Who did the Red Sox think they were, anyway?

Didn't they know that he was *Alex Rodriguez* and that he played for the *Yankees*?

The bluest of the blue collars on the Red Sox, Varitek would have none of it. At the moment Rodriguez glared and shouted at Arroyo, Varitek spun out from his spot behind the plate and faced Rodriguez, standing between the Yankees superstar and his batterymate. It was one of Varitek's standard maneuvers, something he prided himself on. *You're not getting near our pitcher. Not on my watch.* And when the tensions escalated further, when Rodriguez shifted his aggression toward Varitek and challenged the player—"Fuck you! Fuck you! Fuck you!" Rodriguez shouted directly at the Red Sox catcher—Varitek raised his hands and shoved them into Rodriguez' face, looking as if he wanted to stuff his catcher's mitt up the player's nose (it didn't fit) and triggering a bench-clearing scrum that resulted in an array of suspensions and fines for both teams.

Following the game, after reporters cleared from the area near his locker, Varitek acknowledged that Rodriguez' angry words were precipitated by a few of his own.

Said the Red Sox catcher when asked what he said to Rodriguez: "I basically told him to get the fuck down to first base."

At that moment, the century-old rivalry between the Red Sox and Yankees was reduced to its most unfiltered state.

Fuck you.

No, fuck *you.*

Still, while the Red Sox and Yankees rolled around in the mud on July 24, there was a succession of events that made the game important for the Red Sox. In fact, the Red Sox and Yankees endured a 54-minute rain delay at the start of the game, things looking so bleak at one juncture that the Yankees believed the game had been postponed. And while the game was indeed in doubt, while Red Sox officials seemed prepared to reschedule the contest less than 24 hours after the frustrating 8–7 loss to New York, Red Sox players were resolved to play the contest. Varitek was among the chief representatives who walked into manager Terry Francona's office and relayed the players' wishes to immediately go back into battle, and so the Red Sox grounds crew prepared the field after a downpour that had lasted all of Friday night and Saturday morning.

"It became clear that our players really wanted to play," said Sox general manager Theo Epstein. "So we made an extraordinary effort to get the field ready and it worked."

As things turned out, it worked better than the Red Sox possibly could have imagined.

Immediately following the fight between Varitek and Rodriguez, the Red Sox scored four times to take a 4–3 lead. The teams subsequently exchanged blows—9–4 Yankees, 9–8 Yankees, 10–8 Yankees—before the Red Sox won on an improbable, two-run home run by Bill Mueller against the otherworldly Mariano Rivera in the bottom of the ninth inning. The homer sent a Fenway Park crowd of 34,501 into a state of near ecstasy, completing a truly extraordinary game that lasted three hours, 54 minutes and included an off-field dispute (about the effect of the rain), an on-field dispute (between Varitek and Rodriguez), and a heart-stopping finish revealing the vulnerability of arguably the most dominating closer in the history of baseball.

Yes, the Red Sox knew they could beat the great Mariano Rivera.

And in the long run, that was something that would prove invaluable.

Yet, while some New Yorkers obnoxiously suggested that Yankees "woke up" the slumbering Red Sox—even then it was about *them*—the truth was that the Red Sox almost immediately went back to sleep after the Yankees left town. Despite a schedule that included inferior opponents, Baltimore, Tampa, and Detroit, the Red Sox lost five of their next nine games and went a perfectly mediocre 6–6 over the next 12. Several of those contests came even after the club shipped away Nomar Garciaparra at the July 31 trading deadline, suggesting that the immediate impact of that trade, too, was far less significant that many would have liked to believe.

As a result, the most lasting effect of the July series between the Red Sox and Yankees was this: Alex Rodriguez solidified his place as both a prima donna and a villain in the eyes of the Red Sox and their followers. Had Rodriguez simply absorbed the pitch by Arroyo and done what he should have done—trotted to first base—there would have been no conflict, no ejections, no nonsense. The Yankees might have retaliated in conventional form by having starter Sturtze fire a fastball into the ribs of Rodriguez' Red Sox counterpart—namely, Mueller—and there is no telling what might have happened after that. Maybe the umpires would have issued warnings. Maybe Mueller would have charged the mound and been ejected. Maybe, as a result, he would not have been available to bat against Rivera in the bottom of the ninth.

Whatever the alternatives, the fact was that Rodriguez' place with the Yankees was now solidified. He was the *enemy*. Any giddiness Red Sox fans may have felt about the prospect of Rodriguez joining Boston during the off-season was entirely gone, replaced by general and genuine disdain. And in the Red Sox clubhouse, where the inhabitants often chose their words carefully when asked about opposing players—on or off the record—one uniformed member of the Sox described Rodriguez as "queer," which was not meant to be any commentary on the player's sexual orientation (Rodriguez is, in fact, married) or personality quirks as much it was a way to suggest that he was childish, even babylike, downright *soft*. For all of the political correctness that was overtaking the world, locker rooms and clubhouses remained among the few places where manhood was trumpeted, where players were expected to live by a certain code.

And when *anyone* demonstrated even the slightest bit of ego or self-absorption, he would more than likely hear about it, be it from his teammates or anyone else. So whether the culprit was Alex Rodriguez or Kevin Millar—"I think Millar is turning gay," a playful Manny Ramirez once cracked to a reporter during the season when Millar bleached his hair in hopes of ending a slump—was largely irrelevant.

Admittedly, in the case of Rodriguez, he was an easy target. Rodriguez was six foot three and 225 pounds, and he was blessed with extraordinary talent, good looks, the richest contract in the history of professional sports ($252 million) and the political skills of a both a senator and salesman. Rodriguez addressed reporters by their names—even the allegedly shrewd New York media ate it all up, hook, line, and sinker—and he often gave insightful answers. Whether he was honest was another matter entirely, though many reporters, in any town, weren't often interested in the truth. They were interested in the best *quote*, and there were few true superstars who could meaningfully fill a notebook like Rodriguez.

The problem, naturally, was that Rodriguez came off as phony, egomaniacal, self-absorbed, manipulative, calculating, and terribly, terribly vain. That message was conveyed even to opposing players, many of whom resented Rodriguez for everything he possessed, some of whom disliked him for everything he represented.

"Even when he swings and misses it's like, 'Look at me, I'm A-Rod,'" one member of the Red Sox said in the days after the July 24 brawl.

In some corners of New York, however, Rodriguez' actions somehow made him tough, gritty, rugged. When it came to Yankees newcomers, New Yorkers often anticipated that moment when the player completed his transition into pinstripes, as if he were celebrating a baptism or bar mitzvah, a rite of passage. Wearing the uniform was not enough. There had to be some catalytic event, some climax that turned the player from just another free agent into that most celebrated of things, *a Yankee*. The way many New Yorkers often talked about that metamorphosis—*"Tonight was the night Roger Clemens became a Yankee,"* they would say—one would think that a player was being elevated to knighthood, to a place of eternal immunity.

In New York, there were the gods.

And then there were *the Yankees*.

Of course, the same was true in Boston, though the door swung in the other direction. There were countless enemies that had come through Fenway Park over the years, but the ones wearing Yankees grays were the most sinister. In the 1970s, when the rivalry between Boston and New York was most violent, Boston fans threw

THE RIVALRY WITHIN: *Red Sox right-handers Pedro Martinez (foreground) and Curt Schilling share a laugh during spring training. Including the postseason, Martinez and Schilling went a combined 42–17 during the 2004 season, after which Martinez signed as a free agent with the New York Mets.*

MATTHEW WEST/BOSTON HERALD

MATTHEW WEST/BOSTON HERALD

OPPOSITES ATTRACT: *Red Sox shortstop Nomar Garciaparra (left) greets Yankees counterpart Derek Jeter before a spring training game in which an injured Garciaparra did not play. Garciaparra and Jeter served as centerpieces of the Boston–New York rivalry until Garciaparra was traded from the Red Sox on July 31, 2004.*

JOHN WILCOX/BOSTON HERALD

MANAGEMENT TEAM: *Red Sox manager Terry Francona (left) and general manager Theo Epstein confer before the Sox' 7–2 loss to the Baltimore Orioles on Opening Day, April 4. Epstein hired Francona to replace Grady Little, who was fired by the Red Sox following the 2003 American League Championship Series loss to the Yankees.*

MICHAEL SEAMANS/BOSTON HERALD

BALCO BUM: *Jason Giambi, following through on a swing against the Red Sox in April, was rendered useless to the Yankees for much of the season, including the playoffs, because of an intestinal parasite and then a benign tumor, all while denying allegations of steroid use. After the season Giambi was vilified in New York as a liar and a cheat when it was revealed that he'd used steroids for years, according to his testimony before a grand jury in the BALCO case.*

MATTHEW WEST/BOSTON HERALD

CAPTAIN COURAGEOUS: *Yankees' trainer Gene Monahan tries to stop the bleeding from Derek Jeter's chin after the shortstop's famous catch-and-dive into the seats against the Red Sox on July 1. The play knocked a woozy Jeter out of the game but helped the Yankees win a classic, as they finally prevailed 5–4 in 13 innings.*

TARA BRICKING/BOSTON HERALD

IN YOUR FACE: *Red Sox catcher Jason Varitek (right) and Yankees shortstop Alex Rodriguez exchange words and blows on July 24 at Fenway Park, where the Red Sox eventually claimed a dramatic 11–10 victory on Red Sox third baseman Bill Mueller's dramatic home run against Yankees closer Mariano Rivera. Rodriguez was upset after being hit by a pitch thrown by Red Sox pitcher Bronson Arroyo, precipitating a bench-clearing brawl.*

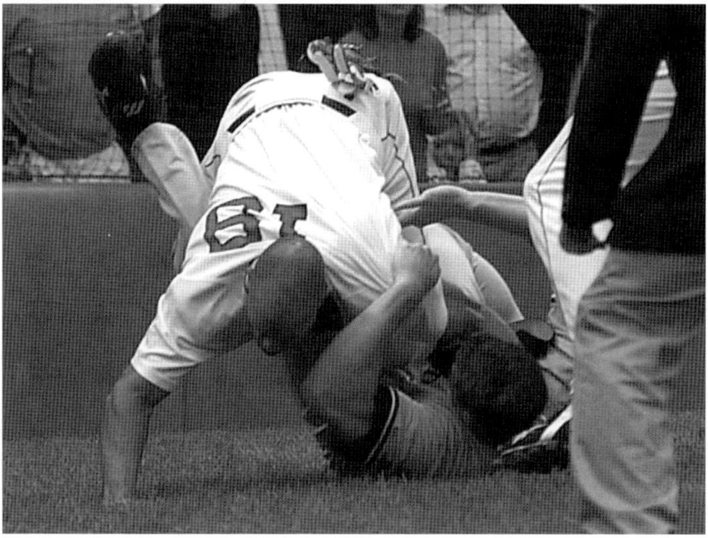

TARA BRICKING/BOSTON HERALD

DRAGGED DOWN INTO THE MUD: *Red Sox outfielder Gabe Kapler (top) and Yankees pitcher Tanyon Sturtze wrestle during the July 24 incident. The brawl between the Red Sox and Yankees was one of the more memorable incidents in the storied history of the two franchises.*

MATT STONE/BOSTON HERALD

LOWE POINT: *Red Sox pitcher Derek Lowe (foreground) sprawls to field a throw at first base during a disastrous outing in a 14–4 loss to the Yankees on September 18. Lowe allowed seven runs in one inning of the game, but rebounded to have a big October.*

MATTHEW WEST/BOSTON HERALD

OCTOBER INTENSITY: *Gary Sheffield surprises Alex Rodriguez with the force of his emotion after scoring in Game 1 of the ALCS against the Red Sox. Sheffield had an MVP-type year in his first season as a Yankee, delivering in the clutch . . . until all the Yankee bats went cold after Game 3.*

MATTHEW WEST/BOSTON HERALD

BUSINESS AS USUAL: *Or so it seemed, as Mariano Rivera accepts congratulations from Jorge Posada after recording a save in Game 2 of the ALCS, his second in two nights. Rivera seemed destined to add to his legend as baseball's greatest postseason closer, but his inability to slam the door in Game 4 gave the Red Sox life that spawned a miracle.*

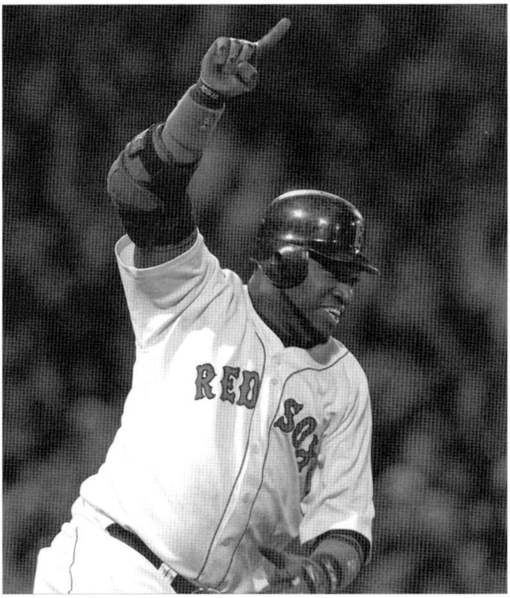

MICHAEL SEAMANS/BOSTON HERALD

MR. OCTOBER: *Red Sox designated hitter David Ortiz celebrates his game-winning single against the Yankees in the 14th inning of Game 5 of the American League Championship Series. The hit, which gave the Red Sox a 5–4 victory, marked the third consecutive Boston win that ended with a swing of Ortiz' bat and sent the teams back to New York for Game 6 with the Yankees holding a 3–2 series edge.*

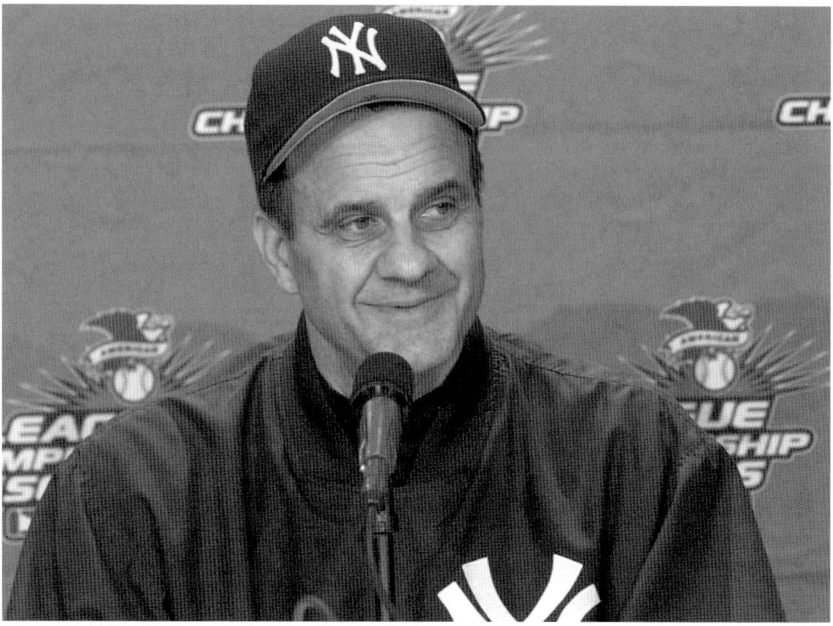

TARA BRICKING/BOSTON HERALD

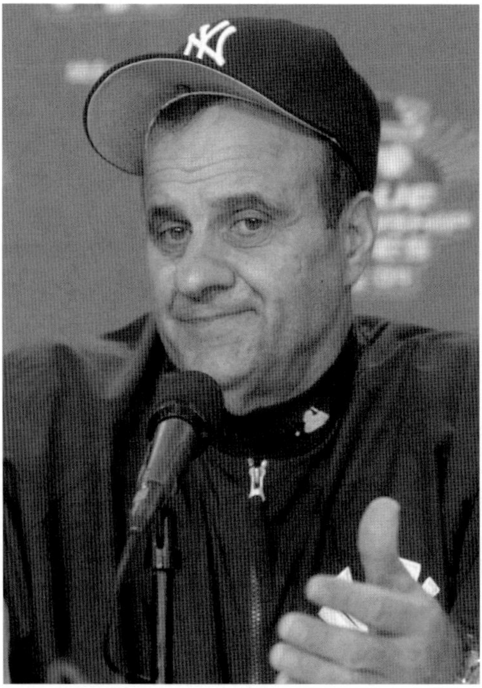

DAVID GOLDMAN/BOSTON HERALD

TORRE TIME: *Yankee manager Joe Torre looks relaxed answering questions at the off-day press conference before Game 3 of the ALCS. His calm demeanor and knack for making the right decisions had come to define Yankee success in October, but when his team blew a 3–0 series lead to the Red Sox, Torre for a change became a focal point of much second-guessing from fans and media.*

NANCY LANE/BOSTON HERALD

A SWIPE OF THE HAND: *Attempting to avoid the tag of Red Sox pitcher Bronson Arroyo (front left), Yankees shortstop Alex Rodriguez swats Arroyo's arm in the eighth inning of Game 6 of the American League Championship Series. Rodriguez was successful in knocking the ball free but was called for interference in an eventual 4–2 Yankees loss. Boston subsequently blew out the Yankees in Game 7, winning 10–3.*

MATT STONE/BOSTON HERALD

KNUCKLING DOWN: *Red Sox pitcher Tim Wakefield, who surrendered Aaron Boone's game-winning homer in Game 7 of the 2003 American League Championship Series, drew the start for Boston in Game 1 of the World Series against the St. Louis Cardinals. Among active Red Sox, Wakefield has the longest run of continuous service time with the team.*

DAVID GOLDMAN/BOSTON HERALD

GLORY DAY: *Red Sox pitcher Pedro Martinez hosts the World Series trophy after the Red Sox completed a four-game sweep of the St. Louis Cardinals with a 3–0 victory. Boston dominated the series with St. Louis, outscoring the Cardinals, 24–12, and never trailing in any game.*

smoke bombs at Yankees center fielder Mickey Rivers following a fight in which Rivers blindsided Red Sox players. (Rivers was a *cheap-shot ah-tist.*) During a brawl in 1976, Yankees third baseman Craig Nettles pinned Sox pitcher Bill Lee to the Yankee Stadium turf, injuring Lee in the process. (Nettles was a *bum.*) And then there were Jeff Nelson and Karim Garcia, the Yankees teammates who beat up on a member of the Fenway grounds crew during Game 3 of the 2003 American League Championship Series, Garcia jumping over the right field wall and into the Yankees bullpen to join the fight. (They were simply *losers.*)

Though the pure venom from the 1970s never has been matched in the rivalry, the more recent history between the clubs—particularly after unbalanced scheduling and realignment allowed the Sox and Yankees to meet in the postseason—brought the intensity of the rivalry to new heights at the turn of the millennium. In 1999, when umpires made a succession of bad calls that went against the Red Sox during the American League Championship Series, fans at Fenway Park littered the Fenway Park lawn with debris during pivotal Game 4. Yankees owner George Steinbrenner later accused then-Sox manager Jimy Williams of inciting the crowd during the incident, though Williams was merely arguing his case at a time when television replays revealed that he was *right* and the umpires were actually *wrong.*

And then, of course, there was Game 3 of the 2003 ALCS, a contest that will live in infamy. Frustrated by his inability to pitch effectively against the Yankees in the top of the fourth inning, Sox bad boy Pedro Martinez whipped a fastball behind the head of Garcia, a move that even Sox players could not defend following the game. Most New Yorkers regarded Martinez as Public Enemy No. 1 even before the desperate act, and his actions only reaffirmed the belief that he was, among all of the accolades, an extremely poor loser. And so as the Yankees (and catcher Jorge Posada, in particular) shouted at Martinez from the dugout bench, Martinez pointed to his temple with his right index finger, a gesture he had made countless times when speaking with reporters in the Red Sox clubhouse throughout his career in Boston. What Martinez was saying, in fact, was that he would *remember* Posada's remarks—"I have a memory like an elephant," Martinez would often tell writers while making the gesture—but New Yorkers understandably interpreted the sign as a threat that Martinez would throw at Posada's head, something that made Martinez even more detestable and contemptible in the eyes of the Yankees and their followers.

In the never-ending war between the Red Sox and Yankees, there were heroes and villains on both sides.

And like Bruce Willis in *The Sixth Sense*, many fans saw only what they wanted to see.

In fact, Martinez' controversial actions in that game were only beginning, the signature moment of Game 4 coming in the bottom of the eventful fourth, when Red Sox slugger Manny Ramirez overreacted to a Roger Clemens fastball that soared out of the strike zone. Replays revealed that the pitch came nowhere near the head of Ramirez, who nonetheless reacted as if Clemens were trying to decapitate him. So when the dugouts emptied again as Clemens and a restrained Ramirez shouted at one another, 72-year-old Yankees bench coach and baseball relic Don Zimmer charged at Martinez, who promptly grabbed the onrushing Zimmer by the handlebars (namely, his ears) and planted the old man into the Fenway Park lawn as if he were a tomato plant pole.

Zimmer was the one at fault in the matter, admitting as much in a tearful apology one night later, prior to a rain-induced postponement of Game 4.

Nonetheless, Martinez was remembered as the bad guy.

Less than a year later, into this reality came Rodriguez, whose career previously had taken him to Seattle and Texas, places where the combined history could not match that of the Red Sox or Yankees alone. So as much as Alex Rodriguez may have believed that he knew what he was getting himself into when he leveraged his way out of a Rangers uniform and into Yankees pinstripes, the reality is that he had no understanding of the cauldron in which he would land, where he would be despised no matter what he did, no matter whom he addressed by name, no matter what he said, and no matter how politically correct he remained.

In fact, in many places, he would be despised even more.

So, while Rodriguez' transgressions on July 24, 2004, were not nearly as severe as many of those involving the Red Sox and Yankees over the course of their history, they were transgressions nonetheless. And by the time the Yankees left Fenway Park as the July 31 trading deadline approached, by the time the Red Sox had won the final two games of a three-game series and seemingly resumed their course toward the postseason, followers of the Red Sox and Yankees could at least agree on one thing.

Alex Rodriguez was *a Yankee*.

Yes, indeed.

There was no longer any doubt about that.

JULY HEAD-TO-HEAD—
DON'T BLAME IT ON ALEX

Willie Randolph wasn't about to pull a Don Zimmer and go charging after Pedro Martinez, but when Alex Rodriguez and Jason Varitek started fighting on the afternoon of July 24, the Yankees' bench coach did go rushing in to try to separate players. And as he wound up on the ground at the bottom of a pileup, Randolph saw 30 years of Yankees–Red Sox hostilities flash before his eyes.

"When something like that starts, I can't help it," Randolph said with a sheepish smile the next day. "Those old feelings about the Red Sox still come out."

Randolph, the Yankees second baseman during the Bronx Zoo days, has a keen eye for such things, and he believes he saw trouble coming before anybody else when he noticed A-Rod slide in hard and wide Friday night in the series opener to take out Bill Mueller on an unorthodox 4–5–3 double play. Mueller was covering second because of the overshift against Jason Giambi, and when he gave A-Rod a glare after managing to complete the double play, Randolph wondered if it would lead to anything.

Of course, Randolph scoffs at the notion that a couple of brawls between these teams suddenly means the rivalry compares in intensity to the late 1970s, partly because he says the game is different now.

"There's no comparison to the way it used to be," Randolph says. "I still see too much fraternization out there. Too much buddy-buddy stuff. Too much la-la-la on the basepaths. I don't want to sound too old-school, but we didn't speak to each other back then. Thurman [Munson] didn't like [Carlton] Fisk, Fisk didn't like Thurman, and down the line. That's when it was real. You could see the hair standing up on the back of our necks when we played each other.

"When things happened, the umpires didn't get involved. We took care of business. If a guy got hit with a pitch he'd go to first base and then try to kill the shortstop or second baseman with a hard take-out slide. Back then, players understood that was part of the game. But now it's like a lost art."

Randolph took his share of hard knocks in such situations, so he was delighted to see A-Rod go in hard against Mueller. It didn't seem to be an issue at the time, but when he was hit by a pitch from Bronson Arroyo the next day, A-Rod reacted angrily because, he said, "something smelled funny about it."

That was his way of saying he thought Arroyo was sending a message, perhaps for the slide at second base. It didn't seem likely that a young pitcher like Arroyo would take such matters into his hands, not with Pedro and Curt Schilling on his staff, but in any case, A-Rod barked at Arroyo as he began walking slowly toward first, yelling at him to "throw the ball over the plate."

Maybe Rodriguez was just putting on a show for his teammates. Maybe he was trying to act as tough as Gary Sheffield, who'd reacted with defiance in June when he was hit with a Pedro Martinez pitch. One thing was for sure: A-Rod wasn't looking for a fight, no matter what Red Sox fans wanted to believe. It's just not his nature. He'd never had a fight in his baseball career, in the majors or the minors, or, for that matter, on the football field in high school in Miami as a highly regarded quarterback. It wouldn't have been good for the A-Rod image, which he had been cultivating carefully since becoming the first player taken in baseball's 1993 amateur draft.

A-Rod wanted to be friends with everyone, and once he even got Derek Jeter in trouble because of it. During a brawl between the Yankees and Seattle Mariners in 1999, when A-Rod was still with his original team, he sought out Jeter, his pal at the time, and began joking with him. Both players were laughing as the brawl broke up in such a manner that then Yankee Chad Curtis confronted Jeter in the dugout, and then again in the clubhouse after the game, with reporters present, to tell him he thought his behavior was inappropriate.

No, A-Rod isn't a fighter. A psychologist might conclude that for all of his fame and fortune, Rodriguez forever wants to be the most popular kid in school, his insecurity going back to a childhood when his father deserted the family in Miami, leaving nine-year-old Alex heartbroken.

"I tried to tell myself it didn't matter," A-Rod told the *Seattle Times* in 1996, "but times when I was alone, I often cried. Where was my father? To this day, I don't really know how a man could do that—turn his back on his family."

It hurt all the more because the father, Victor, once a catcher in the Dominican pro league, had been so good to his youngest son, teaching him how to play baseball and "spoiling me because I was the baby of the family," A-Rod said.

Nine years passed before young Alex heard from his father again, getting a phone call on the day he was drafted, in June of 1993, by the Seattle Mariners. Years later A-Rod would say he could barely remember anything about the phone call, except that his father had said he would like to get to know his son again. Alex himself made no promises, but some 18 months later, in December of 1994, Victor showed up unannounced as Alex was preparing for a winter league game in the Dominican Republic.

"I was taking batting practice," A-Rod recalled years later. "He just bought a ticket and came to the stadium. When he told me who he was, I almost broke down."

Alex agreed to go to lunch with his father the next day, but after tossing and turning in bed that night, as all the old resentment came rushing back, he never went.

"I couldn't just go and see him, just like that," he said.

Periodic phone calls over the years began to thaw the ice a bit, and A-Rod's marriage in 2002 to Cynthia Scurtis, a teacher with a master's degree in psychology, had an impact that led to a reunion with his half brother, Victor Jr., in Dallas in 2003.

Still, in talking to a reporter from the Dallas *Morning News* at the time, A-Rod called his reunion with his half brother "joyous," but made it clear the wounds opened all those years ago by his father's abandonment hadn't healed completely.

"Why open myself up to getting hurt again?" he said. "It's something I find hard to talk about."

Suffice it to say that A-Rod is a sensitive soul who had no intention of starting a brawl with the Red Sox after getting hit by Arroyo. He wanted to vent a little bit, perhaps intimidate a young pitcher along the way, before going on down to first base. But then Varitek intervened and made it personal.

The joke going around in the days after the brawl, told with great delight by Red Sox fans, was that Varitek, commenting on A-Rod's so-so season, had enraged the Yankees superstar by telling him, "We don't throw at .260 hitters."

A-Rod's version of the story seemed more likely. Basically he said that Varitek cursed at him so forcefully that he responded instinctively, cursing back and challenging the Sox catcher to bring it on. The TV cameras left no doubt about A-Rod's harsh language. But the cameras showed Varitek only from behind, and besides, he never took off his mask, so no one knew for sure what he said.

"It was worse than anything I said," A-Rod said when asked about it weeks later. "That's why I reacted the way I did."

His reaction was to invite Varitek with a wave of his hand to make the first move. When the catcher stuffed his glove in A-Rod's face, players came flying from both dugouts to join the brawl. But rather than the usual grabbing and holding from players on both sides, this fight was vicious by baseball standards. Players were being grabbed around the neck, yanked backward, spun around, as the pile of bodies moved in all directions. Yankees pitcher Tanyon Sturtze had Gabe Kapler around the neck when Sox teammates David Ortiz and Trot Nixon jumped in, dragging Sturtze away from the pile where they triple-teamed him in one of the uglier spin-off fights. Meanwhile, in the main event, after the initial blows were thrown, Varitek attempted to pick A-Rod up by the legs, apparently with the intent to body-slam him. But A-Rod, at six foot three, 225 pounds, was stronger than Varitek figured, and so the two men wound up grappling with one another while other players tried to pry them apart. A-Rod took choppy steps as the pile moved, because, he said later, "my biggest fear with all those bodies out there was getting rolled at the knees by somebody in the pile, and getting hurt. So I tried to keep moving. I wasn't worried about Varitek hurting me. And I couldn't hit him because I would have hurt my hand, since he still had his mask on."

That was A-Rod's way of saying he didn't think Varitek was much of a tough guy. Months later, in fact, A-Rod remained bitter toward Varitek. When asked by a Boston reporter before the ALCS if he would talk to the Red Sox catcher and perhaps make peace between them, A-Rod stared hard at the questioner for a few seconds, then said, as coldly as possible: "No, I don't plan to talk to him."

At the time, after the game that day in July, A-Rod didn't allow his anger to show. As usual, he was cool, calm, under control, in keeping with the A-Rod image. All around him, meanwhile, there was mayhem, at least among the media, as reporters found themselves in a scrum trying to get close enough to A-Rod's locker to hear what he was saying. The Red Sox had come back to win the game 11–10 in a most dramatic fashion, rallying in the ninth inning to defeat Mariano Rivera on a walk-off home run by Bill Mueller, but with the Yankees still leading by eight and a half games, the fight was a much bigger story on this day. As always, the number of credentialed media for a Yankees-Red Sox game always made for an adventure in trying to work the locker room, especially in Boston.

Fenway Park opened in 1912, and except for the big-screen TV, you'd swear the visitors' clubhouse looks exactly the same as it did when Ruth and Gehrig were suiting up. Certainly it hasn't been enlarged; Derek Jeter no doubt has bigger closets in his apartment at Trump Tower. By the time you squeeze 25 ballplayers in there along with a handful of coaches and team personnel, and another 40 or so reporters, it feels like the subway at rush hour. At least partly as a result, players routinely grab their clothes after showering and go dress in the trainers' room, which is also small, but at least they're bumping into teammates as they pull their pants on, and not relative strangers. Reporters, meanwhile, have to maneuver around a food spread that is set out in the center of the room for the players after games, and more than once have come away from postgame interviewing to find ziti sauce on the arms of their shirts. In this case A-Rod's locker was across the aisle from the food spread, walled off one side by a pillar, limiting access, which is why reporters were elbowing for position long before he came back from the trainers' room to answer questions.

A-Rod didn't seem fazed by the media frenzy. He answered questions for 10 minutes, and as usual, gave reporters what they wanted—in this case a willingness to admit the fight was more than the usual heat-of-the-moment overreaction, but rather an indication of the hard feelings between the two teams.

"It wasn't your generic fight between New York and Kansas City, or New York and Minnesota," was the way A-Rod put it. "You could tell there was some residual carryover from last year's playoffs. It tells you just how intense this rivalry is right now."

Later, as he was wrapping up the interview session, A-Rod was asked if there was a genuine dislike between the two teams. He paused as he was making his way through the media crowd, smiled, and said rather wryly: "It's not love."

In fact, it was clear the Red Sox now had someone on whom to focus their frustration at finishing second to the Yankees every year. In this era Jeter has always been the object of the Yankee fans' obsession, as evidenced most prominently by the vulgar T-shirts they wear in his honor, but Jeter has never fostered resentment among opposing players. A-Rod was different. He's a little too smooth talking, a little too image conscious in the eyes of some of his peers, and as such he became a convenient face for the Red Sox to attach to the rivalry. Curt Schilling, never at a loss for an opinion, took the lead in that regard, publicly blaming A-Rod for unnecessarily starting the fight with Varitek, and as the season moved along it seemed the Sox hated the Yankee third baseman as much as the Yankees hated Pedro Martinez. All of which added spice to a rivalry that once again was becoming nasty on the field, as well as in the stands. Even Randolph, the old second baseman, had to admit that emotions in the respective dugouts were running hotter than at any time since the Yanks and Sox seemed to fight every other week back in the late '70s.

"I do think the guys are starting to feel what this rivalry is about," Randolph said the day after the A-Rod brawl. "It doesn't have the same edge as in our day, but there's something there. There's no doubt this thing is bigger than ever because of all the media hype. The Red Sox hear about [losing to the Yankees] more than ever, and I kind of felt like that's why Varitek wanted to be a tough guy and start something with A-Rod. He's not the first guy who has tried to spark his team by starting something, but it's not going to affect our team. These guys are very focused on winning."

By winning the Friday night game 8–7, in fact, the Yankees had struck the most significant blow in this series, no matter that they lost the next two games. After all, about the only thing they hadn't done to discourage the Red Sox to that point was beat up on Schilling, so when they did that, leaving him teary-eyed on the bench—where the TV cameras could find him—at game's end, and widened their lead to nine and a half games, the Yankees effectively ruined the summer for New Englanders. A brawl wasn't going to change that.

NEW AND IMPROVED—RED SOX

EVEN BEFORE THE YANKEES CAME AND WENT, RUMORS PERSISTED concerning the future of Nomar Garciaparra. Having agreed to a trade that would have sent Magglio Ordonez to the Red Sox for Garciaparra over the winter, the Chicago White Sox renewed their interest in the shortstop, presumably as part of a multiple-team trade in which the Red Sox would have ended up with a starting pitcher, perhaps even Randy Johnson. The Chicago Cubs also were interested in Garciaparra—reports out of Chicago had Garciaparra being swapped in a deal that would have included right-handed Cubs starter Matt Clement—and Red Sox officials treated each and every question from members of the local media with the response that they had no plans to trade their franchise shortstop.

In the middle of it all stood 30-year-old general manager Theo Epstein, a native of Brookline, Massachusetts, who grew up in the shadow of Fenway Park and understood the history of the Red Sox as well as anyone.

Much to Epstein's chagrin, as things so often did in Boston, the Garciaparra story developed such a life of its own that Red Sox officials felt the need to quash the rumors. It was during a pregame session with the media during the team's West Coast trip in the middle of July that Francona, citing a conversation he had with Epstein earlier in the day, turned the table on reporters and asked them the simplest of questions:

If he told the media definitively that the Red Sox were not going to trade Garciaparra, but that the rumors still persisted, would reporters write them?

When many of the reporters said that they would, a fact that had as much to do with the competition between media outlets and the fear of being scooped, the manager recognized that there was virtually no way to control what was and was not reported, particularly with a player of Nomar Garciaparra's stature. Francona, in fact, had the very same conversation with Garciaparra, which only gave the player more ammunition in his never-ending argument that the media was not culpable. And at the time, for what it's worth, one Cubs official acknowledged that the Cubs did indeed have a serious interest in trading Garciaparra, but that the Red Sox had given no indication to that point that the player would be made available.

What Epstein, Francona, and the rest of the Red Sox were saying seemingly was true.

Nomar Garciaparra wasn't going anywhere.

"I feel bad for Nomar," Francona said prior to a July 15 game at Anaheim that signaled the start of the season's second half. "I'm sure he's tired of it."

As it was, Garciaparra was not alone. Rumors about Lowe had persisted, too, and the pitcher had similarly grown tired of dealing with the uncertainty. Following the July 25 victory over the Yankees, in fact, an obviously sarcastic and bitter Lowe entered a small conference room at Fenway Park, where Sox pitchers typically met the media after their performances. Lowe took his place at a small table in the front of room and immediately addressed reporters as if they were the enemy, blaming them for all that had been written about him in recent weeks concerning trade scenarios that had him being sent to a number of different places.

Such trade talk was part of baseball, of course, but fans and media alike frequently neglected to recognize that the people they covered were, in fact, *people*, and they were susceptible to the same insecurities and uncertainties as anyone else.

"You guys all got me traded, so I was just trying to enjoy my last game as a Red Sox," Lowe grumbled to reporters following the 9–6 win over the Yankees in which he allowed just two earned runs in six and two-thirds innings. "I'm the guy everyone wants to see traded and by winning this game, I'm just trying to enjoy the last Red Sox-Yankees game before I go elsewhere.

"I look at the fact that we're 11–9 in my [starts]," Lowe added. "I know my bad games have been really bad, but if I'm the problem around here then we all need to move on. I don't feel like I need to go out and consistently prove that I deserve the ball the next 11 or 12 times during the year."

That is what the trading deadline could do to people, even ones who had enjoyed success at the highest levels of professional sports.

It made them doubt themselves.

Nonetheless, by the time August was about to dawn, the rumors were not rumors at all. They were real. The Red Sox were 56–45 on the morning of July 31—that made them a remarkably mediocre 41–39 since their 15–6 start—and Epstein was now involved in serious discussions with the Cubs, Montreal Expos, and Minnesota Twins on a four-team trade. The teams ultimately settled on a musical-chairs arrangement in which Garciaparra and minor-league outfielder Matt Murton were sent from Boston to the Cubs while shortstop Orlando Cabrera (from Montreal) and first baseman Doug Mientkiewicz (from Minnesota) arrived in Boston. The young general manager also pulled the trigger on a separate deal, acquiring speedy backup outfielder Dave Roberts from the Los Angeles Dodgers for minor-league outfielder Henri Stanley.

And just like that, after months of contract negotiations, politicking, public sparring, and trade rumors, the Nomar Garciaparra era in Boston came to an extraordinarily abrupt end.

He was gone.

"My initial reaction was, 'Wow,'" Garciaparra told reporters during a three-game series between the Sox and Twins in Minneapolis. "There's been a lot of talk, a lot of speculation, but you don't know. . . . I've been away from it, focused on just playing, because it was out of my control. If it was in my control, I'd still be wearing a Red Sox uniform. That's the place I know, I love, all those fans, I'll always remember, but I'm also going to another good place. I'm going to a phenomenal city with a great tradition as well, with phenomenal fans, a great organization, and I'm excited about that. . . . There's definitely sadness, because I'm leaving a place that I love, a place that's dear to my heart."

Concluded the player: "Every single day I went out there, I was proud to put that uniform on, and what it represented. It meant the world to me [to play for the Red Sox]. I've always said, 'This is the place I started and always wanted to finish.' Obviously, it's not going to happen, but at the same time, they can take the shirt off my back, but they can't take away the memories."

Understandably, in many circles, the trading of Garciaparra was met with disbelief. The trade was front-page news in both major Boston newspapers and was the lead story on television newscasts. For all of the things that had befallen the Red Sox over the course of their history, the team always had a lineage of great players who began and ended their careers in Boston. And while that legacy had come to an end the day Roger Clemens left the Red Sox via free agency to sign with the Toronto Blue Jays on Friday the Thirteenth of December 1996, the idea that the Red Sox would trade a homegrown franchise player and one of the cornerstones of the franchise—and someone still in the prime of his career—seemed utterly preposterous.

The Red Sox, after all, had not traded away a player of Garciaparra's stature since dealing away (gulp) Babe Ruth to the hated Yankees in 1920.

As it turned out, of course, the trading of Ruth was a landmark event that significantly altered the history of both the Red Sox and Yankees, New York winning 26 world titles since the trade to the Red Sox' zero. The deal eventually spawned the cute-but-ridiculous notion that trading away Ruth had resulted in the Red Sox being cursed, which, in turn, became a crutch for some disgruntled Red Sox fans to rely on during decades of anguish. In fact, the notion of a curse became a far more popular topic and media hook in the rest of America than it did in Boston, where most Red Sox fans recognized the simple fact that the Yankees won more championships because they frequently had the better team. In the end, what it would take for the Red Sox to beat the Yankees was a talented team that believed it could win more than it believed in the existence of any curse or supernatural force.

Yet, in the wake of the Garciaparra deal, Epstein's place in history hung in the balance. Were Garciaparra and the Cubs to go on and win the World Series—Chicagoans had their own absurd curse theories to explain the Cubs having gone without a world title since 1908—Epstein might forever be linked with former Sox owner Harry Frazee, the man who made the decision to sell Ruth to the Yankees. Epstein was well aware of that fact, which made his willingness to pull the trigger on the trade all the more courageous.

"The safe thing to do would have been to play it out. The safe thing to do would have been not to touch it," said Epstein, who acknowledged that he subsequently ran into many fans who expressed displeasure with the trade. "But in my mind, we were not going to win the World Series as is."

With the Red Sox still resting seven and a half games behind the Yankees, in fact, there was the very real possibility that Boston would fail *to make the playoffs,* an unnerving reality for club officials who had invested $130 million (there's that number again) into the payroll. And though Sox officials were still saying publicly that the division title was not beyond their grasp—they still had 61 games to play entering the July 31 meeting with the Twins—the reality was that they were focused more on winning an American League wild card race against a number of teams. Most notably, an Anaheim Angels squad that had similarly and freely spent dollars during the off-season, signing outfielders Vladimir Guerrero and Jose Guillen along with pitchers Bartolo Colon and Kelvim Escobar in hopes of contending for the World Series.

From purely a baseball perspective, the Red Sox felt that by trading Garciaparra they could improve their depth, team speed, and shoddy defense, the latter of which was still haunting the team.

"If we're going to beat Anaheim," Epstein said during one private moment in which he acknowledged that the Yankees appeared beyond his team's reach, "then we needed to improve our defense."

Had that been the focus of the discussion over the next few days and weeks, Nomar Garciaparra's departure from Boston might have been more pleasant, though even then the idea of a cordial separation might have been naive. As the media picked up the pieces after the deal, Sox officials suggested that they had no choice but to trade Garciaparra, who forced his way out of town by threatening to go on the disabled list in August and September—the most important months of the season—if team officials did not trade him. Then Sox officials leaked to the *Globe* that Garciaparra actually injured his Achilles playing soccer before spring training—not during camp, as had been suggested—further attempting to smear the player's reputation. The entire matter was further clouded by the club's relationship with the *Globe*, which was owned by the *New York Times*, which had the second-largest share of ownership in the Sox next to John Henry himself.

All around, there were alliances and allegiances being upheld, all of which made the truth impossible to decipher, particularly when Garciaparra offered a side to the stories that completely contradicted what was suggested by Sox officials.

Ultimately and inevitably, of course, the attention turned back to the field, where the Red Sox still had time to make up for weeks of ineptitude. But on the night of July 31, after the eventful trades of the day, the Sox went out and dropped a 5–4 decision to the Twins. The next day, with Cabrera at shortstop—he homered in his first at-bat—the Sox suffered a 4–3 defeat that dropped their record to 56–47, meaning that they had gone a perfectly mediocre 41–41 over an 82-game stretch that had begun on May 1.

Given that reality, the Red Sox were looking very much like a Fortune 500 company.

They cost a fortune.

And they played .500.

In the first two weeks after Theo Epstein traded away the best shortstop ever to wear a Boston uniform, the reality is that the Red Sox did not improve much. The Sox went 4–4 in their first eight games after the trade, 8–7 in their first 15. By then, their deficit in the American League East had mushroomed to a season-high 10½ games with a mere 46 games to play, making any chance of catching the division-leading New York Yankees a virtual impossibility.

And then, as if waiting for that stage of the baseball season where the games truly meant something, the Red Sox took off on of the most impressive, extraordinary, and downright inspiring winning streaks of their considerable history.

In the span of one month—from August 16 through September 15—the Red Sox won 25 of the 30 games they played, assembling winning streaks of six games, 10 games, and four games during a truly remarkable stretch in which they won 16-of-17 and 20-of-22. The stretch began with a three-game sweep over the Toronto Blue Jays in Boston and ended with the Sox taking 2-of-3 from the Tampa Bay Devil Rays at Fenway Park, and along the way the Red Sox took complete command of the American League wild card race by going a sterling 8–1 in nine games against the Texas Rangers, Anaheim Angels and Oakland A's, three playoff contenders from the American League West with whom the Red Sox were competing for the fourth and final playoff position in the American League.

Of particular importance was the series against the Angels, on whom Epstein, in particular, had set his sights at the time of the Garciaparra deal. Anaheim had arrived in Boston just one and a half games behind the Sox in the wild card race and was simultaneously making a run at the West Division title, and the series drew additional attention in Boston because the Sox had been beating up on weak sisters like Toronto, Chicago, and Detroit. So in came the Angels, whom many believed would provide a true test for the new-and-improved Red Sox, and the result was Boston victories by the scores of 10–7, 12–7, and 4–3, the latter a classic one-run game pitched by a rejuvenated Lowe, who improved to 4–1 since surviving the trading deadline.

From top to bottom, the Red Sox were clicking, playing with both conviction and unbridled confidence.

"No disrespect to the teams that we've played, but everyone kept saying, 'They've won a lot of games, but look who they've played,'" noted center fielder Johnny Damon. "Now we're playing the Anaheim Angels, who had won the same amount of games that we had, and then we win three in a row. I hope people start giving us credit because this is a very special run that we are going on."

Said closer Keith Foulke: "For $150 million, this is how we're supposed to play."

Offered Lowe: "It's just confidence. People remember August and September—that's what I kept telling myself early in the year. No one remembers what you did at the beginning of the year. People want to know what you do down the stretch run."

After sweeping the Angels, the Sox took 2-of-3 from the Texas Rangers, then went into Oakland for a three-game series against the A's, who were competing with Anaheim for the AL West Division title. In what proved to be a thorough dismantling, the Red Sox won by scores of 8–3, 7–1, and 8–3, improving to 8–1 against the A's on the season, 11–1 since falling behind to Oakland, 2–0, after the first two games of the 2003 AL Division Series. That, too, was significant, particularly if the Sox were to end up meeting the A's again in the first round of the 2004 playoffs.

Of the three victories over Oakland, none was more symbolic than the middle one, a contest in which the Red Sox played flawlessly. Once again stationed behind Lowe, the Sox stifled Oakland rallies in the second and eighth innings with, of all things, defense, allowing their offense time to build on an early 3–0. By the end of the series with the A's, the same Sox team that had been generously handing out unearned runs in May and June was now among the stingiest teams in the American League in the category—the Sox also ranked among the American League leaders in fielding percentage since August 1, when Cabrera joined the team—and their formula for winning was right out of a Baseball 101 textbook: get an early lead, play solid defense and, of course, get good, stable, reliable pitching both at the beginning of the game and at the end.

The A's, who had become one of the best home teams in baseball during the tenure of revolutionary general manager Billy Beane, simply were no match for them.

"We played our asses off tonight," a beaming Epstein said after the second of the three Oakland victories.

Said Francona: "We've been making teams beat us. We didn't necessarily do that [earlier in the season]. We were giving teams extra outs and giving them more opportunities. Teams had more opportunities to beat us than they do."

By the time the Red Sox got to Seattle, their August run was being compared with the greatest streaks in club history, most notably an infamous stretch during the 1988 season forever known as "Morgan Magic." Having struggled for much of the 1988 season under then manager John McNamara, the Sox began the second half of the season under longtime minor league skipper Joe Morgan, who took over as interim manager when the crusty McNamara was fired. Playing as if liberated from the rule of a tyrant, the 1988 Sox won 12 straight and 19-of-20 to thrust themselves back into contention, ultimately winning the American League East before a swift, four-game sweep at the hands of the A's in the American League Championship Series.

But unlike 1988, where the Red Sox won games in dramatic and sometimes peculiar fashion, the 2004 Sox relied on no such luck. Their overall play was simply masterful, the kind of baseball that many expected when the club left spring training, assuming the Sox had been able to function with a healthy Garciaparra and Nixon. As it was, this streak took place without Garciaparra, who had been traded, and largely without Nixon, who returned to the club only in a limited role at the beginning of September after reinjuring his left quadriceps muscle late in July. At the time, Nixon feared that he would not play again at all in 2004.

Now, with less than a month remaining in the regular season, Nixon was eyeing a trip to the playoffs and all of New England was once again caught up in Red Sox hysteria.

"Everybody's hitting and everything's falling in line," said Morgan, a Walpole, Massachusetts native whose winning streak turned him from an interim hire into the Sox manager through the 1991 season. "It's pretty much the same thing [as in 1988]. The only difference is it's not the interim manager."

Already armed with a contract through the 2006 season, Terry Francona was not complaining.

After romping through Oakland, the Red Sox arrived in Seattle on September 9 with a five-game lead over Anaheim in the American League wild card race and with an 84–54 record, a startling 30 games over .500. There were a mere 24 games remaining in the season and, coupled with the fact that Oakland, Texas, and Anaheim were due to face one another in the final two weeks of the regular season, the increasing likelihood was that the Red Sox were once again going to the playoffs. The question was whether the Red Sox would be going as the American League wild card entry or as the champions of the American League East, all because an extraordinary thing had happened on the way from July to August to September.

The Red Sox had moved to within just two games of the mighty Yankees.

During the month of August, in particular, the greatest difference between the Red Sox and Yankees once again was coming to light. While the Red Sox were methodically and systematically dispatching opponents, the Yankees were plodding along at a mediocre pace. From August 16 through September 8, while the Red Sox were going 20–2, the Yankees went 11–10, surrendering a remarkable eight and a half games in the standings in the span of just 24 days. And while there was some panic in New York concerning the play of the Yankees, the reality was that New York's bottom-line won-lost record was not poor as much as it was average. The Red Sox, on the other hand, were playing at an otherworldly pace that had the entire baseball world awestruck for the simplest of reasons.

Baseball was a game built on failure. In any 10-game stretch, to win six was considered a notable achievement. And when you got right down to it, the difference between a good team and an average team was roughly one win every 10 games, which introduced a wide range of variables—including luck—into the equation.

As a result, baseball officials and executives were careful to avoid what Epstein liked to call "snapshot evaluations," simple cross-sections that revealed only a part of the more accurate picture. Lots of teams—or, for that matter, players—had stellar games, weeks, or months, but baseball, in particular, was a game best measured over time. (Worcester *Telegram* reporter Bill Ballou, a veteran writer who covered the Red Sox, often described baseball as "a game of exposure.") During longer stretches, strengths and weaknesses were respectively reaffirmed or exposed, providing a much more accurate representation of the facts. So while fans liked to project data from small samples—if backup catcher Doug Mirabelli could hit five home runs in 10 games, didn't it stand to reason that he could hit 50 home runs in 100 games?—such leaps in logic were impossible (and dangerous) to make because there was nothing more deceiving than a streak of any kind.

In baseball, nobody was ever as good as he looked during a hot streak or as bad he looked during a slump.

And the same was true of teams.

Nonetheless, it was the *manner* in which the Red Sox were dispatching opponents that had baseball observers truly impressed and that had many convinced that the Red Sox were better than the Yankees, that Boston ultimately would catch New York and win the American League East. On that topic, too, there was considerable debate as to the real value of a division championship—if both the Red Sox and Yankees qualified for the playoffs, what did it matter?—but at the very least it was something else for Bostonians and New Yorkers to disagree on. Given the success of the Oakland A's under the guidance of Billy Beane, there had developed a theory in baseball that the best teams were actually determined over the course of the regular season, that the playoffs were more difficult to predict because, over a shorter span, success was arbitrary. But over the marathon that was the regular season, the cream inevitably rose to the top, and so in some convoluted manner it actually meant more to win a division title than it did to win a World Series.

Whatever the ultimate logic, the difference between the Red Sox and Yankees was now becoming clear to everyone: the Red Sox had better pitching, particularly in the starting rotation. During the pivotal month of August, Red Sox starters went a combined 19–6 with a 3.66 ERA, numbers that dwarfed the totals of their Yankees counterparts, who went 9–10 with a 5.15 ERA.

Lowe (3–1, 4.19 ERA during the month) had rediscovered his form from 2002, when he was a 21-game winner, and both Bronson Arroyo (3–2, 4.01) and Tim Wakefield (5–1) had been giving the Red Sox consistent outings. All three of those pitchers served as excellent complements to Schilling and Martinez, who, in tandem, were firing on all cylinders to give the Red Sox the kind of prolific one-two punch that general manager Epstein had envisioned when he acquired Schilling from the Arizona Diamondbacks the previous November.

The Yankees? Their starters were failing. After losing pillars Roger Clemens, Andy Pettitte, and David Wells to free agency, the Yankees acquired Kevin Brown and Javier Vazquez during the off-season to step into sizable holes. But by early September, when the hot-headed Brown broke his left hand punching a wall in frustration as the Yankees' lead in the American League East slowly and steadily and slipped away, the Yankees were faced with the reality that Vazquez was coming off an August in which he went 1–2 with a 7.43 ERA and staff ace Mike Mussina was reeling from a month during which he went 0–2 with a 7.04 ERA.

Were it not for the resurrected Orlando Hernandez, the Yankees might have already lost their grip on the American League East.

At least that's the way Red Sox fans saw it.

As for the Red Sox, the consistency and dependability of their starting rotation was beginning to reveal itself as the foundation on which their success was built. Epstein was fond of pooh-poohing the long-standing belief that championships were won with pitching and defense—"Unlike a lot of people, I don't think that pitching is 90 percent of the game," said the young general manager—but the bulk of his maneuvers since the end of the 2003 campaign were committed to improving those two specific areas. He traded for Schilling. He signed Foulke. And at the trading deadline, he chose to jettison Garciaparra, whose offensive upside was higher than that of Cabrera and Mientkiewicz, for better depth and defense at two positions on the field where the team's inability to make plays was proving costly.

At the time, in fact, it seemed as if everything for the Red Sox was going according to plan. While Byung-Hyun Kim had long since fallen off the map—even during spring training, players were privately lobbying for Arroyo over Kim, whom they found to be eccentric and unwilling to assimilate—the

Red Sox could not have asked for a better outcome with their pitching. Early on in spring training, pitching coach Dave Wallace had stressed that the club's greatest concern entering the season was depth, in large part because the Sox did not have a strong pool of pitchers to draw from at Triple-A, which effectively served as a taxi squad for the major league team.

"My biggest concern is health and depth," said Wallace, a baseball veteran who had worked as both and coach and executive with organizations including the Los Angeles Dodgers and New York Mets. "You're going to need pitchers during the year. For me, that's a major concern."

As it turned out—and for the Red Sox, this was an enormous stroke of good fortune—the Red Sox did not need many pitchers at all. After Arroyo replaced the enigmatic Kim early in the year, Red Sox starters did not miss a single start during the entire regular season as a result of injury. *Not one.* The Sox summoned minor-league left-hander Abe Alvarez from their Double-A affiliate in Portland, Maine, because they needed an additional starter for a doubleheader against the Baltimore Orioles in July, but Schilling, Martinez, Lowe, Wakefield,and Arroyo never once failed "to go to the post," as the pitchers termed it.

In this day and age, especially, that was an extraordinary achievement. In the entire major leagues during the 2004 season, 309 pitchers started games, an average of slightly more than 10 per team. Of those 309, only 79—or roughly 25 percent, an average of slightly more than two per team—were healthy and effective enough to make at least 29 starts. But the Red Sox had *five* starters who made at least 29 starts, meaning there were no unexpected surprises during the course of the season. Francona never had to juggle his rotation or unnecessarily tax his bullpen because of an injury to a starting pitcher. No starter went to the disabled list, which would have forced the Red Sox to summon depth from the minor leagues that Wallace feared was not there.

Red Sox officials partially credited this phenomenon to staff management on the part of their manager, pitching coach, and medical personnel, but the reality is that luck was a huge part of it, too. There wasn't a team in baseball that handled its pitchers with the hope that the club *would* have to make adjustments on the fly, but injuries were a part of the game for everyone. For the 2004 Red Sox—at least on the pitching staff—injuries never became a factor. And when Arroyo eclipsed 175 innings pitched late in the year, the Sox had five starters with 175 or more innings for the first time since 1929, the beginning of the Great Depression.

That achievement, in retrospect, was nothing short of extraordinary.

"We tried to be careful because we really didn't have a lot of starting pitching at Triple-A," Francona said late in the year, echoing Wallace's remarks from spring training. "We set things up at the All-Star break and we tried to set guys up so they could be healthy and productive. I think you've heard me say that a million times."

Along the way, Francona also modified his offensive approach, introducing the elements of speed and fundamentals into a Red Sox attack that was astonishingly uncreative during the first four months of the season. From April through July, in fact, the Red Sox rarely tried to steal bases, seldom attempted the hit-and-run, and almost never bunted. At times, Epstein and Francona seemed so committed to baseball's trendy new "Moneyball" approach—the philosophy took the name from a Michael Lewis book about Beane and his revolutionary statistical approach to baseball—that Epstein and Francona often seemed to be making a political statement as much as they were overseeing a baseball team. They sometimes seemed so committed to the strategy, so downright blind, that they eschewed some of the long-accepted practices of the game on the field (namely, the bunt) even when it was the right thing to do.

Throughout baseball, in fact, the entire "Moneyball" strategy had become a controversial topic. As the general manager of the small-market A's, Beane had developed a system that allowed Oakland to win despite limited resources. In short, the A's invested most of their limited player payroll in pitching—there simply was no way around it: you had to pay for pitching—and built an offense around cheaper, more affordable players based largely on their on-base percentage. The strategy, quite simply, was that the more baserunners you had, the more runs you would score, which was especially true if you did not have the money to pay expensive run producers like first baseman Jason Giambi and shortstop Miguel Tejada, former winners of the Most Valuable Player award who left the A's via free agency when the team was no longer able to afford them. And along with that strategy, Beane incorporated the use of sabermetrics, statistical studies that showed it was generally inefficient to bunt or to attempt stolen bases, plays that could produce unnecessary outs and effectively disarm potentially the most damaging weapon on the field, the hitter.

If you had a lineup filled with men who could hit or work their way onto the bases, after all, why not let them do it?

And for the A's, in particular, the philosophy worked.

By the end of August, however—and after the arrivals of Cabrera, Mientkiewicz, and Roberts—the Red Sox had added some creativity, some *baseball,* to what had a been a dull, stagnant, attack. They bunted when the situation called for it. They executed the hit-and-run on occasion. And they stole bases more frequently, adding more balance to their attack and greater dimension to their arsenal, falling somewhere between the philosophies of the A's and, say, the Minnesota Twins, another successful small-market team that had succeeded with an approach almost entirely different to that of Oakland's.

The bottom line was that there was more than one way to skin a cat, and when it came to offensive baseball, the more ways the better.

Francona, for his part, attributed a large part of the team's modified approach to the change in personnel, but the reality was that the Red Sox altered their strategy, too. And somewhere between the new "Moneyball" style of play and the old, outdated beliefs of traditional, old-school baseball, the 2004 Red Sox found a very, very happy medium.

"I think you try to manage your personnel to their strengths, and I think we have different people here than we had before," Francona said. "We're catching the ball, we're pitching and we're getting timely hitting. We're doing a lot of different things."

More specifically, the Red Sox were capable of winning in a lot of different ways, offering a big reason why they were rumbling through the most challenging part of the season with extraordinary ease and efficiency.

And so for the final time during the 2004 regular season, the Red Sox prepared to take on the Yankees, this time for the right to stake claim to the American League East.

And the Red Sox team that the Yankees were about to see in New York was unlike any the Yankees had encountered during this season.

THE STEINBRENNER WATCH—YANKEES

GEORGE STEINBRENNER CAME BOUNDING DOWN THE STEPS FROM the Stadium Club door to the street, on his way to his waiting Lincoln Town Car. As usual, reporters were poised to intercept him. They expected nothing particularly interesting, certainly nothing inflammatory. The Yankee owner hadn't turned on his team in classic Boss fashion all season, and now, on August 9, the Yankees had a 10½-game lead on the Red Sox.

But you never know with George, which is why the *Post* and the *Daily News*, and sometimes other newspapers covering the Yankees, assign a reporter just to cover the owner whenever he flies in from his home in Tampa.

There was a time when an irate Steinbrenner might say or do anything after a tough loss, from firing the manager to demoting a pitcher who had "spit the bit," as he would say. Reporters were always on the lookout for him, but usually they didn't have to look far, as he couldn't wait to vent publicly, and often came storming into the back of the press box to alert everyone that Hurricane George was about to blow.

Ah, but age and four championships in six seasons combined to take most of the bite out of the Boss as he entered his 70s. Even when he criticized his team, it was mild compared to the old days, and he no longer made himself easily available when his temper sent him into a rage. As a result, by the dawn of the new millennium, reporters only went looking for him at Yankee Stadium when a crisis was at hand.

But then Leon Carter, to the chagrin of many a sportswriter, changed all of that. The *Daily News* sports editor since 1999, Carter is responsible for what is widely known around the stadium as the Steinbrenner Watch, since he's the one who began ordering reporters from his newspaper to stake out the Yankee owner anytime he was in town. That, in turn, eventually forced other newspapers to do likewise.

As Carter tells it, the idea for the Steinbrenner Watch goes back to 2001, when the Yankees were routed 12–2 on August 2 by the Texas Rangers, immediately after Texas owner Tom Hicks had popped off in the Fort Worth *Star-Telegram*. At the time the Yankees were well on their way to a fourth straight AL East title, but Hicks was quoted saying "these aren't the same Yankees" who had won four championships in six years.

After the loss, Carter asked *Daily News* baseball columnist Bill Madden to call Steinbrenner in Tampa and get a reaction to both the loss and Hicks' comments.

Steinbrenner took Madden's call and delivered a back-page headline, accusing his team of "laying down and dying," while also making a point to remind Hicks that his Rangers, with Alex Rodriguez in his first year in Texas, were in last place.

"Our back page was 'STEAMED,'" Carter recalls. "Everyone else dealt with the loss. We had George with the kind of quotes you can't buy."

In New York, of course, the back page often sells the paper on newsstands all over the city, no small matter since the *Daily News* and the *Post* are always competing for readers—and more to the point, for circulation figures that are the basis for selling advertising space.

In any case, Carter says it was after the "STEAMED" back page that Steinbrenner began making himself less available to reporters, especially by phone. As a result, Carter put his reporters on Steinbrenner alert in 2002, making sure they knew when he was in town, ready to track him down at the first hint of trouble. It was a quiet season on that front, but then when the Yankees were bounced out of the playoffs by the Anaheim Angels, Carter sent feature writer Wayne Coffey to Tampa in December for a sit-down interview, and hit the jackpot when Steinbrenner took swipes at Joe Torre and his coaches, and even—gasp—Derek Jeter, accusing his star shortstop of partying too much.

The criticism infuriated both Torre and Jeter, creating the first real chaos of the Torre era, and plenty of follow-up stories.

Carter loved it, naturally, and decided to make the Steinbrenner Watch an official assignment for the 2003 season.

Or, as one reporter with experience on the Watch calls it: waiting for George to say something really moronic.

Carter doesn't put it quite like that. But neither does he try to pretend otherwise.

"Because he has taken to releasing most of his public comments through [Manhattan publicist] Howard Rubenstein in recent years," Carter says, "you don't really get the real Steinbrenner. His comments are measured. We want to get his true thoughts. I think fans want to hear from him, especially after a loss, because he's like one of them. Even if the Yankees are in first place, when they lose a game, to George it's like the end of the world.

"We don't stake out [Mets' owner] Fred Wilpon or [Jets' owner] Woody Johnson or [Giants' owner] Wellington Mara. But because of his history, we do stake out Steinbrenner. Part of it is for competitive reasons. If he says something outrageous, I don't want to read it somewhere else."

Since 2003, then, anytime Steinbrenner is in town, Carter has assigned one of his reporters to wait outside the stadium after the game, win or lose, and to try to get a reaction from George as he leaves. Sometimes he's out the door in five minutes, sometimes it can be well over an hour.

At first the *Daily News* reporter usually would be waiting by himself. But since Memorial Day of 2003, when Steinbrenner criticized his team at length to the *News*' Christian Red—as well as the Newark *Star-Ledger*'s Larry Rocca—after Roger Clemens' first failed attempt at career victory No. 300, other newspapers were forced to react. The *Post* began assigning a reporter to the same duty, and, after important losses, reporters from other papers often hurried outside as well.

It's not exactly a plum assignment. The reporter usually doesn't get to write a baseball story that night, since it's often too late to get locker room reaction to the game by the time Steinbrenner departs. And often he or she winds up writing no more than a few paragraphs after the Boss says something innocuous as Yankee security people hustle him into the backseat of the Town Car.

Beyond that, sportswriters in general are tired of Steinbrenner. When he does criticize his team, his rants are as dim-witted as ever, proof that after all these years, he still doesn't understand baseball, still thinks problems can be solved with football solutions—harder workouts, better play-calling, et cetera. Likewise, then, after all these years, you have to ask: who cares?

Carter believes fans care. He believes people react strongly to Steinbrenner, one way or the other. So even though the Yankees owner rarely provides back-page material anymore, the Watch is nonnegotiable, win or lose.

"No matter what he says, we want it," says Carter.

For four months in 2004, the stakeout had been mostly a waste of time. But on August 9, after a 5–4 loss to the Blue Jays on a Monday afternoon, the Boss stopped as he reached his car and began answering questions from two reporters, the *Daily News*' Kristie Ackert and the *Post*'s Evan Grossman, both of whom had drawn Watch duty that day.

Steinbrenner hadn't clashed with Torre all season, but on this day he was furious that the manager had played Kenny Lofton in right field. Torre had given sore-shouldered Gary Sheffield a rest, using him as the DH, and Lofton had made an error, approaching Reed Johnson's single tentatively, then having it kick off his leg. The error allowed a run to score, but the play happened in the second inning, so it didn't stand out as crucial.

Nevertheless, someone obviously had told Steinbrenner that this was the first time Lofton had started a game in right field, and that was all the ammunition he needed to unload on Torre.

"I don't want to see Lofton in right field," Steinbrenner barked when asked what he thought of the loss. "I think two things: the error wouldn't have been made out there if Sheffield had been out there. And I think he might have caught that home run [in the sixth inning by Gabe Gross]. That home run barely got in. Sheffield goes right up after it. The defense wasn't good. That's what worries me."

Finally, the Steinbrenner Watch had paid dividends. This was back-page stuff, the owner attacking the manager for the first time since they'd kissed and made up in the spring. Never mind that, as usual, Steinbrenner's criticism was mindless. With a double-digit lead in the standings, Torre was smartly managing with the big picture in mind, trying to make sure that Sheffield's season-long shoulder pain didn't reach the point where it forced him out of the lineup by, say, October.

Second, while it was true that Gross' home run barely cleared the 10-foot right field wall, it also got out of the park in the blink of an eye, a laser toward the foul line that was in the seats before Lofton could get anywhere near it. Sheffield, who isn't as fast or as agile as Lofton, had as much chance of catching it from his seat in the dugout as he would have had in right field.

It was enough to make a manager bang his head against the dugout wall. However, Torre, with his $19.1 million contract extension long since signed and sealed, seemed completely unfazed when asked about the criticism the next day. If anything, he seemed somewhat amused, much the way he had always reacted before things got personal between him and the owner in 2003.

"He's George, he's going to say things," said Torre. "Last year, I thought maybe the eight years were enough, maybe we were tired of each other. But after this spring, that changed, obviously, with the new contract and everything. It changed my whole perspective. It's different in my brain now. That didn't bother me."

And, by the way, Torre noted: he wouldn't hesitate to use Lofton in right field again if he thought it necessary, and, in fact, did play him there a couple of more times during the season to give Sheffield a rest.

Of course, a 10½-game lead made it easier to laugh off criticism. At the time, in fact, the Yankees were enjoying perhaps their most stress-free days of the season. Not only did they have the big lead, but they had a five-game winning streak coming into that game with the Blue Jays, and over four consecutive days they'd received eight-inning gems from starting pitchers Kevin Brown, Javier Vazquez, El Duque Hernandez, and Jon Lieber, something Yankee pitchers hadn't done in four years.

And Steinbrenner picks this time to take on his manager? Even for him, irrational and impulsive as he is, it seemed a bit over the top. So what was eating George? That was the real question, and it wasn't hard to figure out the answer. Steinbrenner is accustomed to getting what he wants as Yankee owner, since money can buy just about anything in a sport without a salary cap. But in this case, it couldn't help him acquire Randy Johnson at the trading deadline, and Steinbrenner had been on the prowl since the July 31 deadline came and went without a deal.

The Boss had wanted Johnson badly. As early as June 30, while the Yankees were in the midst of sweeping the Red Sox to take an eight-and-a-half-game lead in the AL East, Steinbrenner did a radio interview on The Sporting News network, where he shocked baseball people by openly lusting for The Big Unit.

"God, who wouldn't love to have Randy Johnson?" he said when asked about the possibility of Johnson being available. "He is a great lefthander. He is probably one of the greatest pitchers the game has ever seen. He's a dominator and we'd love to have him. Anybody would love to have him, but I also know that Jerry Colangelo is not going to give him away. We'll have to wait and see what happens as the deadline gets closer."

Steinbrenner seemed to be daring Bud Selig to fine him, considering his answer amounted to the very definition of tampering with a player under contract with another team, which is forbidden in baseball. But Selig, who picks his fights judiciously with Steinbrenner in return for his support on various matters, looked the other way. Meanwhile, the blatant courting of Johnson by the Yankees continued, as Yankee players sweet-talked the 41-year-old lefthander at the All-Star game in Houston. Even the normally reserved Mariano Rivera kidded with reporters that maybe he could talk Bernie Williams into giving up Johnson's No. 51 if he became a Yankee.

Talking Johnson into waiving his no-trade clause wasn't the problem, however. The Yankees were the one team for whom he was willing to leave the desert, and the Diamondbacks, with the worst record in the majors at the time, were ready to unload his huge salary as part of a rebuilding process. The hang-up was that the Yankees didn't have the kind of major-league-ready prospects in their farm system, or even inexpensive young major-leaguers with a future, to entice Arizona.

It's easy to forget, considering the enormity of the Yankee payroll, that this run of championships and near-championships since 1996 was launched by a farm system that produced a great nucleus—Derek Jeter, Mariano Rivera, Andy Pettitte, Bernie Williams, and Jorge Posada. But all of those players were signed or drafted by 1992, and since then the farm system has contributed precious little to the Yankees cause. If you don't count Alfonso Soriano, for whom the Yankees outbid other teams to sign when he forced his way out of a contract in Japan, the last player to come out of their farm system and have a significant impact was Posada, who was a rookie in 1997.

Over the years the Yankees have been notorious for trading away prospects to acquire veteran talent, but by 2004 the problem was more the result of a decade of bad drafting. Since drafting Jeter in 1992, 13 players had been selected in the first-round of the June amateur draft by the Yankes, and only two of them had reached the majors—neither as Yankees. Left-hander Eric Milton was traded as a minor-leaguer in 1998 as part of a deal for Minnesota Twins' second baseman Chuck Knoblauch, while right-hander Mark Prior turned down the Yankees' offer when he was drafted out of high school in 1998, choosing to go to USC instead, before being drafted three years later by the Cubs. Finally, even with resources to outbid other teams on international players who aren't subject to the draft, the Yankees have wasted big money on the likes of Andy Morales, Katsuhiro Maeda, and Jackson Melian.

The problem isn't that Steinbrenner skimps on scouting as a way to help pay his millionaire ballplayers. For years now, Yankee scouts just haven't done a good job of identifying and projecting big-league ability, and hard as it may seem to believe, other executives around the majors think a big part of the problem is that Steinbrenner is too . . . soft? Apparently the same guy who is notoriously tough on his employees, from secretaries in Tampa to his GM, Cashman, in New York, hasn't been nearly tough enough on his scouting and personnel department.

"He should have cleaned out that whole Tampa office by now, based on their development record," an American League GM said during the 2004 season. "If his major-league executives performed the same way, he'd be firing people left and right. But all he's done is shuffle some titles around with his scouting operation. Nobody can figure it out."

Steinbrenner did some more shuffling just before the trading deadline, growing angry as he kept hearing that his farm system had nothing the Diamondbacks—or other teams—wanted. He demoted scouting director Lin Garrett, shifting his responsibilities to international scouting, and put Damon Oppenheimer, VP of player development, in charge of amateur scouting. But for the most part he has had the same people running his Tampa operation for nearly a decade, and has little in the way of major-league talent to show for it.

As a result, the Yankees never got close to making a deal at the trading deadline for Johnson. The D-Backs had scouts watching the Yankees' Triple-A and Double-A teams in the minors for weeks, but couldn't find players they considered the type of big-time prospects they would need to justify trading The Big Unit. As a result, conversations between Cashman and Arizona GM Joe Garagiola Jr. never went very far.

"We tried to get creative," said Cashman, "and get another team involved that might match up better with what they were looking for. But nothing worked."

Cashman did make a trade at the deadline, sending Jose Contreras to the Chicago White Sox for Esteban Loaiza, a journeyman who'd struck gold in 2003 when a newly developed cut fastball helped him go 21–9, but then seemed to lose the magic as quickly as he'd found it. Loaiza had been pitching poorly for weeks, and while the Yankees were hoping to revive him, they made the deal mostly because they'd given up on Contreras. Indeed, to get rid of him they agreed to pay $8 million of the $17 million remaining on the famous four-year, $32 million contract with which the Yankees outbid the Red Sox and prompted the more famous "Evil Empire" line from Sox president Larry Lucchino.

"We still think he's got a lot of talent," Cashman said of Contreras. "But it just wasn't going to happen for him in New York."

That was a nice way of saying Contreras couldn't handle the pressure of pitching for the Yankees, a conclusion that everyone in the organization had reached. He wound up pitching better for the White Sox, but still nothing like the Yankee scouts had envisioned. And so the Contreras signing was still another black eye for the organization's scouting and development department, and finally it was costing the Yankees dearly.

Loaiza was no Big Unit, everyone knew that, but when he turned out to be worse than Contreras in his first handful of starts for the Yankees, concern about the starting rotation continued to linger. After the flurry of strong outings that preceded Steinbrenner's Kenny Lofton outburst, the Yankees sagged through the dog days of August, losing six of seven at one point, including an embarrassing sweep in the Bronx at the hands of the Anaheim Angels. Suddenly their lead was shrinking, as the Red Sox finally had gotten hot, and with Mike Mussina just back after a month on the disabled list with a sore elbow, the Yankees were waiting for someone to step forward as an ace.

That it turned out to be Orlando Hernandez was the surprise of the season. Actually, for a month or so El Duque seemed to be keeping the Yankees in first place single-handedly, and the irony was that for all the money Steinbrenner had spent, the Cuban right-hander had cost the owner pennies in comparison to the rest of the roster. For that matter, he was a Yankee only because he desperately had wanted to wear the pinstripes again.

In fact, the Yankees had washed their hands of El Duque when they traded him to the Montreal Expos after the 2002 season, as part of a three-way trade that sent Bartolo Colon from Montreal to the Chicago White Sox. The Yankees made the trade at least partly to keep the Red Sox from getting Colon, but they had also grown tired of El Duque's act. As injuries limited his effectiveness, the Yankees began to regard him not as the clutch postseason pitcher he had been for them after defecting from Cuba in 1998, but a hot-tempered, high-maintenance employee who complained too much, whether about being asked to pitch in relief, or about relatively minor clubhouse issues. At one point, as punishment for El Duque's behavior, Cashman took his interpreter, Leo Astacio, away from him, and forced the Spanish-speaking pitcher to fend for himself with the press. Eventually Cashman relented on the interpreter, but as Hernandez continued to be hindered by injuries, the Yankees were looking for a reason to move him.

El Duque never did pitch for the Expos, missing the entire 2003 season because of a rotator cuff tear in his right shoulder that required surgery, and he became a free agent when the Expos made no attempt to re-sign him. By January of 2004 his agent, Jeff Moorad, was shopping Hernandez around, with the promise that the pitcher would show that his arm was sound at an open workout before spring training camps opened. At the time, the Red Sox had more interest in taking a chance on the right-hander than did the Yankees.

The workout, at the University of Miami, was attended by scouts from several teams, but the scouts came away from it feeling as if they'd been played for fools. Four other unemployed Moorad clients, including Donovan Osborne and Randy Keisler, threw first. El Duque then took the mound and threw 35 pitches, several of which were looping curveballs, and his fastball topped out at 78 mph on their radar guns.

"It was a joke," one scout said months later. "His arm strength wasn't back, and the feeling there was that he wasn't even trying because he didn't want to sign with anybody but the Yankees."

Red Sox officials had the same feeling, especially when El Duque declined their request for a private workout in February. They were further convinced when, as GM Theo Epstein would say months later, Moorad told him that to sign El Duque, the Red Sox offer would have to "far exceed" that of the Yankees. No one was willing to guarantee too much money because there was no way to know what to expect from El Duque. Though he lists his birth date as October 11, 1969, baseball people suspected he was closer to 40 than 35, and he hadn't pitched in 18 months.

Finally, at the urging of organizational pitching guru Billy Connors, the Yankees signed Hernandez in March to a one-year contract that guaranteed him $500,000, plus $45,000 for every start he made. He spent the the first half of the season continuing to rebuild arm strength, and then, with Kevin Brown and Mike Mussina both sidelined at midseason, El Duque made his first start for the Yankees on July 11. He picked up a win when he allowed two runs over five innings against the Tampa Bay Devil Rays, and soon he was proving to be the bargain of the year.

"I wish we could have gotten him," Epstein admitted to reporters as El Duque began piling up the wins.

By the middle of August, Hernandez was 5–0, and still the Yankees were struggling enough to allow the streaking Red Sox to close the gap on them quickly. The Sox cut five games off of a 10½-game lead in the space of seven days, and suddenly everyone in New York was nervously watching the scoreboard. The Yankees then went 5–2 on a road trip to Cleveland and Toronto and still lost another game in the standings, before returning home to play the Cleveland Indians on August 31 with a four-and-a-half-game lead.

Predictions of doom were coming fast and furious now on the talk shows, but not even the most pessimistic of fans could have imagined the nightmare that would unfold in the opener to an 11-game home stand, as the Yankees were massacred 22–0 by the Indians. The score represented the worst loss in the history of baseball's most decorated franchise, and it tied the worst shutout defeat in all of Major League Baseball since 1900. As such, the beating would have been terribly humiliating under any circumstances, but given the way their lead in the AL East was evaporating, it made the Yankees look as if they weren't just collapsing, but choking.

Any mention of the Red Sox by reporters was met with defiance rather than the Yankees' usual practiced indifference. At his pregame press session even before the 22–0 loss, the normally unflappable Torre cut off a question about "the streaking Red Sox" with a curt reply that seemed to be revealing of the pressure the Yankees were feeling.

"Your job is to be negative, to look at the dark side," said Torre, speaking of the media. "In this clubhouse we don't do that."

There was no bright side on this night, however, and afterward Torre's own defiance melted.

"Whatever you want to write," he said with a shrug in his office after the game, "we deserve it."

Perhaps worst of all, the night had a symbolism the Yankees couldn't escape. Because while Javier Vazquez, who hadn't pitched well since the All-Star break, was getting tattooed by Cleveland, lasting only one and one-third innings, Curt Schilling was beating the Anaheim Angels in Boston, cutting still another game off the Yankees' lead, earning the 18th of his 21 wins for the season. Surely the juxtaposition caused Yankee decision makers to wonder about what might have been, though probably not for the first time.

At baseball's general managers' meetings in Scottsdale, Arizona, the previous November, the Yankees had made the decision to cut off trade discussions with the Arizona Diamondbacks for Schilling and pursue a trade for the younger Vazquez instead. At the time the Diamondbacks were asking for Nick Johnson and Alfonso Soriano, plus prospects, in a 5-for-1 deal for Schilling, and though GM Brian Cashman knew such a demand would be lowered eventually, he also believed there was no urgency to act. Based on what he was reading in the Phoenix-area newspapers where Schilling lived, Cashman believed the veteran pitcher would only waive his no-trade clause to go to the Yankees or, his old team, the Phillies. He didn't anticipate the emergence of Terry Francona as a Red Sox managerial candidate changing Schilling's mind, leading to a deal with the Red Sox by Thanksgiving.

"I assessed that wrong," Cashman would say at season's end. "What was unanticipated was the Red Sox swooping in the way they did."

Had Vazquez blossomed into a No. 1-type starter, as the Yankees hoped, at least it would have justified their preference at the time for a younger arm. But after a strong first half Vazquez fell into a prolonged slump that mystified everyone around the Yankees, because, somewhat like Jose Contreras, he could look so dominant at times. The difference was that where Joe Torre all but admitted he could see fear in Contreras' eyes at times, the manager was convinced that Vazquez didn't scare, and continued to believe he would be OK. However, others worried that he was having a confidence crisis he might not survive. His catcher, Jorge Posada, told reporters he hoped that in a strange way, taking the loss in the 22–0 game would make him tougher mentally.

"He looks tough," Posada said, "but he's not tough at times."

Vazquez at least was tough enough to answer reporters' questions at his locker after the mother of all blowouts, but the shell-shocked look on his face didn't bode well for the coming weeks, and sure enough, his problems would continue.

On this night, however, reporters weren't as interested in the reaction of Vazquez or any of the Yankee players as they were that of the owner. By about the third inning, everyone was on the Steinbrenner Watch, first keeping an eye out for one of his old back-of-the-press-box eruptions, and when that didn't materialize, joining the postgame stakeout outside the stadium.

It was an hour after the game when he emerged from the Stadium Club exit, and apparently was afraid of what he might say. He'd obviously told Yankees officials he wasn't talking, because his chauffer pulled the Town Car right in front of waiting reporters, blocking their path to Steinbrenner, who then jumped into the backseat while ignoring questions being shouted at him.

As it turned out, the 22–0 loss, combined with the specter of the charging Red Sox, was too cataclysmic for a George tantrum. Instead it brought out the old football coach in him—as he pictured it, a cross between Knute Rockne and Vince Lombardi.

So the next day he issued a press release through publicist Howard Rubenstein, reassuring the citizens of New York that his boys would make a goal-line stand against the invaders from the north.

"We all know that New Yorkers never quit," it read in part, "and we reflect the spirit of New York."

Then he ordered messages put on the marquee boards outside the stadium that usually only list that day's opponent and the time of game:

"Quitters never win. Winners never quit."

On scoreboards inside the stadium read still another message: "When the goin' gets tough, the tough get goin'." Farcically, the old Billy Ocean song by the same name played through the stadium speakers as the Yankees took batting practice.

It all began to feel like some *Saturday Night Live* skit, especially when Steinbrenner appeared in his private box during batting practice, two and a half hours before game time, and watched from above, apparently with the idea of inspiring his players. What it inspired mostly, however, was giggling. A-Rod compared it to "the principal watching class. It was pretty funny."

Of course, he said that only after El Duque Hernandez pitched the Yankees to a 5–3 victory that night, further cementing his new-found status as staff ace, while allowing everyone in the Bronx to breathe again. Somewhere, Knute Steinbrenner was surely congratulating himself for rescuing his team with his motivational methods.

Out on the George Watch, however, he wasn't taking any credit publicly.

"I don't mean to be rude," he said to reporters as he waved off questions while getting into his car. "Just savor the victory."

He said it as if it were a gift he'd personally delivered to the city.

Five days later, however, the owner wasn't feeling so benevolent. The Yankees had lost two of three to the Baltimore Orioles over the weekend, and their lead had been cut to two and a half games. The Yankees had looked tight, scoring only five runs in three games. In their entire history the Yankees had never blown a lead of more than six games in the standings, but now it looked like just a matter of time before the Red Sox caught them, and Steinbrenner was "freaking out at the very thought of it," as one Yankee employee put it at the time. The whole city was on George Watch by now. Everyone expected something, but no one expected him to resort to begging for a forfeit, which is what he did on Monday, September 6, the day the Tampa Bay Devil Rays showed up at 6 P.M. for a 1 P.M. doubleheader.

Hurricane Frances caused travel problems for the Devil Rays, forcing the doubleheader to be downsized to one game. The Yankees, who treated fans waiting all day at the stadium to free hot dogs and sodas, had a right to be upset. All indications were that the Devil Rays had disregarded directives from Major League Baseball to leave Tampa two days earlier, after weekend games with the Detroit Tigers were canceled because of the impending hurricane. Citing family concerns, the Devil Rays didn't want to leave before the hurricane hit, and then couldn't get out of Tampa on Monday until midafternoon. At the very least, MLB did a poor job of communicating with the Yankees on the situation, inconveniencing them and their fans. But Steinbrenner, who detests D-Rays' owner Vince Naimoli, made a serious misjudgment in sending team president Randy Levine onto the field to publicly call for a forfeit.

"We were here, ready to play, the Devil Rays weren't," Levine told a group of reporters late that afternoon. "The rule states if your team is here and ready to play, and the other team isn't here, there should be a forfeit."

Everyone listening knew that Levine—Steinbrenner's underboss, as *Daily News* columnist Mike Lupica calls him—was speaking for the Yankee owner. And considering that Hurricane Frances had caused much devastation in Florida, where the owner lived, Steinbrenner looked small and callous in calling for a forfeit. Not to mention scared of the Red Sox. After all, if the Yankees needed a forfeit from the lowly Devil Rays to win the AL East, they were really in trouble. Predictably, Steinbrenner was slammed by the newspapers for his stance, and just as predictably he then backpedaled, insisting through Levine and Cashman the next day that the Yankees hadn't actually asked for a forfeit; they only wanted to be treated fairly by MLB. Toward that end, they made the point that league officials had forced them against their wishes to play a game with the Orioles a year earlier when a hurricane was bearing down on Baltimore.

Steinbrenner himself invited a *New York Times* reporter into his office at the stadium to make his case: "You reach a point where everyone is against the Yankees, including the commissioner, and that just shouldn't be."

One MLB official laughed when he saw the quote.

"Poor George," the official said sarcastically. "The deck is really stacked against him, isn't? He makes you wish we had a salary cap, just to see how he'd do on a level playing field. He complains about every little thing, and always thinks he's getting screwed. He doesn't remember that Bud just did him a big favor by not slapping him with a fine for tampering after his Randy Johnson comments. He's unbelievable."

As it turned out, Steinbrenner should have just been happy the Devil Rays showed up at all, as the Yankees swept four games from them—and later a fifth, when the game the Yankees had wanted forfeited was made up on September 23—to restore their confidence and enable them to maintain a three-and-a-half-game lead as they began six final regular-season games with the Red Sox.

By then the intrigue was growing by the minute. On the field, as well as on the Steinbrenner Watch.

SEPTEMBER HEAD-TO-HEAD—MIND GAMES

Try to think of it in these terms: no matter your age, how mature you have become, how much you have learned or accomplished or endured, your parents always possess that uncanny ability to strip away your confidence, to lure you to into second-guessing yourself, to reduce you, ultimately, into the child that did not know any better than to follow their every command and instruction.

Then ask yourself the following:

Who's your daddy?

So it was for Bostonians, even late in the 2004 season, when the revamped, high-powered and well-oiled Red Sox machine renewed acquaintances with the New York Yankees with the American League East Division title still very much in play. Entering Yankee Stadium on the weekend of September 17–19, the Red Sox were 88–57, a season-high 31 games over .500, and within three and a half games of the Yankees in the American League East. Of the Red Sox' final 17 regular season games, six were against New York, including a three-game series at Fenway Park the following weekend, September 24–26. There seemed little doubt that the Red Sox had all the momentum, that they had worked out the kinks, that they had truly discovered themselves entering the final stages of the schedule and approaching that time of year that all baseball players and teams strived to reach.

October.

And so it all began, the final tussle for the 2004 American League East, though there remained the possibility that the Red Sox and Yankees would meet again in the playoffs a month later for the right to go to the World Series. Because major league rules prohibited division rivals from meeting in the first round of the playoffs, any such encounter would be forced to take place once again in the AL Championship Series, where the Yankees and Red Sox, like the branches of the Mafia in *The Godfather*, seemingly had settled all family business only a year earlier. Yet the idea of another potential seven-game series between the Sox and Yanks already was seeping into the minds of fans from both cities, leading to some speculation that the games at the end of the regular season would not have as much meaning. There were still things to be decided, of course—the winner of the AL East would have, among others, home field advantage—but the bigger picture revealed that both the Red Sox and Yankees would be among the four American League teams participating in the postseason.

All that remained to be determined were the precise matchups—who would play whom . . . and when . . . and where.

Nonetheless, the obvious truth was that the Red Sox and Yankees never needed *any* reason to play, something that once again came to light in yet another epic contest on Friday night, September 17, in the first of the final six head-to-head meetings. Before a Yankee Stadium crowd of 55,128, the Red Sox rallied for two runs in the ninth inning against the normally unflappable Mariano Rivera, who uncharacteristically threw his hands up in frustration when Johnny Damon's game-winning single fell in front of inexplicably passive Yankees center fielder Kenny Lofton. (Lofton, who nonchalantly pursued the ball as if he were participating in a pickup softball game at a Labor Day weekend barbecue, did not play in the subsequent games of the series and disappeared faster than Jimmy Hoffa, raising the question as to whether his New York teammates had him bumped off.) The sign of Rivera losing his cool was truly warming to the hearts of the Red Sox and their followers, who had seen that kind of look before, albeit on the faces of their own players. The entire series of events demonstrated that even iceman Rivera had a breaking point, a theme that would remain constant (for both teams) throughout their final regular season meetings.

But for now, at least, the end result was that the Red Sox were a mere two and a half games out with 16 games to play, a fact that had the Yankees nervously looking over their shoulders, particularly with the Red Sox once again demonstrating that New York's surefire problem-solver, the great Rivera himself, was indisputably flawed when it came to pitching against Boston. Going back to Bill Mueller's dramatic home run against Rivera on July 24—the same day Alex Rodriguez picked a fight with Jason Varitek—Rivera's last two save opportunities against the Red Sox had turned into crushing Yankees defeats.

For the Red Sox, how sweet it was.

"Without question, this is a blow to their ego," said Red Sox right-hander Bronson Arroyo, who had served as the Sox' starting pitcher in the 3–2 victory. "You start getting a little closer (in the standings) and people start doubting themselves a little bit."

Given that reality, the Yankees and their media corps resorted to a familiar and theretofore unfailing tactic against the Red Sox:

Psychological warfare.

Whether such tactics were necessary against Derek Lowe at the time was debatable, particularly with the events that took place on Saturday, September 18, with the Yankees seemingly on their heels. With a chance to move the Sox within one and a half games of the Yankees in the division, Lowe came out and walked leadoff man Derek Jeter in the bottom of the first inning, an annoying development for Red Sox followers given the inspiring manner in which the previous game had ended. By the time Lowe walked off the mound roughly an inning later, he had turned in a performance as wretched as his July 4 outing in Atlanta, a game that similarly cut the legs out from under the Red Sox. In one very ineffective inning against the Yankees, Lowe allowed four hits, three walks, and seven runs, helping the Yankees to a 9–0 lead that ended the game before it began. Lowe retired just three of the 11 batters he faced, looking so completely inept that one had to wonder about the effect such an outing would have on his confidence.

That was bad enough.

But what happened in the immediate aftermath of the eventual 14–4 annihilation was even more unnerving.

Following the game, after reporters had cleared the clubhouses and congregated in the dungeon/workroom at Yankee Stadium, at least one member of the New York media scurried around the room and began whispering in the ears of Boston reporters: *was it true that Lowe was out drinking early into the morning on the day of his scheduled start?* Such an occurrence was extremely difficult to prove, of course, and most members of the media shrewdly discounted the rumor as nothing more than industry gossip. Nonetheless, the seed was planted, and the information stuck in the heads of many members of the media, an industry ripe with rumormongers and cattier than any suburban wives' book club or mothers' group.

Reporters talked—about the subjects they covered, about each other, about everyone and everything. And in an age of supersaturated media—newspapers, magazines, cable television, Internet and, above all else, radio—there were countless members of the press who did not have particularly good reporting skills, who could not determine fact from fiction, who did not follow up *what* they had learned with the question of *why* they had learned it. That reality inevitably led to sloppy reporting and tabloid journalism, though the tabloids had moved up significantly on the media food chain as cable television, radio, and Internet outlets began buying into a shock jock mentality.

Beyond that, there was also this issue: even if Lowe had been drinking, was there any way to prove that it had affected his performance? New York Yankees outfielder Mickey Mantle was the greatest example of this reality, having built a Hall of Fame career and a reputation as perhaps the greatest player ever despite a never-ending, well-known fight with alcoholism that eventually claimed his life. Unbeknownst to the media, how many players had gone out the night before games and performed well? How many failed? In this case, too, there was simply no way to connect A to L (as in loss) without making a succession of jumps and assumptions along the way.

As a result, most reporters recognized that, when it came to evaluating performance, the best thing to do was to minimize the excuses and explanations unless the evidence suggested doing otherwise

And this was not one of those cases.

"I looked like a rookie, like it was my first game," admitted Lowe, who had gone an encouraging 7–2 over his previous nine decisions. "There was no reason for this game to happen. Everything was in line to pitch a good game and it was a disastrous game from the first batter."

Added the pitcher: "I'm not an excuse guy, but believe me: If I could find one right now, I'd throw it at you."

Obviously, that was the way this series was going: with first Rivera—and then Lowe—showing signs of cracking under pressure.

But if emotional and mental breakdowns were to be the common theme of these final regular season meetings between the Red Sox and Yankees, the most compelling example was yet to come. One day after Lowe imploded on the Yankee Stadium mound, the typically steely-eyed Pedro Martinez similarly threw up on himself. Martinez allowed eight hits, eight runs, three walks, and three home runs in five innings—the final score this time was 11–1—allowing the Yankees actually to increase their lead during the series from three and a half games to four and a half games despite the potentially devastating loss behind Rivera in the Friday night opener.

Martinez, like Lowe, did not make excuses—"The ball never felt right in my hand," said the pitcher—though he did not seem particularly alarmed, either. The Red

Sox still had three games to play with the Yankees, beginning in five days, meaning Martinez would be on the mound again when the teams met for their final regular season series of 2004.

It was then that Pedro Martinez entirely cracked.

And his manager was right there alongside him.

So while four days passed before the Red Sox and Yankees met again—New York's lead in the American League East remained unchanged at four and a half games, effectively putting the Sox in need of a three-game series sweep—it soon became apparent that Pedro Martinez felt more frustration than he had shown following his loss at Yankee Stadium on the previous Sunday afternoon. Martinez' inability to defeat the Yankees had been well documented during recent years, and he took the mound at Fenway Park on Friday night, September 24, looking more determined than ever. Martinez allowed a pair of runs to the Yankees in the third inning and another in the sixth, but he was nonetheless positioned for a victory when, after Martinez held the Yankees scoreless in the seventh, Damon hit a two-out solo home run against reliever Tom Gordon that had given the Red Sox a 4–3 lead heading into the eighth.

Inexplicably, and without warning, Francona then broke from a pattern he had established all year and sent Martinez back out for the eighth inning. To that point, the Red Sox had managed Martinez with remarkable consistency, frequently limiting the pitcher to seven innings and/or 105 pitches, numbers that generally went hand in hand. Early in the season, Francona even had publicly stated that Martinez would be handled in such a manner, something that was not terribly surprising given the fate that befell his predecessor, Grady Little, who lost his job when he chose to go with his gut and send Martinez out for the eighth inning of Game 7 of the 2003 American League Championship Series at Yankee Stadium.

Now, 11 months later, here was Francona doing the same thing, albeit in a game of far less significance.

Naturally—as was often the case when the Red Sox slipped up against the Yankees—the roof caved in. Entrusted with a 4–3 lead in the eighth, Martinez allowed a game-tying home run on the second pitch to the first batter he faced, the underrated Hideki Matsui, that left the pitcher standing on the back of the Fenway Park mound with an unforgettable look of frustration and exasperation on his face. (It was Rivera Redux.) Bernie Williams quickly followed with a double. And two batters later, ancient designated hitter Ruben Sierra punched a single to right center field that scored Williams and gave the Yankees a 5–4 lead, finally drawing Francona from the dugout amid cascading boos from a Fenway Park crowd that had just witnessed the ghost of Grady Little.

Francona seemed somewhat miffed at the inevitable second-guessing that took place after the 6–4 loss, but even some of his players and high-ranking Sox officials privately wondered how the manager could experience such a brain cramp when the very scenario in which Francona had just failed had been presented to him during his job interview. He had passed the test then. But with the Yankees in town now, in late September, before a full house at Fenway Park and with a division title potentially at stake, Terry Francona out and out wilted.

Ugh.

"If I had thought he was losing it, I would have taken him out. In my opinion, he still had good stuff. . . . I wouldn't have left him in if I thought he was out of gas," said Francona, sounding a great deal like Little following Game 7.

Added the manager: "If I run out after two pitches [and the Matsui home run], it would look like I wasn't making a very good decision before the inning. We put a lot of thought into what we're doing. I'm just saying that I thought [Martinez] was in command of what he was doing. I thought he deserved to stay out there and, actually, I thought the reason he deserved to stay out there was because he was going to get them out."

That last response, in particular, drew the manager criticism. *It would look like I wasn't making a good decision before the inning.* In professional sports, admissions like this were terribly unusual. Managers, coaches, and players had answers and excuses for just about everything, but rarely did they ever acknowledge that they made a decision because *of what it might look like*. Ideally, that shouldn't matter. Managers, in particular, were supposed to make decisions with conviction, and if they failed they were supposed to adjust and make the necessary changes. They were never, ever, supposed to worry about *what they looked like*. To do so would be to suggest that they were making decisions more for self-preservation or to placate the public (or their bosses) rather than doing what best served the team, and as soon as that motive was compromised, it was inevitably time to go.

For Francona, his job was safe. But while Red Sox fans never had the chance to boo Grady Little for his Game 7 mistake—the game was played in New York and Little was subsequently fired—Francona's blunder nearly a year later allowed Sox fans to boo Little in effigy. In that way, Terry Francona was serving as a scapegoat for something that had happened 11 months earlier, and the entire episode only raised the question of how Francona would perform in the postseason when faced with decisions that would only be more difficult.

During Francona's first year in Boston, never were the boos louder than on the night of September 24.

"I guess there was a time they were calling me Fran*coma*," the manager would say weeks after the season, chuckling. "I didn't know that."

Still, the poster boy for frustration became Martinez, even beyond the weekend, which ended with a pair of too-little, too-late Red Sox victories (by lopsided scores of 12–5 and 11–4, counterbalancing the events from the previous weekend) that left the Sox three and a half games behind the Yankees with seven games to play in the regular season. The victories moved the Red Sox to the cusp of a playoff berth as the team departed for a seven-game road trip to Tampa Bay and Baltimore to conclude the regular season.

Yet while the Red Sox prepared to officially purchase their ticket to October, Martinez appeared as fragile as ever, though it had nothing to do with his physical health. New York's victory in the series opener had continued an alarming trend (at least for the Red Sox) during Martinez' career in Boston in which the Yankees routinely found a way to defeat him. Including the postseason, Martinez had made 30 career starts against the Yankees in his Red Sox career, posting an 11–10 record. But all nine no-decisions had swung in favor of the Yankees, meaning New York was a remarkable 19–11 in games started against them by a pitcher who was considered among the greatest of all time and one of the most dominating of his era.

There were many reasons for New York's success against Martinez, many of which had nothing to do with the pitcher himself. After the September 24 defeat, Martinez' career ERA against the Yankees was 3.24, a number that included one career start (a victory) as a member of the Montreal Expos. That ERA suggested that Martinez had pitched well against the Yankees, but also that New York had the quality pitching to match Martinez through the early and middle parts of games, particularly while Martinez was in Boston. Typically, Yankees hitters wore down Martinez, making him throw more pitches than usual, forcing Red Sox managers (from Jimy Williams and Joe Kerrigan to Little and Francona) to lift him from games earlier than they would have liked, thereby turning the game over to a bullpen that frequently could not match up with the Yankees and Rivera.

Over and over and over, it was a formula that worked for New York.

That was all very hard to swallow for a man like Martinez, who was not accustomed to playing opponents to a draw. He was used to *winning*. And time after time after time, when he left the mound during a game with the Yankees only to end up with a defeat or a no-decision, the frustration inside of him built as he was asked, over and over again, the same question by members of the relentless media corps from both Boston and New York.

Pedro, why can't you beat the Yankees?

"What can I do but tip my cap and call the Yankees my daddy right now? I can't find a way to beat them at this point," Martinez said after the September 24 failure.

He added: "It's frustrating for me after my teammates picked me up so many times. It's all me. I wanted to bury myself on the mound."

Ever the opportunists, reporters seized on Martinez' words and turned them into back-page stories and headlines for days to come. Martinez' teammates were asked if the pitcher was mentally defeated, if he was conceding defeat to the Yankees. In the frenzy that followed a remark made in the heat of the moment, Martinez' psyche was analyzed and dissected by reporters in both cities as if they were performing psychotherapy. Most of them overlooked the simple fact that Pedro Martinez was frustrated, that he was a human being, that he would forever remain a proud and fierce competitor who would never concede anything to anyone because it simply was not part of his nature.

Naturally, as is often the case, we all missed the bigger point. As the Red Sox and Yankees parted ways wondering whether they would meet again in 2004, there was more than Martinez to question. Francona's impact on the coming weeks would be looked at, too. And for all of the scrutiny being directed at the Red Sox, who were on their way to a seventh consecutive second-place finish in the American League East, also overlooked was the simple fact that the Red Sox had the same spell over Mariano Rivera that the Yankees seemed to have cast over the great Pedro Martinez.

Which begs the question:

When the Red Sox defeated Mariano Rivera in New York on September 17, how come nobody from New York wondered if Rivera had been out drinking the night before?

SEPTEMBER HEAD-TO-HEAD—KARMA AND THE COSMOS

All year I'd thought the Red Sox were trying a little too hard to be different. The hair, the beards, the frat-house atmosphere in the clubhouse, it all seemed to be the Sox' way of trying to convince the world how much fun they were having, even if the Yankees had broken their hearts in 2003, even if history said it would happen again in 2004. Massarotti kept telling me it was no act, that they reveled in their wackiness, and naturally I thought he was just drinking the Kool-Aid again, seeing what the Sox fan deep inside of him wanted to see. But now the Sox were charging at the Yankees, and with pennant-race pressure hanging over their final six meetings of the season, it was hard not to notice how comfortable they seemed in this environment. As they took batting practice, they played hockey with the bats and balls; as each new hitter would begin his BP round by putting down a bunt, two on-deck hitters would take positions in front of the plate, use their bats as sticks to field the bunt, pass it between them, and finally shoot to score against the hitter-turned-goalie. Goals and/or saves were met with roars of delight, and as I watched from behind the batting cage, I had to admit, it was hard to fake this kind of fun, especially on September 16, as a capacity crowd filed into Yankee Stadium.

Still, it made you wonder: did it speak to their closeness as a team or just their free-spirited personality? And in either case, would such camaraderie play a role in ultimately determining a winner between these two teams?

Certainly this was the time of year when you started asking those kind of questions. Especially now that the changing nature of the race in the AL East made you take a harder look at the Yankees. All season the starting pitching had made fans nervous, but now there were big games to play, and so the Yankees were being asked to prove they had the stuff of champions. Their $184 million payroll all but assured them of getting to the playoffs, as they simply overwhelmed most American League teams with their depth of talent. But could they win the big ones? They would find out in back-to-back weekends with the Red Sox, and then October baseball, the drama that determines success or failure every year for this franchise. And while the Red Sox had added a proven postseason pitcher in Curt Schilling to a team that had taken the Yankees to the absolute limit a year earlier, the Yankees had a host of players who hadn't been through this before—at least not while carrying the huge expectations that came with playing in the Bronx at this time of year.

In fact, it had to be hard to fathom for the holdovers from '96, but only five players in pinstripes at the moment had won a World Series as Yankees—Jeter, Bernie, Posada, Rivera, and El Duque. At times Jeter, the captain and by now unquestioned leader, and Posada, perhaps the most passionate of all the Yankees, had publicly questioned whether the teams of '02 and '03, the teams missing the likes of Tino Martinez, Paul O'Neill, Scott Brosius, Chuck Knoblauch, David Cone, Joe Girardi, and even Luis Sojo, had the grit, the heart, or whatever it was that enabled the old Yankees to win four championships in six seasons.

Jeter, who never forgave Steinbrenner for pushing Martinez out the door after the '01 season, could be blunt and harsh on the subject. More than once after a tough playoff loss he had stopped a reporter in midsentence whenever a question would begin with "This team has won championships before, so . . ."

"This group hasn't," Jeter would interject, making a point that sounded like an indictment of sorts. "We've got to prove we can do it."

Such talk always raised the question of just what role intangibles, chemistry, karma, all those hard-to-define elements that go into the makeup of a team, play in surviving the crapshoot—as baseball people like to call it—that is October baseball, with its three rounds of playoff series. The Yankee teams of the last few years have had more overall talent than the championship clubs, yet they had come up short for one reason or another.

As for this team, whatever questions lingered about pitching, it had more position-by-position talent than any of Joe Torre's teams, and surely its record-setting number of comeback victories was proof of a strong and healthy heart. But what about the camaraderie factor? Goofy as they acted sometimes, the Red Sox clearly were very much united in their quest to beat the Yankees. Maybe they weren't quite the Miracle-

On-Ice underdogs that the Boston media sometimes liked to portray, but they seemed to be about as close in spirit as a major league team of millionaires can be these days.

The Yankees, meanwhile, certainly got along fine, but seemingly more as neighbors than brothers in arms. It wasn't anything like the old line about 25 cabs for 25 players, but neither was there much socializing together. Jeter, Posada, and Williams would go to dinner together on the road, joined occasionally by Ruben Sierra. A few of the Latin guys would hang out, but as the Yankees have continued to add superstars in recent years, they have become more and more distant as a group. In their clubhouse, in fact, some of the lockers may as well be islands.

Mike Mussina was one of the first big free-agent signees to be added to the championship mix, coming aboard after the 2000 season, and he has never been one of the boys, largely because he is smarter than the average ballplayer. That's not always good for bonding. Indeed, Mussina is a graduate of Stanford who can be condescending with the media and aloof in his own clubhouse. Keeping reporters at arm's length hardly makes him unique in the Yankees clubhouse, but Mussina might be the only player who is not on speaking terms with team broadcaster Michael Kay.

Kay has been around the Yankees since covering the team as a newspaper reporter in the late 1980s, and even after becoming a broadcaster, first on radio, now on TV, he has continued to be a near-daily presence in the clubhouse. Combining an upbeat personality with a talent for schmoozing, Kay has been a friend to most Yankees over the years, yet he hasn't spoken to Mussina in three years.

The way Kay tells it, he approached Mussina the day after the right-hander had pitched a good game in 2001, and asked him if he would do a taped three-minute interview for the pregame radio broadcast that night—*The Kay Korner*, as it was called.

Mussina rolled his eyes, according to Kay, reluctantly agreed, then answered questions in a manner that Kay found insulting.

"When I turned the recorder off," Kay recalled years later, "I said, 'You know, Mike, you don't ever have to worry about doing this show again. You could pitch a perfect game and I'll still never talk to you again.'"

Kay said Mussina was a bit taken aback, but not enough to apologize. Meanwhile, Kay's vow was nearly put to the ultimate test a couple of months later, when Mussina came within one out of pitching a perfect game against the Red Sox, but in any case, Kay says he has remained true to his word.

"I haven't spoken to him since then," he says.

The year after Mussina signed, Jason Giambi was the Yankees' big-ticket free agent, and while friendly, he has never become anything like the leader he was in the Oakland A's rowdy clubhouse. If anything, Giambi made himself something of an outcast by insisting as part of his deal that his personal trainer, Bob Alejo, be allowed to travel with the team and dress in the locker room like one of the players. It was a bad precedent, obviously, since any number of Yankee stars could have demanded similar privileges, but what made it particularly galling to teammates was that Alejo didn't seem to know his place, and, according to other players, walked and talked with too much swagger for their liking.

For that and other reasons, GM Brian Cashman has since limited Alejo's access, keeping him out of the locker room. But Alejo has continued to travel with the Yankees, and has remained Giambi's constant—and only—companion away from the ballpark.

In 2003 the Yankees added two more big free agents, Hideki Matsui and Jose Contreras. Matsui was friendly and likeable from the start, but he also didn't speak English. As a result, he became another free agent who kept to himself, socializing with his interpreter, Roger Kahlon. Contreras, a sensitive soul who missed the family he left behind in Cuba, also kept company almost exclusively with his interpreter, Leo Astacio.

In 2004 more islands formed in the clubhouse. Gone were buddies and workout fanatics Roger Clemens and Andy Pettitte, both of whom added presence and personality to the locker room. In their place were Kevin Brown, practically the definition of a loner, and Javier Vazquez, a nice but quiet guy who kept a very low profile in his first year in the Yankees clubhouse.

Finally, there were the highest-profile additions, Gary Sheffield and Alex Rodriguez. Sheffield fit in quickly as a no-nonsense gamer who won teammates over with a clutch bat and his willingness to play with an injured shoulder all season, but he was another player who kept to himself off the field, surrounded by his own friends and associates, including a personal publicist. On the road he was often joined by Meade Chasky, a card-show promoter who handled Sheffield's marketing affairs.

Then there was A-Rod, once a close friend of Jeter's before the fallout over the infamous *Esquire* magazine article in 2001. As teammates for the first time, they put on a good show publicly, always throwing together during warm-ups before games, talking in between innings while taking ground balls, but off the field they went their separate ways. One person close to the situation said A-Rod made attempts early in the season to break through into Jeter's inner circle, but Jeter made it clear they were no longer tight, and that was that. While Jeter continued to hang out mostly with Posada, A-Rod brought his wife on most road trips, spending his time away from the ballpark with her. If his wife wasn't with him, often Eddy Rodriguez (no relation), his longtime mentor who coached him as a kid at the Miami Boys and Girls Club, would keep him company. If A-Rod went out socially with anyone from the Yankees, it was usually bullpen catcher Mike Borzello, who was also Mussina's closest friend on the ballclub.

None of this made the Yankees dysfunctional in any way. More than anything, it was just a sign of the times, as so many major-leaguers are mini corporations in this huge-money era, often talking more on their cell phones to their "people," as they say, than with teammates during the course of the day. But with all of these islands in the clubhouse, it was obvious the Yankees weren't as close as a group as they'd been in the late '90s; whether it chipped away at their resolve in some immeasurable way, or made them any more vulnerable at crunch time, was a matter for sports psychologists and talk-show callers to debate.

But in any case, the time had come to prove it one way or the other. And when the Red Sox rallied from a run behind in the ninth inning against Mariano Rivera to defeat the Yankees 3–2 on Friday night at Yankee Stadium, cutting their deficit to two and a half games, it was more cause to wonder about intangibles as opposed to a certain Curse. But before anyone had time to conclude that perhaps the Red Sox' intangibles would help them finally overcome history, the Yankees made any such talk seem laughable by routing the Sox in the next two games, pounding on Derek Lowe and Pedro Martinez in winning 14–4 and then 11–1. The lead was back to four and a half games, and it remained there as the Yankees invaded Fenway Park the following Friday. With only a week remaining in the season, it was obvious the Sox needed to sweep to have any real shot at catching the Yankees in the division race. The Yankees knew one win would essentially clinch the division for them, and so, if one game could sum up the history between these teams, both recent and ancient, it was Friday night's 6–4 Yankee victory. Not only did the New Yorkers find a way to beat Pedro again, but they did it in a fashion that was eerily similar to Game 7 of the 2003 ALCS, rallying in the eighth inning against him, as Terry Francona pulled a Grady Little and left him in to blow the game.

Joe Torre had taken the opposite tack, going to his setup reliever, Tom Gordon, early, for Mike Mussina when the game was tied 3–3 after six innings. It was a bold and risky move, especially because Torre knew it meant he wouldn't be able to use Gordon on Saturday. But he decided it was time to go for the kill, understanding what it would mean to beat Pedro again—psychologically as well as in the standings.

"With Pedro on the mound," Torre said afterward, "you come out to try and win the game, not to beat Pedro. So when you get to the sixth, seventh, eighth inning and you're right there, it becomes a must-win. That's why I decided to go to Gordon there."

When Johnny Damon hit a tie-breaking home run off Gordon in the seventh, it looked as if Torre's strategy would backfire. But his moves always seem to work against the Red Sox, and sure enough, Gordon and Mariano Rivera closed the door from there while the Yankees rallied against Pedro.

So the lead was five and a half games, and it didn't matter even a little bit that the Sox won the next two games. Both teams knew the race was over; it ended with Pedro publicly surrendering, calling the Yankees "my daddy," and Torre managing with the golden touch he has had in so many postseasons. In some ways it was the perfect snapshot of the last seven seasons, all ending with the Yankees in first, the Red Sox in second.

Of course, 2003 was all the proof either side needed to know it wasn't necessarily over between them. So the Sox continued to play hockey during batting practice in the last week of the season, having as much fun as MLB law allowed. The Yankees continued to go their separate ways for dinner, living on their private islands. Watching the way September had been going, I had started to believe that intangibles, chemistry, and karma would change the course of this rivalry. I'd forgotten about the cosmic order of the universe.

TO HELL AND BACK—RED SOX

WITH THE NEW YORK YANKEES IN THEIR REARVIEW MIRROR, THE Red Sox wasted no time moving on. The Sox opened a three-game series at Tampa Bay on September 27 with a 7–3 victory behind the braided cornrows of Bronson Arroyo, whose 10th victory gave the Sox five pitchers with 10 or more wins for the first time since 1979. And after a season that essentially began almost a year earlier at the moment that Aaron Boone homered against Tim Wakefield, the win officially secured for the Sox the American League wildcard berth, ensuring that there would be fall baseball in New England.

Division title or not, the Red Sox were going back to the playoffs.

And they were more determined than ever.

"This is the beginning," declared manager Terry Francona. "I think the players feel that way, too."

Said pitcher Pedro Martinez, who already seemed to have forgotten his struggles against the Yankees: "I'm expecting to go further and further. I don't want anymore of [just] clinching the wildcard. I want to go further and I'm pretty sure the whole team feels the same way."

A year earlier, the 2003 Red Sox drew criticism upon qualifying for the playoffs, many suggesting that a rowdy on-field celebration indicated the team was happy to merely reach the postseason. Sox players celebrated with fans at Fenway Park, where the Sox had clinched against the Baltimore Orioles, and a handful of players ran along the streets outside Fenway to a nearby bar, The Baseball Tavern, to join fans in celebrating what was the Red Sox' first playoff appearance since 1999, the third in six years. Then the Sox went out and dropped the first two games of the AL Division Series against the Oakland A's, rekindling speculation about the extent of their hunger, before they rallied to beat Oakland and advance to the historic ALCS against the Yankees.

In 2004, in Tampa, the celebration was far more restrained, though there were moments when the clubhouse felt like the basement of a fraternity house at the conclusion of exam week. The Sox sprayed champagne on one another, something that did not the least bit bother Francona, who felt that in order to win in a cramped, intense environment like Boston, the players needed their room to vent. So the players cracked open beers and poured them on one another, and at one point in the middle of standard champagne fights—think of them as squirt guns for grown-ups—the gregarious David Ortiz threatened to go nuclear, hooking up a hose to a bathroom faucet and striding into the center of the clubhouse as if preparing to put out a fire.

As teammates scattered, Ortiz—in a hilarious garb that included goggles—roared with laughter.

That was the kind of environment the Red Sox clubhouse had become.

In the coming days, while waiting to learn whether they would face the Minnesota Twins, Anaheim Angels, or Oakland A's in the first round of the playoffs, the Red Sox returned to business. Francona insisted that the Sox still had not ruled out the division title because the Sox had not been mathematically eliminated in the American League East, but that was just rhetoric. With a week before the start of the postseason, the Red Sox had the luxury of setting up their pitching rotation and resting their starters, something that was of tremendous benefit given the length of the regular season. The Red Sox had reported to spring training roughly seven months earlier and, like every team, had stopped to catch their breath only briefly during the regular season, so the rest now was invaluable. Sox officials never would admit it publicly given the presumed response of fans and the media, but at this stage of this season, it was more important for them to align their pitching rotation than it was to beat the Yankees.

The ultimate goal, after all, was to beat New York when it truly counted.

In October.

Though Francona indicated that the Sox would make no immediate announcements concerning the pitching staff, Martinez pressed the issue. One night prior to a very lackluster performance in the finale of the Tampa series—the game meant nothing, but Martinez' apathy irked Sox officials nonetheless—Martinez wanted to know where he stood in the projected playoff rotation. Out of respect for the player, Francona told Martinez that he would be pitching the second game of the division series—that meant Schilling would go Game 1—and the pitcher slipped out of the clubhouse without addressing reporters. But the next night, after his uninspired effort, Martinez *volunteered* to reporters the information that he would be pitching Game 2, a curious maneuver given that players typically told the media nothing about such matters. Yet Martinez clearly wanted it known that the decision had been made—again, he wanted control over the dispensation of the information—and he did not sound especially happy about the decision, no matter what he said publicly.

In fact, a week earlier, Martinez had told *Boston Herald* reporter Karen Guregian that he was not sure how the Red Sox would have the heart to inform him that he would be pitching Game 2 given all that he had done for the franchise.

But following the Tampa game, Martinez was far more diplomatic.

"I'm not angry," Martinez said, though his expression belied his words. "[Schilling] was the No. 1 starter from the get-go and he deserves to be the No. 1 starter in any game. . . . It's proper. Without a doubt he deserves to be the No. 1 starter in that game. I hope he pitches as he has. You need to respect that guy. He's been better than anybody. He's been better than Pedro Martinez."

There was no disputing that, really, and even Martinez knew that he did not have a case based on the statistics. To that point in the season, Schilling had more victories (21 to 16), a better ERA (3.26 to 3.90) and had walked nearly half as many batters per nine innings (1.39 to 2.53). Most important of all, the Red Sox were 24–7 in Schilling's 31 starts as opposed to 19–14 in Martinez' 33 outings, and Schilling had been invaluable during the stretch run, winning his final eight decisions while the Red Sox won each of his last nine starts. Everybody from Boston to Baja knew that Schilling had established himself as the ace of the staff, that he deserved to pitch Game 1 of the playoffs, though one couldn't help but wonder if Martinez felt deep down that the deck had been stacked against him from the start.

In the complex mind of Pedro Martinez, the pitcher somehow felt as if he had been disrespected.

Schilling was the No. 1 starter from the get-go.

In reality, of course, that had not been true. Martinez pitched Opening Day. Martinez was the highest-paid pitcher of the roster. But after Schilling joined the team, Martinez was put in the unfamiliar (and undesired) position of having to fight for his throne, and the indisputable truth was that Curt Schilling wrested the crown away from him during the regular season. The bottom line was that Pedro Martinez was pitching the second game because he was the second-best pitcher on the 2004 Red Sox, though that did not stop Martinez from revealing a bit of his displeasure—"I could actually pitch fifth or not at all in the playoffs if I continue to pitch the way I am," he said sarcastically—with a sharp response that provided a glimpse at his wounded pride.

Still, with Martinez, it was often hard to tell. Extremely temperamental to begin with, Martinez was particularly edgy when he was not pitching well. And over his final three starts of the regular season—the two games against the Yankees and the lethargic performance against the Devil Rays—Martinez had allowed 27 hits and posted a 9.35 ERA in 17⅓ innings. He finished the year with a 3.90 ERA that was the highest of his career. His nine losses were his most since 1996. And the 26 home runs he allowed were more than the combined total from his previous *three* seasons, 2001–2003, when he surrendered, in order, five, 13, and seven home runs for a total of 25.

And through it all, he was approaching free agency, something of which everyone was extremely well aware.

Said one Sox official after Martinez' poor outing in Tampa: "I think everything he has done this whole season has been about his contract."

Whatever the explanation, the entire matter demonstrated the subtlety with which Francona had to tread. All players, no matter how experienced or accomplished, had egos and insecurities. They needed to be reassured. They needed to be reminded that they had value and that they were appreciated. They needed to know that they were part of something, that they were not taken for granted, something that ultimately made them no different from any employee who was part of any department for any company in the world.

Even professional athletes, no matter how many zeroes in their paychecks, had to feel needed.

With the issue of Games 1 and 2 resolved, the Red Sox traveled to Baltimore for a season-ending four-game series with the Baltimore Orioles. Like any playoff team, the Sox had some minor roster issues to deal with, but the biggest question remaining involved Francona's starters for Games 3 and 4 of the postseason. Every team in baseball operated with a five-man pitching rotation during the regular season, but the presence of travel days during the off-season meant that, barring rainouts, no team ever would be asked to play more than three days in a row. So most teams went to a four-man rotation, which, in the case of the Red Sox, meant that only two pitchers from the group of Derek Lowe, Tim Wakefield, and Bronson Arroyo would be allowed to start games in the postseason.

Francona had a choice to make.

No matter what he did, he was going to disappoint somebody.

And long after he had led his players onto the sun-baked fields of Florida for their first workouts of spring training, his words were ringing true.

Part of the reason you try to build relationships is because there comes a time when you're going to have to tell someone something they don't want to hear.

That someone was Derek Lowe.

Like many people facing difficult circumstances, Derek Lowe refused to admit to himself what he knew to be true: over the second half of the season, Bronson Arroyo had pitched better. That simple fact proved to be Lowe's undoing, at least when it came time for the Red Sox to name their four-man rotation for the postseason. And so by the time Lowe emerged from the manager's office during the final weekend of the regular season and slinked out a back door of the visiting clubhouse to avoid facing reporters at Baltimore's Camden Yards, the decision had been made.

Bronson Arroyo and Tim Wakefield were in.

Derek Lowe was out.

As was the case at Turner Field in Atlanta on the Fourth of July, Lowe's reluctance to face the media suggested an unwillingness to cope, at least for the time being. He went into a cocoon. He began feeling sorry for himself. Lowe had a lot on his mind, and he was also hearing from friends who had told him of cable television and Internet speculation that Lowe had been out partying before his start at Yankee Stadium in mid-September. That further irked the pitcher, who, like most players, felt the media was never held accountable for anything. Reporters and broadcasters could write or say just about anything they wanted—even if they were wrong—and apologies or corrections did little to minimize the damage. Once something was *out there*, once a player had been tagged with a label, it was part of the player's record forever, rightly or wrongly.

So after the Red Sox arrived in Anaheim, where they were scheduled to begin the American League Division Series, on October 5, Lowe needed to vent. Sitting in a corner of the visiting clubhouse at Angel Stadium, Lowe summoned a *Herald* reporter and wanted to know: Where did these reports come from? How did they start? How was it that the media could report something that was inaccurate and get away with it? Lowe was sprawled in a chair and had an edge in his voice, but he was also somewhat playful. It was the passive manner in which he dealt with anger. At his core, Lowe was extremely good-natured and disliked confrontation, and he was rarely—if ever—seen raising his voice. For all that Derek Lowe had endured during his career in Boston—the ups and downs as a setup man, closer, and starter—he had never really exploded at a member of the media. Lowe often jabbed with reporters and seemed to enjoy the banter, but where many players ultimately would turn their frustration on the media, Lowe would frequently turn inward and focus on himself.

Given Lowe's contributions to the Red Sox in October 2003, it was difficult to explain how he ended up here, in a confidence crisis, only a year later. With the Red Sox facing a 2–0 series deficit against the Oakland A's in the 2003 AL Division Series, it was Lowe who started a do-or-die Game 3 at Fenway Park, giving the Red Sox seven superb innings (zero earned runs) in an eventual 3–1 Sox win that ended with a dramatic, two-run home run by Trot Nixon in the bottom of the 11th inning. Two days later, after the Red Sox had similarly won Game 4 in breathtaking fashion, Lowe was asked to come out of the bullpen (on one day of rest!) to close Game 5 under the most difficult circumstances. With the Red Sox clinging to a 4–3 lead in the bottom of the ninth, Lowe entered with nobody out and runners at first and second. After a sacrifice bunt put runners at second and third, Lowe faced three consecutive left-handed hitters in pinch-hitter Adam Melhuse, outfielder Chris Singleton, and pinch-hitter Terrence Long.

Lowe struck out Melhuse. He walked Singleton. And then he struck out Long with a banana-bending sinker that started in the left-handed batter's box and tailed back over the plate, locking the knees of the stunned Long, who took the final pitch of the 2004 Oakland A's season for called strike three.

At that instant, Derek Lowe was everything he thought he could ever be—and more than the Red Sox ever could have hoped for when they acquired him and Jason Varitek for Heathcliff Slocumb in July 1997.

"If you had any doubts about his heart, there are absolutely no doubts now," general manager Theo Epstein said at the time. "That was as clutch as you can possibly be. I don't know how many pitchers in the game have the guts to make those pitches."

Said Varitek of Lowe's final offering to Long: "That strike three pitch was the best pitch he's ever made."

For the Red Sox, all of that only made it more maddening when Lowe had the kind of year he had in 2004, when there was just no way of predicting what he would give them. On some days, Lowe looked like a 20-game winner. On others, he looked like Jimmy Anderson, a journeyman left-hander who joined the Sox during the middle of the 2004 campaign and who looked more like a gas station attendant or garbage collector than a big-league pitcher. It was Anderson to whom one radio personality compared Lowe during the middle of the season, after Lowe's meltdown in Atlanta and when even Francona seemed to have lost hope in the right-hander. Lowe remembered the remark and stored it away until just before the playoffs, when he jabbed with the media member and pointed out that Jimmy Anderson had long since been sent on his way.

"Now *there's* somebody who knows the game," Lowe cracked, referring to the radio voice.

By the time the playoffs were set to begin, even the speculation about Lowe's alleged partying in New York had mushroomed into a bigger issue. Following Lowe's last regular season start in Tampa—like Martinez, Lowe performed poorly in the series—there were whispers within the organization that Lowe had been "unprepared," suggesting that he had celebrated too long with teammates following the wildcard clincher, which had taken place the previous night. Lowe challenged those allegations, too. But regardless of what was true and what was not, there was no disputing the fact that Derek Lowe's reputation had taken a major hit during the 2004 season, both on the field and off. And so the pitcher, who had turned down a three-year, $27 million offer from the Red Sox during spring training, was faced with the reality that the 2004 season had likely cost him a great deal of money given that he was preparing to enter free agency as soon as the postseason was complete.

But for Lowe, at least, that wasn't even the worst part of it.

The worst part was that the playoffs were about to begin and he was buried in the bullpen.

Of all the teams participating in the postseason, none may have had more momentum than the Anaheim Angels. Behind the sizzling bat of MVP candidate Vladimir Guerrero, Anaheim had won 5-of-6 to pull into a tie with the Oakland A's atop the American League West entering the final weekend of the regular season. That was when the Angels arrived at the Oakland Coliseum for a three-game series under the simplest of scenarios: the winner of the series was going to the playoffs, the loser was going home. The Angels subsequently took the first two games to wrap up the AL West and, coupled with a loss by the AL Central Division champion Minnesota Twins on the final day of the season—the Red Sox watched the final outs of the Twins game on a clubhouse television in Baltimore—ensured that they would open the playoffs at home against the Red Sox instead of on the road against the Yankees.

Still, for all of the momentum the Angels had generated during the final three weeks of the season, the matchup with the Red Sox presented an obvious problem for them. While the Angels possessed one of the most dominating bullpens in baseball, their starting pitching left something to be desired, particularly when matched against a group like Boston's. The Red Sox would open the series by throwing Schilling and Martinez, and there was not a single pitcher on the Anaheim staff that could match up with either Sox starter, let alone both. On top of it all, the Angels were playing without second baseman Adam Kennedy, who was lost to injury late in the season, and insubordinate outfielder Jose Guillen, whom manager Mike Scioscia had suspended for the balance of the season late in the year. The Guillen decision drew the Angels praise from all corners of the baseball world, but the impact on the field was that without Guillen and Kennedy (the Most Valuable Player of the 2002 AL Championship Series), an intimidating Anaheim lineup had been shortened considerably.

Against the Red Sox, then, the Angels' strategy was obvious:

Stay close early, pit your bullpen against theirs, win late.

It was Anaheim's only hope.

For Boston, the absences of Kennedy and Guillen were a stroke of good fortune, though the Sox were due more than their share of good breaks, particularly in the postseason. Each of the last three times the Sox had reached the World Series, they had done so despite losing a key contributor late in the season. In 1967, with the Sox in a heated playoff race in August, the club lost the services of charismatic young power hitter Tony Conigliaro, who was hit in the face by pitch in one of the most horrific baseball injuries ever; Conigliaro's life was never really the same. In 1975, it was another young power hitter, Jim Rice, who was lost for the playoffs when a pitch broke his wrist. And in 1986, in an admittedly lesser misfortune, the Sox went to the playoffs without veteran pitcher Tom Seaver, who had been acquired in a late-season trade with the Chicago White Sox to help solidify the middle and end of the Red Sox rotation.

At the start of the 2004 postseason, however, it was *the other guys* who had to deal with the reality of playing at something less than full strength. And in addition to playing without two starters, the Angels had not been able to align their pitching rotation because they had to play meaningful games on the final weekend of the regular season.

And so those were the conditions under which the Red Sox began the 2004 postseason behind Schilling, whom they confidently sent to the mound. Game 1 subsequently developed precisely how the Red Sox had hoped, Boston scoring once in the first inning against ineffective Anaheim starter Jarrod Washburn, then exploding for seven more runs in the fourth against Washburn and reliever Scot Shields. By the time the Angels scored on a Troy Glaus homer against Schilling in the bottom of the fourth, the Red Sox already had built an enormous 8–0 advantage, a lead that would be difficult to threaten for a lineup operating without Guillen and Kennedy, particularly against a pitcher as experienced and immune to pressure as the cold-blooded Schilling. Meanwhile, the vaunted Anaheim bullpen effectively had been taken out of the game, denied the opportunity to pitch in situations of any consequence thanks to the ineptitude of the Anaheim starter.

As it was, the result was a lopsided 9–3 Sox victory, though the win did not come without its share of Sox concern. It was late in the game that Schilling fielded a dribbler by Guerrero and threw sloppily to first, triggering a brief Anaheim rally that ultimately meant nothing. And while even some Sox teammates questioned whether the image-conscious Schilling was playing to the cameras when he winced and reached for his right ankle following the misplay—the timing of the injury *was* convenient, after all—the Red Sox soon pulled the pitcher from the mound and arranged for him to have an MRI exam immediately after the game. Schilling had long since spoken with reporters in a formal press conference and was getting dressed at his locker following the game, when a reporter approached and asked about the status of Schilling's ankle.

"Honestly?" said the pitcher. "We're going to find out."

Nonetheless, not long after Schilling hobbled out the clubhouse door accompanied by trainer Jim Rowe, the Red Sox were on their way back in again, this time for Game 2. By that point, much of the focus had shifted to Martinez, whose struggles at the end of the regular season raised serious questions about his state of mind. Prior to Game 1, in fact, Martinez boycotted the customary press conferences reserved for the next day's starters—such gatherings would allow reporters to have stories about the Game 2 starters in the paper on the day of Game 2—a decision that was met with predictable disapproval from many members of the national media. But whatever Martinez' reasons for failing to attend—and with him, there was never any real way to know what was eating at him—the obvious truth was that the pitcher saw Game 2 as a challenge and that he would need to pitch well.

As it was, Martinez trailed the Angels and fellow Dominican Republic native Bartolo Colon by a 3–1 score entering the top of the sixth, giving the Angels and manager Mike Scioscia precisely the situation *they* had hoped for. The bases were empty with two outs when Colon allowed a single to Kevin Millar and a game-tying home run to catcher Jason Varitek, the latter of which would prove to be the most important hit of the series. Martinez followed Varitek's homer by retiring the final six Anaheim batters he faced, all while the Sox improbably scored one run in the seventh and four runs in the ninth against a pair of Anaheim's overpowering relievers, veteran right-hander Brendan Donnelly and flamboyant phenom Francisco Rodriguez. And so while Anaheim led by a 3–1 score after five innings entering a part of the game that was supposed to be an Angels strength, the Red Sox outscored Anaheim by a 7–0 score over the final four innings with Boston relievers Mike Timlin, Mike Myers, and Keith Foulke joining Martinez to retire 13 of the final 14 Angels batters of the game.

"I was a No. 1 today. That's all that matters to me," said Martinez, clearly still focused on the fact that he did not pitch Game 1. "I don't care what all the experts out there have to say. I just do my job. I let go of my ego. I swallowed it because, to me, anytime they give me the ball I'll pitch. I'm special. I'm a No. 1. I don't care how many games I have to wait."

Still, if all of that reflected some level of bitterness in the pitcher, it also demonstrated this: Pedro was back. Martinez' struggles at the end of the season had concerned both him and Red Sox officials, who frequently wondered if the pitcher was more focused on himself than on the team. But in the short term, at least, Game 2 of the AL Division Series demonstrated that Martinez was as healthy as ever—the pitcher's final 16 fastballs of the game all registered between 92 and 95 miles per hour on the stadium radar gun—and that he was once again *focused*, intent on proving to the world that yes, he still had it, that he could win big games, that he could pitch in pressure situations, and that he could rise to the occasion.

That he was still *an ace*.

Two days later, after the Angels and Red Sox traveled across the country to resume the series in Boston, the Red Sox dispatched the Angels again—and for good, clinching the series—though the game possessed far more drama than it should have. While Arroyo mystified the Angels by changing both speeds and arm angles on his curveball, the Sox scored two in the third, three in the fourth, and one in the fifth to take a 6–1 advantage into the seventh. It was then that Francona suspiciously lifted Arroyo after a leadoff walk to Jeff DaVanon—Arroyo had thrown only 91 pitches—turning the game over to his bullpen in hopes of closing out the series. But six batters after Arroyo's departure, veteran Timlin allowed a game-tying grand slam to the superhuman Guerrero, knotting the score at 6 and sending the game into extra innings, once again matching the Red Sox bullpen with that of the Angels.

Having already used Myers, Timlin, Alan Embree, and Foulke through nine innings, Francona had little choice in the 10th but to turn to the embattled Lowe, who allowed a walk and an infield hit before escaping the inning without any damage. Scioscia then made a similar move in the bottom of the inning, calling upon left-hander Washburn (the Game 1 starter) to face the left-handed-hitting David Ortiz with two outs and a runner on base. The result was a series-clinching, two-run home that landed in the trendy "Monster seats" above Fenway's fabled left field wall—while baseball fans throughout America referred to the left field wall as the "Green Monster," most New Englanders acknowledged it simply as "The Wall"—and that sent the customary, capacity crowd at Fenway into a state of bliss.

Once again, there was joy in the Red Sox clubhouse after the game, though this time Ortiz did not emerge from the showers toting a hose. Instead, a bratty Martinez took a cooler filled with water and soaked a small cluster of reporters, undoubtedly taking out his frustrations on the easiest of targets: the media. Still, the celebration was noticeably restrained, at times seeming almost manufactured or prearranged. In fact, throughout much of decisive Game 3, the crowd at Fenway had been surprisingly passive, as if unimpressed with the remarkable ease with which the Red Sox were handling the Angels. At times, it all seemed too easy, at least until Guerrero homered in the seventh inning, awakening the crowd for the final stages of the game and adding some much-needed drama to the moments leading up to Ortiz' heroics.

Still, to suggest that the Red Sox had reason to be satisfied was something of a stretch, particularly because the Sox had succeeded only in reaching the same destination as they had in 2003. They were in the American League Championship Series. They were waiting to play either the Yankees or the Minnesota Twins. And while Sox players said the right things about having no preference when it came to facing either the Twins or the Yankees, their competitiveness was seeping to the surface. Privately, some Sox players acknowledged that they would love another crack at the Yankees, whom many had felt were no better than the Sox a year earlier. And, in fact, since the start of 2003, the Red Sox and Yankees had played 45 games through the end of the 2004 regular season, the Red Sox holding the slightest edge in victories, 23–22.

"If we're ever going to win this thing," said reliever Embree, "it's probably fitting that we do it going through [New York]."

While the Red Sox eventually got their wish—the Yankees defeated the Twins in four games, winning three straight after losing the series opener—there was another story developing within the walls of the Red Sox clubhouse. Amid the celebration following Game 3, Schilling quietly sat at his locker and acknowledged that, earlier in the day, he had visited with foot and ankle specialist George Theodore of the renowned Mass General Hospital. Theodore had made the trip to Fenway Park at the request of Sox owner John Henry, who encouraged the club to get another opinion on Schilling's ailing right ankle. And so while the Red Sox were suggesting publicly that Schilling was fine following his Game 1 mishap and that he could continue pitching with only the same problems that had nagged him during the regular season, there was reason to believe that the Red Sox possessed growing concerns about their staff ace.

Now, they were bringing in *specialists.*

Wasn't this a cause for worry, particularly among a Red Sox following that had seen the team lose key players at the most pivotal times throughout their history?

Replied Schilling when asked how the problem compared to his difficulties earlier in the season: "I don't know that I have any more concern."

And so one year later, after Aaron Boone and Alex Rodriguez and Schilling and Foulke and all that had happened between Boston and New York, the two most intense baseball cities in America were exactly where they had started.

Face-to-face.

In the American League Championship Series.

Four wins away from a trip to the World Series.

Incredibly, the Red Sox were favored. According to an assortment of oddsmakers in Las Vegas, the Red Sox were the more popular choice to advance to the World Series. This was an astonishing development, really, given all of the elements that could be taken into account. Over an 86-year span beginning with the 1919 season, the Yankees had won 26 world championships and the Red Sox had won zero. In 2004, New York had won the American League East, defeating the Red Sox by three games. And as a result, New York had home field advantage, meaning the Red Sox would have to win at least once at Yankee Stadium and that, in all probability, the Red Sox would have to win either Game 6 or Game 7—or both—on the hallowed ground of the *House That Ruth Built,* where the Yankees had so often proven unbeatable at the most important of times.

Despite all of that, most people liked the Red Sox.

And the primary reason was Curt Schilling.

Of course, the most compelling aspect of sports is the sheer unpredictability, the astonishing manner in which things can so swiftly and thoroughly turn. And so it was in the 2004 American League Championship Series between the Red Sox and New York Yankees, at least from the perspective of so many New Englanders. Pitching with a supportive splint on his right ankle, Schilling went out in Game 1 and allowed two runs in the first inning, four more in the third. Schilling's fastball, normally clocked anywhere from 93 to 96 miles per hour, was hovering between 88 and 90, and he looked incapable of driving off the stadium mound with his right foot. He walked two batters and struck out only one, marking the first time in six years that he finished a game with more walks than strikeouts. And after leaving the mound following the third inning, Schilling disappeared down the dugout steps and up the runway to the Red Sox clubhouse.

When he did not return, many justifiably believed that the Red Sox' championship hopes went with him.

As usual, the game also dealt Schilling and the Red Sox their usual dose of humility, mostly the result of the loose-lipped Schilling's remarks prior to Game 1. During a press conference with the national media on the day before the series opener, Schilling spoke of the thrill at pitching at a place like Yankee Stadium, of the satisfaction that could come from making "55,000 New Yorkers shut up." It was the kind of contrived remark that Schilling loved to make, one that would get ample play in the New York City tabloids and placed on him even more pressure, which he was truly immune to. In fact, Schilling liked the give-and-take. The last time Schilling had faced the Yankees in the postseason—as a member of the Arizona Diamondbacks in the 2001 World Series—Schilling was asked about the aura and mystique that a franchise like the Yankees possessed, and he responded with a remark that forever earned a place in baseball annals.

Said the talkative right-hander: "Mystique and Aura are dancers at a nightclub."

On a national stage, especially, that was how Curt Schilling operated.

Frequently, one had to wonder how much time he spent thinking the stuff up.

In some ways, Game 1 proved a cross-section for what the entire series would become. Facing an 8–0 deficit after six innings and with their staff ace hobbled, the Red Sox had yet to even manage a baserunner against Yankees starter Mike Mussina. They were the victims of a *perfect game*, for goodness sake, a threat that finally was quashed when second baseman Mark Bellhorn doubled with one out in the seventh. Pitching from the stretch for the first time all night, a machinelike Mussina subsequently allowed hits to three of the next four batters he faced, departing with an 8–3 lead as reliever Tanyon Sturtze entered to face Jason Varitek with a man on in the top of the seventh.

Incredibly, before long, the score was 8–7. Sturtze allowed a two-run home run to Varitek, then finished the seventh before giving way to right-hander Tom Gordon at the start of the eighth. Gordon sandwiched two outs between two singles before allowing a skyscraping two-run triple to Ortiz that struck the top of the wall in left field, nearly a home run that would have tied the game. With the Red Sox now within a run and the tying run on third base, Yankees manager Joe Torre summoned typically unflappable closer Mariano Rivera, who retired the overmatched Kevin Millar on a pop to short. And after the Yankees extended their lead to 10–7 in the bottom of the eighth, Rivera allowed two more Sox baserunners in the ninth before finally ending the game on a double play hit by Bill Mueller, who had homered against Rivera during the unforgettable July 24 meeting that also featured the fight between Varitek and Yankees third baseman Alex Rodriguez.

In the end, the Yankees won Game 1 by a 10–7 score.

But in the process, what appeared to be a terribly one-sided fight had morphed into another epic struggle between Boston and New York that was decided by the slimmest of margins—the distance between Ortiz' triple and a home run.

Still, for the Red Sox, the lasting effect seemed damning. As encouraging as the final innings of the game had become, the injury to Schilling loomed. While a testy Francona declined to address his plans if Schilling could not make his next start, scheduled for Game 5—"It's way too early," snarled the manager—Schilling stood in the center of the visiting clubhouse and took a far more realistic stance. Yes, his ankle was bothering him. Yes, it affected his delivery. Yes, there was little question that he was so badly impaired that even he questioned whether he would be able to pitch again in the series.

And even if he could, he wondered whether he would be able to pitch effectively.

"If I can't go out there with something better than I had [in Game 1], I'm not going back out there," Schilling said quite emphatically. "This isn't about me. It's about winning a world championship. If I can't do better than I did, I won't take the ball again."

With those words, the championship hopes of the 2004 Boston Red Sox seemed to sink like a stone.

And so it was, one day later, that the Red Sox preempted a charade and acknowledged what most everyone already knew: Curt Schilling was probably done for the season. The Sox conducted a press conference prior to Game 2 in which team doctor Bill Morgan detailed Schilling's precise injury—the pitcher had a dislocated tendon, said Morgan—and revealed that the injury was causing instability in Schilling's right ankle. While medication prevented Schilling from feeling much pain on the mound during his delivery, the tendon was moving back and forth across the outside of his ankle bone, resulting in a *popping* or *snapping* sensation each time Schilling tried to deliver a pitch. The entire news conference was a somewhat startling revelation for a professional team, particularly in an age when many teams treated any news concerning injuries as highly classified information.

If the Red Sox were being so open now—after only one game—it was not a good sign.

"We decided to go with the truth," general manager Theo Epstein said somewhat begrudgingly as he departed from the unusual gathering.

So it was that the Red Sox handed the ball to Martinez for Game 2 under the most ironic of circumstances. *They needed him to be their ace.* But even with Schilling's status in serious doubt, the Red Sox still believed they had a chance, largely because they had both Martinez and the enigmatic Lowe, who had combined for 41 victories during the 2002 season. Unlike many clubs, who had a tremendous shortage of pitching, the Red Sox had in Lowe a pitcher who had won 52 games over a span of three seasons, from 2002–2004. Lowe had struggled badly in September and was entirely unpredictable, but the good news is there was also the chance he could pitch *well.* Certainly, he was no worse than Yankees pitcher Jon Lieber, who was facing Martinez in the second game of the series. And if the Red Sox had Martinez, Lowe, Arroyo, and Wakefield, they still had a chance of competing against a Yankees team that was short on starting pitching, particularly given the uncertainty of Yankees starter Orlando Hernandez, who had been nursing a sore arm.

Predictably, from the start of Game 2, the capacity crowd at Yankee Stadium taunted Martinez, who was serenaded at every opportune moment with melodic chants of "*Who's your dad-dy?*" And while Martinez struggled at the outset, issuing a walk, hit batter, and run-scoring single to the first three batters he faced, he settled down nicely in the subsequent innings, allowing the Yankees only the one run through the first five frames. Following the RBI single (by longtime Martinez adversary Gary Sheffield), Martinez allowed just two hits to the next 20 Yankees batters—a one-out single to No. 9 hitter Kenny Lofton in the second and an infield single to Rodriguez in the top of the fifth.

The problem, once again, was a Red Sox lineup proving embarrassingly inept against Lieber, who was nearly duplicating Mussina's performance from a night earlier. Lieber retired 19 of the first 21 Red Sox batters of the game, allowing only a leadoff walk to Ortiz (in the second) and a leadoff single to shortstop Orlando Cabrera (in the third). Red Sox hitters looked so clueless that the game seemed entirely beyond their reach when Martinez made a careless pitch to John Olerud in the sixth—the well-past-his-prime Olerud yanked the ill-placed offering into the right field seats for a two-run home run—giving the Yankees a commanding 3–0 lead on a night when the Red Sox had thus far advanced only one runner beyond first base.

Martinez, in fact, gave the Red Sox precisely the same outing he had turned in during Game 2 of the American League Division Series against Anaheim—seven innings, three runs—though the result this time was markedly different. And before Martinez departed the game in the bottom of the seventh, Lieber had breezed through the top of the inning. The Red Sox went on to scrape out a run against the struggling Gordon in the eighth, making the score 3–1 before Torre again summoned sure-thing Rivera, who sealed the door on another Yankees victory.

Following the game, Martinez downplayed the chants of Yankees fans, attempting to trivialize the taunts by putting them into perspective. And while one embarrassing member of the New York press corps actually *thanked* Martinez for his candor during the middle of the press conference, the remarks came off as contrived, terribly obvious, and downright bizarre.

"It actually made me feel really, really good," Martinez said, drawing chuckles from assembled media who thought he was being sarcastic. "I don't know why you guys laugh. I wasn't done with my answer. I actually realized that I was somebody important because I got the attention of 60,000 people and all of you. If you reverse time to 15 years ago, I was under a mango tree without 50 cents to pay for a bus. [In Game 2], I had the attention of 60,000 people. I thank God for that."

Just the same—whether they were using baseballs, mangoes, or papayas—things on paper began to look ominous for the Red Sox. While dropping the first two games of the series to New York, the Sox had done so despite pitching their vaunted one-two punch of Schilling and Martinez. Now Schilling was hurt and Martinez would not be able to pitch again until at least Game 6, and the Sox had to turn to the 27-year-old Arroyo, whose only other career playoff start had come against the Angels, in a best-of-5 series, with the Sox *ahead* by a 2–0 series score. This time, the circumstances were different. As opposed to the division series, when the Sox effectively played Game 3 at triple-match point—a loss still would have left them with two more chances to advance to the ALCS—Arroyo had to take the mound knowing that he had almost no margin for error. He *had* to pitch well. A defeat would leave the Sox with a 3–0 series deficit against the most accomplished franchise in the history of professional sports, and no team in baseball history ever had overcome a 3–0 series deficit.

On top of it all, the Red Sox had to deal with a masochistic fan base whose insecurities shot directly to the surface anytime there was adversity, particularly against the Yankees. While the Sox lost both Schilling and Game 1 in the series opener, the Game 2 defeat was, in many ways, much more frustrating. The matchup of Martinez against Lieber was a clear advantage for the Red Sox, but the Boston lineup looked lost against the Yankees' Game 2 starter. Yet if the Red Sox truly were going to exploit the New York pitching staff, they would do so as the series progressed, as New York was forced to go deeper into a rotation that was noticeably shallower than in years past.

Nonetheless, when it came to the Yankees, Red Sox fans understandably needed convincing.

So what about those who already believed the Red Sox were defeated?

"They don't need to watch the game," snapped outfielder Johnny Damon. "We have a game to play. It's unfortunate if they feel that way. They've seen it in the past but this team is different. We know we can do it—it's just a matter of doing it."

As it turned out, much to the dismay of Damon and the Red Sox, many Red Sox fans wished they had *not* watched the third game of the series. Though rain initially postponed Game 3 and allowed for two days off instead of one—that fact introduced the possibility that Schilling might be able to return—the game was played on Saturday, October 15, under the Fenway Park lights on a comfortable 57–degree night. An extremely ineffective Arroyo allowed three runs in the first and three more in the third, the latter during which he failed to record an out. And just eight days after mesmerizing the Angels, the stringy right-hander retired just five of the 13 batters he faced, surrendering six hits, six runs, two walks, and two home runs before suffering the greatest indignity of all.

He was replaced by Ramiro Mendoza, the former Yankee whose career in Boston had theretofore been a complete disaster and who had been added to the playoff roster only for the most desperate occasions.

On the postseason pitching staff of the 2004 Red Sox, Ramiro Mendoza was the panic button.

Remarkably, despite the failure of Arroyo, the Red Sox still had a chance in Game 3. Prior to Arroyo's departure, the Red Sox had scored four runs in the second inning against equally ineffective Yankees starter Kevin Brown, who never came out for the bottom of the third. (Arroyo actually outlasted Brown in the game.) The Sox then greeted Brown's replacement, Javier Vazquez, with a two-run rally in his first inning of work, leaving the teams tied at 6 after just three innings of play.

At that point, what had been billed as a matchup of Bronson Arroyo and Kevin Brown had turned into a meeting of Ramiro Mendoza and Javier Vazquez, and that was the kind of scenario that neither Sox manager Terry Francona nor Yankees skipper Joe Torre wanted to see.

As things turned out, the sight was more horrific for Francona. Though Mendoza made it through his first inning without incident, the pitcher opened the fourth by hitting No. 9 hitter Miguel Cairo, prompting Francona to immediately summon right-hander Curtis Leskanic. Leskanic lasted only four batters, allowing a walk, home run, and double to the final three, leaving the score at 9–6. So out went Leskanic and in came knuckleballer Wakefield, who originally was scheduled to start Game 4. And by the time Wakefield walked off the mound at the end of the fourth—finally the Sox had recorded three outs—the Yankees had an 11–6 lead and were en route to a lopsided 19–8 beating that gave them a commanding 3–0 series advantage and left the Red Sox laying bloodied and beaten, like carcasses in the desert.

The buzzards were circling.

Or so it seemed.

"It's definitely embarrassing," admitted the shell-shocked Arroyo. "You try to forget about it during the regular season, but when it's crunch time, to get destroyed like that and have a football score up there, it's definitely embarrassing."

Said Damon: "We all had the belief that this team was a team that could go out and do it. We haven't done it. It's not fun."

Noted manager Francona, albeit weeks later: "If I was on a radio talk show, I would have said the Yankees were going to win. You had to."

It was, after all, the logical thing to do.

In the wake of Game 3, the Red Sox were roundly criticized, most notably for the manner in which they carried themselves. Once praised for being a collection of free spirits who grew their hair long and thrived on lawlessness, the Sox were now viewed as being undisciplined, immature, unmotivated. They were drinkers and they were partiers, nothing like the corporate and clean-cut Yankees, who functioned efficiently and professionally at the most critical of times. The Red Sox were very much living up to the nickname given them by bearded center fielder Damon, whose mountain-man look had made him a cult hero but who was 1-for-13 with five strikeouts through the first three games of the series.

"We're just a bunch of idiots," Damon had cracked.

And after Game 3, he never appeared more right.

Following the debacle, frustration grew so high in some corners that the players' wives and girlfriends had to be restrained from one another. Earlier in the playoffs, both for good luck and as a sign of solidarity, Schilling's wife, Shonda, had bought a collection of scarves and handed them out to the other wives and girlfriends. Damon's fiancée, Michelle Mangum, had refrained from wearing hers, however, and it was following the 19–8 defeat to the Yankees that Mangum entered the family waiting room following Game 3 and struck a nerve in Shonda Schilling.

"A lot of good those fucking scarves have done," said Mangum.

Countered Shonda Schilling: "Well if you were wearing one, maybe your fiancée wouldn't be 0-for-16."

The two women ultimately had to be separated from one another, though the good news for Red Sox followers is that the tension among the players never reached such heights. For all of the criticisms promoted by their carefree nature, the 2004 Red Sox proved capable of functioning in Boston precisely for the same reason. Things inevitably became tense for all teams at some point during a baseball season—there were more untold stories of clubhouse fights and encounters than the media and fans ever knew—and many players did not know how to cope with failure. To do so required a unique perspective, an understanding that there truly was no pressure because there was really nothing to lose.

Baseball was a game, after all.

Even if it hardly seemed it.

Still, in a place like Boston, people had long since lost perspective. Fans and media put so much pressure on the team to win that it became virtually impossible for the players to simply *play*, a reality that created a spiraling paradox. The harder the players tried, the worse they played, the more they lost. In Boston, more than any other place in professional sports, what was required to win was a team that had no fear of losing, that had no concerns about being lumped in with the succession of Red Sox teams that had failed to win a World Series over the 86-year span beginning in 1918. Where most Sox teams feared being lumped into the past, the 2004 Red Sox seemed to recognize that they would truly be no worse off than any other collection of players to have worn the uniform since the days of World War I.

They were *expected* to lose.

And so in the wake of Game 3, just one defeat away from a truly humiliating sweep at the hands of the hated Yankees, the 2004 Red Sox seemed to come to a startling conclusion.

They had been freed.

All they had to do was play.

In that way, especially, Damon had become the poster boy for the entire team. Not long after the start of the season, after Damon had reported to spring training with flowing locks and hair on his face, some Fenway fans began showing up at the ballpark in wigs and fake beards, playing off media references to *The Passion of the Christ* and dubbing themselves *Damon's Disciples*. The player became instantly identifiable both on the road and at home, his look growing so familiar to fans that, during the season, he had his beard publicly shaved for charity. His face then clean, Damon immediately grew back the beard, continuing to play throughout the season with a consistent productivity and efficiency that had not been apparent to that point in his Red Sox career.

Johnny Damon may have looked like Charles Manson, but he was playing like an All-Star.

Nonetheless, from the start of Damon's career to the end of the 2004 season, the metamorphosis was extraordinary. Damon began his career with the Kansas City Royals as speedy outfielder who was literally and figuratively groomed, coming through the Kansas City system with closely cropped hair and a boyish charm. He had married his longtime girlfriend and was painfully shy, speaking with a stutter that he would eventually overcome.

After five years with the Royals and a subsequent stint with the Oakland A's, Damon was not much different when he signed a four-year, $31 million contract with the Red Sox prior to the 2002 season, when he had a sensational first half of the season and represented the Red Sox at the All-Star Game. But his play slipped steadily in the second half of that season and he went through a divorce that winter, and by the time he showed up for Spring Training 2003, he was acting like a man in a midlife crisis. Red Sox officials grew so concerned about Damon's off-field habits that then manager Grady Little confronted the player about partying too much, a concern that had not entirely dissolved by the start of 2004.

By then, too, the once soft-spoken Damon had emerged as a quote machine for hungry members of the media, who were routinely flocking to his locker after games because they knew Damon would be there.

Said one Red Sox official early in the season, when Damon went through one of his rare slumps of 2004: "Our center fielder needs to stop talking and start getting some hits."

Still, however disturbingly liberated Damon had become both on the field and off, the effect on his game was proving too beneficial for anyone to tinker with. By the end of the 2004 season, Damon had enjoyed his best season as a member of the Red Sox, finishing with a .304 batting average, 20 home runs, and 94 RBI, the latter an astonishing amount for a leadoff hitter. He scored 123 runs, one behind Anaheim outfielder Vladimir Guerrero for most in the American League. And he had been such a catalyst for a Red Sox offense that led the major leagues in runs scored for a second consecutive season that he was being mentioned as a candidate for the AL Most Valuable Player award, even if nobody expected him to cop the honor.

In the Anaheim series, too, Damon had been an absolute force. In the Red Sox' three-game sweep of the Angels, Damon had gone 7-for-15 (a sparkling

.467 average) with four runs scored and three stolen bases. He had scored at least once in all three series victories and joined No. 2 hitter Mark Bellhorn in placing such relentless pressure on the Anaheim pitching staff that the Angels were forced to confront the fearsome middle of the Red Sox batting order.

Yet by the time the Yankees series began, Damon showed no hint of the same magic. He struck out all four times he came to bat in the series opener and went 0-for-4 again in Game 2, only once managing to hit the ball out of the infield. He had an RBI single in the second inning of wild Game 3 but stranded five baserunners in his final three plate appearances, finishing 1-for-5 in the game and bringing his series totals to 1-for-13. So while Damon was not the 0-for-16 that an annoyed Shonda Schilling had alleged, he had hardly been the kind of factor that the Red Sox had expected in their return trip to the American League Championship Series after Boston's frustrating loss to New York in 2003.

Suddenly, an unshaven Johnny Damon looked very much like the idiot he professed to be.

And as was often the case in baseball, the Red Sox were falling into line behind their hard-living leadoff man.

In most every important baseball game, there comes that pivotal moment when the entire contest turns. On the larger scale that was the 2004 American League Championship Series, that moment was Game 4.

Faced with the prospect of elimination and stationed behind the self-pitying Lowe, the Red Sox took the field for Game 4 under the direst of circumstances. They needed not only to win that night, but also the night after that . . . and the night after that . . . and the night after that. The initial postponement of Game 3 had resulted in the elimination of a day off between Games 5 and 6, meaning the last five games of the series would be played on five consecutive days, assuming the Red Sox could make it that far. And if the Sox were to do that, they would have to start by winning Game 4 behind Lowe, who had not started a game since October 3, the regular season finale at Baltimore in which he was limited to just two innings.

In the two weeks since, Derek Lowe had pitched the grand total of one inning, in the 10th inning of Game 3 of the AL Division Series clincher against Anaheim.

"I think he's going to respond well, but we *need* him to respond well for us," Damon said of his teammate.

To his credit, Lowe did not sulk. The right-hander set the Yankees down in order in the top of the first inning—the first time all series that the Red Sox had held the Yankees scoreless to open the game. Lowe teetered briefly when, with two outs in the third, he allowed a single to Jeter and home run to Alex Rodriguez, but the Red Sox responded with three runs in the bottom of the fifth against Yankees starter Orlando Hernandez, who was similarly coming off a long layoff. The Yankees then chased Lowe in the sixth with a pair of runs (one against Mike Timlin) that gave New York a 4–3 advantage, but after the debacle that was Game 3, Lowe's performance was invaluable, particularly when the need to use Wakefield in relief during the third game forced Lowe into the rotation.

With Lowe and Hernandez gone, the score remained 4–3 through the sixth and seventh, into the eighth. Sensing an opportunity to close out the Red Sox, Yankees manager Joe Torre once again called upon Rivera, who allowed a leadoff single to Manny Ramirez before setting down the next three batters.

So, roughly eight months after Red Sox pitchers and catchers reported to spring training, after going 17–12–1 in 30 spring training games and 98–64 in 162 regular season contests, after sweeping the Anaheim Angels in the first round of the playoffs and dropping the first three games of a best-of-7 series against the Yankees, this is what the 2004 baseball season in Boston came down to:

Trailing 4–3 in the ninth inning against the great Mariano in their 199th game of the year, the Red Sox needed to score.

Or it was over.

Had the Red Sox looked at it in those daunting terms, of course, what ended up happening might never have taken place. Exactly one month to the day after Sox outfielder Trot Nixon began a game-winning rally against Rivera by drawing a walk, Sox first baseman Kevin Millar did the same in the ninth inning of Game 4. Francona promptly replaced the heavy-legged Millar with the speedy Dave Roberts, who took off for a second on a fastball high and off the plate. Presented with the ideal circumstances for throwing out a base stealer, Yankees catcher Jorge Posada sprung from his crouch behind the plate and made a strong throw to shortstop Derek Jeter, who quickly applied the tag. Veteran umpire Joe West stood over the play as Roberts dived headfirst into the bag, slipping his hand just beneath Jeter's tag.

The umpire called safe.

At that moment, had things gone differently, there is no telling what would have become of the 2004 Boston Red Sox. But almost immediately after Roberts' successful steal, third baseman Bill Mueller punched a single to center that allowed Roberts to score easily from second base, tying the game at 4. Rivera avoided further damage in the inning despite a costly error from first baseman Tony Clark and the Yankees subsequently failed to score in the 10th, 11th, and 12th innings, leaving five men on base, including the bases loaded in the top of the 11th. Finally, after Red Sox outfielder Manny Ramirez led off the bottom of the 12th with a single against reliever Paul Quantrill, big bear Ortiz ripped a two-run home run into the Yankees bullpen that gave the Red Sox a dramatic 6–4 victory and thrust a Fenway Park crowd of 34,826 into a glorious celebration.

In Boston, the baseball season continued.

There would be a fifth game.

"Things can change," said Ortiz, whose homer, going back to the conclusion of the Anaheim series, marked the second consecutive Red Sox victory that concluded with him hitting one out of the park. "You never know what can happen from now on. We played a really good game [in Game 4]. It was a totally different game than the one we played in [Game 3]."

Even before Game 4, in fact, the Red Sox' fortunes had begun to turn. Because of the rainout, the Sox had the opportunity to pitch Martinez in Game 5 instead of Game 6. That fact loomed larger with the news that the Sox were seriously considering Schilling for Game 6 at Yankee Stadium, something the Sox confirmed even before Game 5 was played. The announcement that Schilling would pitch Game 6 seemed like psychological warfare at the time, an attempt to plant in the minds of the Yankees (and New Yorkers) the idea that trouble loomed if New York similarly failed to close out the Red Sox in the fifth game. Yet the reality was that the Red Sox were very serious about the prospect of pitching Schilling, thanks largely to an ingenious idea by Sox team doctor Bill Morgan, who proposed a radical manner in which to treat the dislocated tendon in Schilling's ankle.

But for any of it to truly have value, the Sox first had to win Game 5.

Like the fourth game—and, for that matter, so many of the previous affairs between the Red Sox and Yankees—Game 5 was a positively riveting epic from which no true baseball fan could peel his eyes. The game began with a matchup of Martinez and Mike Mussina, the masterful right-hander who took a perfect game into the seventh inning of Game 1. And by the time the game ended in the 14th inning, the Red Sox and Yankees had played for five hours and 49 minutes, the longest postseason game in baseball history. Combined, the Red Sox and Yankees entertained America with a total of 10 hours and 51 minutes of unparalleled competition and drama in Games 4 and 5 alone.

Unlike Game 1, the Sox this time wasted no time getting to Mussina, scoring a pair of runs in the bottom of the first. The Yankees countered with a run in the second and three more in the sixth—the final three scored on a three-run double by the unshakeable Jeter—to take a 4–2 advantage. The Yankees held the same margin entering the eighth, when Torre summoned setup man Tom Gordon who allowed a home run, walk, and single to the first three batters he faced. The score was 4–3 and there was nobody out with runners on first and third when Torre once again called upon Rivera in a save situation with the Yankees clinging to a 4–3 lead.

Faced with a virtually impossible task, Rivera allowed a sacrifice fly to the first batter he faced—Varitek—that tied the game at 4. The Yankees closer subsequently made it through the remainder of the eighth and the entire ninth without allowing another run, but the damage once again had been done. While Rivera had been the possessor of just one blown save in his postseason career entering the 2004 playoffs, the Red Sox had scored the game-tying run against him on consecutive nights with their season at stake. At that moment, at least in Boston, nobody was talking about Pedro Martinez' inability to beat the Yankees as much as they were about Mariano Rivera's inability to close the door on the Red Sox.

And so the game went on to the 10th, 11th, 12th, and 13th. Still there was no winner. And every time the Yankees threatened, the Red Sox would benefit from some extraordinary twist of good fortune. Earlier in the game, for example, New York had a runner at first with two outs in the ninth when No. 8 hitter Tony Clark pulled a line drive into the right field corner for certain extra bases. The ball struck the right field warning track and hopped into the crowd—missing the top of the right field wall by inches—resulting in a ground-rule double that required the baserunner, Ruben Sierra, to advance no farther than third base. With two outs, especially, Sierra was breaking on contact and would have scored easily, but the ground-rule double required him to stop at third. Sox closer Keith Foulke then retired No. 9 hitter Miguel Cairo on a foul pop to first to end the inning.

It was the kind of break that so often went against the Red Sox, particularly in games against the Yankees.

Five innings later, in the 13th, the Sox uncovered further evidence that their luck was changing. Called upon to pitch in relief for a second straight night, Wakefield set the Yankees down in the 12th before his dancing knuckleball began to work against him. Wakefield struck out Gary Sheffield to start the 13th, but catcher Varitek was unable to handle the third strike, resulting in a passed ball that allowed Sheffield to reach first. Three batters later, with two outs and Hideki Matsui (fielder's choice) at first, Varitek failed to handle two more Wakefield pitches, allowing Matsui to advance to third. Fearing another passed ball—this one would have scored Matsui from third—a crowd of 35,120 had a lump in its collective throat as Wakefield intentionally walked Jorge Posada before striking out Sierra, the final pitch a darting knuckleball that a sprawling Varitek speared in self-defense.

Strike three.

Disaster avoided.

At that moment, in particular, Red Sox fans should have recognized that their karma had changed. Varitek, in fact, had not caught Wakefield for much of the regular season, the responsibility typically falling upon backup catcher Doug Mirabelli, who effectively had served as Wakefield's personal assistant. And it had been only one year earlier, of course, that Wakefield had walked off the Yankee Stadium field after allowing the game-winning home run to Boone in Game 7, another extra-inning affair and one that had ended the Red Sox' season.

In 2004, in Game 5, there was every opportunity for history to repeat itself.

Instead, after Wakefield made it through the 14th—his third inning of relief—the Red Sox put a pair of runners on against right-hander Esteban Loaiza in the bottom of the 14th. Up again came Ortiz, who fouled off a succession of pitches from Loaiza before muscling the 10th and final offering of the at-bat into center field for a single. The hit scored Johnny Damon from second base to give the Red Sox a 5–4 victory and send the series back to New York, altering the course of the series and significantly shifting the momentum in the direction of the Red Sox.

With one more loss, after all, the Yankees would be forced to play a seventh game.

In the history of Major League Baseball, no team holding a 3–0 series in a best-of-7 contest ever had been forced to that limit.

The pressure was on the Yankees.

"Even before, the way I look at it, the pressure's all on them," said Foulke. "They put us in a hole and it's their job to put us away. Nobody's ever come back from a 3–0 deficit and that's what we've talked about—changing history. The pressure's on them."

In reality, of course, the Red Sox still had a greater challenge than the Yankees—Boston needed to win two more games, the Yankees just one—though the Red Sox were indeed beginning to regain their swagger. Before Game 4, when the Yankees were leading the series, 3–0, some Red Sox players had responded angrily to a Sheffield quote that appeared in the *Herald* and described the Red Sox as being "a mess." Sheffield denied making the comment and, in a sense, he was right, the remark having been lifted from a story that had appeared in *Baseball Weekly* during the middle of the season. Nonetheless, Red Sox players clearly took note of the comment, in which Sheffield similarly questioned the team's toughness. The Sox posted the quote in their clubhouse, though many teams in the past had done similar things only to go out on the field and get their brains beaten in.

Regardless, by the time Game 5 had been completed—the series now 3–2—there was no disputing the toughness of the Red Sox. While 30-year-old Red Sox general manager Theo Epstein suggested that Game 5 might have been "the greatest game that's ever been played"—Epstein was not yet two years old when, during the 1975 World Series, former Red Sox catcher Carlton Fisk homered in the 12th inning of Game 6, believed by many to be the greatest game ever played—but his point was noted. Whenever the Red Sox traveled deep into October or whenever they played the Yankees—and in this case, both things were true—there was always the possibility that history would be made, as it had been during Game 6 of the 1975 World Series or during Game 5 of the 1986 American League Championship Series, the latter the occasion when then-Sox outfielder Dave Henderson hit a season-saving, two-run home run with two outs in the bottom of the ninth inning that eventually allowed the Red Sox to overcome a 3–1 series deficit and advance to the World Series.

Soon thereafter, the Sox played yet another October classic, ending up on wrong end of a 6–5 loss to the New York Mets when the ball went through first baseman Bill Buckner's legs on the final play of Game 6 of the 1986 World Series. The moment was among the darkest in Red Sox history, but the game was a classic nonetheless.

And so, joining the list was Game 5 of the 2004 ALCS, a drama only intensified by the heroics of Ortiz, whose game-winning hit marked the third consecutive Red Sox victory that ended with a swing of his mighty bat.

"What David Ortiz has done has been phenomenal," wide-eyed Red Sox outfielder Gabe Kapler said in an electric Red Sox clubhouse following Game 5. "He's carried us. It's not easy to go up with the game on the line and produce like he has consistently.

"I'm not sure how they're feeling now or how they'll be feeling after they get on the bus," Kapler continued, speaking of the Yankees. "But I will say this: This team has done something the last two days that should go down in history as an incredible accomplishment. To battle like we've battled is unheard of. It would have been easy for us to quit."

That point was accentuated further less than 24 hours later, when Schilling took the mound at Yankee Stadium for Game 6. Showing no signs of pain or discomfort, Schilling retired the first eight Yankees batters of the night and nine of the first 10. By the time he allowed a run—on a solo home run by Bernie Williams in the bottom of the seventh inning—the Red Sox already had scored four times against Yankees starter Jon Lieber, who had shut down Boston in Game 2. Lieber, too, had pitched quite well, but he had been victimized by No. 9 hitter and second baseman Mark Bellhorn, who completed a four-run Red Sox rally in the fourth inning with a three-run home run into the first row of the left field seats. Umpires originally had ruled the play a double but, to their credit, correctly changed the call after conferring on the Yankee Stadium turf. Again, it was the kind of call that so often had gone against the Red Sox.

Prior to the home run, Bellhorn had been 3-for-21 with nine strikeouts in the series, including an 0-for-3 performance (one strikeout) in Game 2. And despite media speculation that manager Terry Francona might pull Bellhorn from the lineup in favor of the defensively superior Pokey Reese, Francona had only moved Bellhorn down in the batting order. So, after the Red Sox loaded the bases after there were two outs and no one aboard, it was Bellhorn who came to the plate instead of a the offensively challenged Reese.

Four innings after Bellhorn's homer—after Schilling had departed with a 4–1 advantage—the bounces all continued to go the Red Sox' way. With one out against Arroyo, Cairo doubled and Jeter singled, making the score 4–2 and bringing Alex Rodriguez to the plate. Rodriguez hit a soft bouncer up the first baseline that Arroyo fielded before attempting to tag Rodriguez, and the play looked like an easy out until the ball shot out of Arroyo's glove and trickled down the right field line. Jeter scored and Rodriguez ended up on second base, and the Red Sox appeared on the verge of unraveling as a typically bloodthirsty crowd at Yankee Stadium offered deafening roars of approval.

And then, as Arroyo pleaded his case with first base umpire Randy Marsh, 86 years of Red Sox misfortune continued to right itself.

For the second time in the game, the umpires conferred before coming to a dramatic, rightful conclusion: Rodriguez had been guilty of interference. Replays revealed that Rodriguez had forced the ball loose with a swipe at Arroyo's glove, a baseball no-no in both technical and ethical terms. Rodriguez was called out. Jeter was ordered to return to second base. And with a Yankee Stadium crowd of 56,128 crying foul—in New York, of all places—Arroyo retired Sheffield on a foul pop-up to catcher Jason Varitek before closer Foulke came in for the ninth and did what Rivera had been unable to do in Games 4 and 5.

He closed the door.

Following the game, Schilling detailed the process by which he was able to pitch, explaining how Morgan, the team doctor, had prevented the dislocated tendon from moving by placing sutures in the pitcher's right ankle. What Morgan did, in fact, was position Schilling's tendon out of its torn sheath, then place stitches in the pitcher's ankle so that the tendon could not snap back and forth, in and out of place. It was that movement that had caused Schilling discomfort in Game 1, so Morgan proposed the idea of an invasive procedure that might allow Schilling to get back on the mound. Prior to Game 5 at Fenway Park—and in large part because Schilling wanted to get accustomed to the stitches in his ankle—Morgan inserted the sutures, after which Schilling went out on the Fenway lawn and played catch.

Incredibly, the idea worked.

A night later, after Schilling had silenced the Yankees in Game 6, most of the discussion in the Boston clubhouse focused on the play of Rodriguez, whose action was seen nationally (and internationally) as a sign of desperation. Red Sox players privately pulled aside reporters and begged them to emphasize the play—"He needs to be called out—and loudly," one Sox player told a *Herald* reporter—and the Sox elected chatty first baseman Kevin Millar as their official spokesman on the topic.

"It was a classless play. Unprofessional," Millar said of Rodriguez' swipe at Arroyo. "That's just as unprofessional as you're going to see. Play the game hard and play the game right. He's got to brush his teeth looking in the mirror, not with his head down."

Schilling, too, would publicly criticize Rodriguez, his comments coming after an overly dramatic press conference in which he heaped praise upon himself. Still, there was no disputing what Schilling had done on the mound, essentially on one leg, nor the lengths to which he was willing to go in order to win. Because of the threat of infection, Schilling said at his locker after the game, the sutures would be removed from his ankle the following day, prior to climactic Game 7 between the Red Sox and Yankees. And as Schilling gathered his belongings and departed Yankee Stadium following the game, he offered succinct, sincere praise for Morgan, who came up with the idea of using the sutures in the first place.

"Our team doctor is a fucking genius," Schilling said.

With that, Schilling hobbled out of the visiting clubhouse at Yankee Stadium and out to the team buses, where the rest of the Red Sox were waiting.

Improbably, the American league Championship Series was now tied at three games apiece.

Incredibly, for the second straight season, there would be a climactic seventh game between the Red Sox and New York Yankees.

As it turned out, Game 7 really was no contest at all. Standing in the hallway outside the Red Sox clubhouse before the game, Sox executive vice president of public affairs Charles Steinberg suggested that Boston's only chance at a victory would be to score early and get a big lead, fearing that a close, tightly-contested affair at Yankee Stadium would inevitably result in a heartbreaking Red Sox defeat, as it had in 2003.

Steinberg, for what it's worth, possessed a degree in dentistry.

And for the Red Sox, for the second time in two days, a team doctor was absolutely right.

Following Game 6, in a demonstration of pure gamesmanship, neither Yankees manager Joe Torre nor Sox manager Terry Francona opted to disclose a starter for Game 7, though Francona's refusal came only after Torre played coy. ("I saw Joe's press conference, too," Francona cracked.) In fact, the Red Sox already had decided they would give the ball to Lowe, a fitting bit of irony given that Lowe would be pitching on just two days of rest. Bumped out of the starting rotation at the start of the playoffs, Lowe had started in Game 4 only out of desperation, and he had done so on two *weeks* of rest. Now the Red Sox were entrusting him with their season, in Game 7 of the American League Championship Series, in their house of horrors known as Yankee Stadium.

It was all too perfect.

Torre, as it was, opted for Kevin Brown, whom the Red Sox had abused in the embarrassing 19–8 loss in Game 3, though Brown had skated free from that game thanks to the performance of an explosive Yankees lineup. In Game 7, he was not so lucky. After Red Sox leadoff hitter Johnny Damon was thrown out at home plate in the first inning—again, it was an opportunity for the Yankees to seize momentum—Brown allowed a two-run home run *on the next pitch* to—who else?—Ortiz, who yanked a heat-seeking liner into the right field seats for an immediate 2–0 Red Sox advantage.

Three innings later, the game was completely out of hand. After the Red Sox loaded the bases against Brown in the second, Torre desperately turned to right-hander Javier Vazquez, who allowed a grand slam to Damon that landed in the same area in right field. Damon added a two-run homer against Vazquez in the fourth inning—apparently, Damon's fiancée had begun wearing Shonda Schilling's gifted scarf—giving the Red Sox a whopping 8–1 advantage that held up through the sixth.

Lowe, meanwhile, was absolutely brilliant, giving the Red Sox more than they possibly could have bargained for. Entering the contest, manager Francona and pitching coach Dave Wallace believed that, in a best-case scenario, Lowe could give them five good innings, but the surging right-hander went one better, giving them six. And while the Yankees rallied briefly against Pedro Martinez in the seventh—New York score twice to close the gap to 8–3—

the Red Sox were never really in jeopardy, scoring once more in the eighth and again in the ninth en route to a thunderous 10–3 victory.

Now, just four days after the Sox trailed the Yankees by a 3–0 series score, it was the Yankees who were in a complete state of disarray. New York's first two pitchers in Game 7—Brown and Vazquez—were the principal off-season replacements for Roger Clemens and Andy Pettitte, who had backboned the Yankees' success of previous years and who had departed the team via free agency. (It was also the kind of thing that typically happened to the Red Sox.) And the Red Sox finished with four home runs in the game—all from left-handed hitters—suggesting Boston was more suited than the Yankees to play in *The House That Ruth Built*, where a parade of Yankees hitters from Babe Ruth to Lou Gehrig to the switch-hitting Mickey Mantle had taken advantage of the proximity of the right field stands.

In 2004, however, it was the Red Sox who had the better left-handed hitters.

In the Boston clubhouse following the game, no one was more genuinely affected than knuckleballer Tim Wakefield, who had allowed the home run to Boone during Game 7 a year earlier. Standing in the middle of a champagne celebration that truly *meant something* this time—no one was suggesting that the Red Sox celebrated too much on this occasion—Wakefield recounted how he had felt after Game 7 in 2003, how he believed he had been forever tainted in Boston, how he had gone to the Baseball Writers dinner in February after the home run by Boone and been welcomed with cheers. How he, like his teammates, had overcome it all.

"When we got that final out, I wanted to stand on that mound as long as I could and relish the fact that I got to walk off the field a winner this time," said a teary-eyed Wakefield. "For us to win four in a row from these guys really shows the determination and the guts we had in this clubhouse.

"This is as big as the World Series," he added. "To be down 3–0, losing Game 3 the way we lost it, with the way we won Game 4 and the way we won Game 5, then coming back and winning Game 6 and Game 7 here, it's tremendous, not only for this organization, but for the city and the fans that stuck around through thick and thin for us."

Said part owner Tom Werner: "To win in Yankee Stadium, where we have so many bad memories and nights of restless sleeping, we couldn't ask for anything more. The World Series is great, but we've done something historic."

Outside, on the field just in front of the Red Sox dugout, Red Sox players, officials, and coaches gathered with their friends and families to celebrate what many regarded as the greatest moment in the history of the franchise. Red Sox fans who had made the trip down from Boston had clustered behind the third base dugout, cheering for their heroes and mocking the Yankees and chanting the names of any player to walk by.

At that moment, the identity of the Red Sox changed forever.

Boston was a winner.

The Yankees were history.

IN SEARCH OF AURA AND MYSTIQUE—YANKEES

GARY SHEFFIELD ALWAYS WANTED TO BE ON THE COVER OF *Sports Illustrated.* From the time his uncle, Dwight Gooden, was featured on the magazine's cover in 1985 as a 20-year-old phenom with the Mets, Sheffield told friends he would have his own cover someday. In 2004 Sheffield was 35 years old, and he had the big money, the huge house, the luxury cars; he even had the ring, having won a championship with the 1997 Florida Marlins. But he'd never been the subject of a cover story for *Sports Illustrated*, and the kid inside of him still wanted it as a celebration of his star status. Sheffield was having a magazine-cover type of season, making people take notice of his first year as a Yankee by delivering clutch hits night after night, playing the leading-man role that everyone expected fellow newcomer Alex Rodriguez to fill. In addition, Sheffield was sitting on a bombshell story, as one of a few high-profile major-leaguers known to have testified before a grand jury in the federal government's investigation into steroids as they pertained to the Bay Area Laboratory Co-Operative—BALCO, as it was known all too widely by now.

So it was that sometime in August, Ray Negron, a friend of Sheffield's, contacted *Sports Illustrated*'s senior baseball writer, Tom Verducci, and told him of Sheffield's longtime desire to make the cover. Verducci saw it as a natural, since the American League MVP race was an intriguing story in itself, with Sheffield, Manny Ramirez, David Ortiz, and Vladimir Guerrero all staking claims to the award as the season hit the home stretch. Negron later said no promises were made as to what Sheffield might or might not say about steroids, but Verducci made it clear the questions would be asked as part of the interview.

Likewise, Verducci made no promises about the cover, but pitched it to his editors at *SI*, who were open to the possibility. As a result, a photo shoot took place, at which Sheffield posed in an unbuttoned, dirtied-up Yankee jersey, the idea being to make him look old-school tough and defiant.

Then Verducci interviewed Sheffield in his hotel room in Baltimore in early September during a Yankees-Orioles series, and Sheffield delivered a story more explosive than even Verducci ever imagined. In fact, it turned out to be two stories. The main story was a profile of Sheffield chronicling his sometimes controversial career and his superb season with the Yankees, a story in which Sheffield offered unfiltered opinions on a variety of subjects, and also threatened to do damage of some kind to Pedro Martinez should the Red Sox' right-hander hit him with a pitch again, as he'd done in June. The sidebar, meanwhile, became the talk of the baseball world: not only did Sheffield admit to unwittingly using a steroid cream provided to him by BALCO while he was working out with Barry Bonds in San Francisco in January of 2002, but he shredded Bonds' character, portraying him as an impossibly arrogant control freak, even among friends, and told of how Bonds even went behind his back to steal his personal chef, who came with Sheffield from Miami and cooked for both of the players during their stay in San Francisco. "That's the kind of person I found out I was dealing with," Sheffield said of Bonds in the story. "To me, I don't want friends like that. I never will have friends like that."

In addition, Sheffield left little doubt that he believed Bonds had used steroids to artificially pump up his home run totals in recent years, including his record-setting 2001 season in which he hit 73.

"I know guys are not that much better than me naturally," Sheffield told Verducci. "There's no way possible. I'm not going to say any names, but six years ago I had the same number of home runs as another player, and I have had my best [home run] years since then. And you mean to tell me he out-homered me by 250? No way possible. Ain't no one in the world who can convince me that is possible."

Verducci came away from the interview thinking Sheffield had cemented his status as the cover subject with such strong comments about Bonds, the biggest name in baseball, as well as his admission to using the steroid cream.

"I knew it would get people talking," Verducci said weeks later.

However, the hook for the story, as Verducci put it, was still the AL MVP race, so it was slotted to run in the first week of October, just after the regular season ended. Meantime, the magazine's editors put Albert Pujols on the cover the week before the Sheffield story would run, as part of a story about the St. Louis Cardinals, the team with the best record in baseball, and they had the magazine's 50th anniversary edition planned for the week after, with a mosaic-type painting on the cover. Worried about going three consecutive weeks in the fall without a football presence on the cover, according to Verducci, the *SI* editors opted to preview the Oklahoma-Texas college football game on the cover of the Sheffield issue, featuring a picture of Oklahoma's freshman running back, Adrian Peterson. Sheffield did get a tiny piece of the cover, as he was pictured along the top, with the headline tease: Sheffield Speaks His Mind. But it wasn't the cover treatment he had envisioned. Nor did Verducci think it was good editorial judgment.

"I thought our magazine dropped the ball on it, to be honest," Verducci said. "It was a story that created a real buzz."

The buzz was heightened by the timing. *SI* put the story on its Web site on Tuesday, October 5, one day before the magazine hit newsstands, and also the day that baseball's playoffs were starting. The Yankees were hosting the Twins, and as word of the story spread, a media frenzy ensued. Verducci was covering the series, and as he arrived at Yankee Stadium at about 3:30 in the afternoon, he heard that Sheffield was doing an interview on ESPN at 4 o'clock. His first instinct was to fear that Sheffield was backing away from the story, doing damage control by going on TV to say that either he was misquoted or his comments were taken out of context, as players often do when they suddenly realize what an uproar they've caused, and what it might cost them in terms of image. Sheffield, however, confirmed his comments, repeating many of them for ESPN, and didn't deny any of them when surrounded by the print media on the field before the game (locker rooms aren't open to the press before games in the postseason). Sheffield did say he wasn't happy about the timing of the story, since he'd made his comments three weeks earlier, and he didn't really want to deal with it as the playoffs were starting, but he wasn't trying to make it go away by suggesting in any way that he hadn't meant what he said. And for that Verducci was grateful, especially since Sheffield hadn't gotten the cover he'd wanted.

"I heard second-hand that Gary was disappointed about the cover," Verducci said. "But he never ran from the story or the fallout from it. In my eyes he's a real stand-up guy for that. But that's part of his reputation. He speaks his mind and he doesn't have an agenda when he does it. He says things that are controversial, but I defy anybody who's played with him to say he's a bad guy."

In one sense, the timing of the story helped it pass quickly from the headlines, especially when Major League Baseball said it wouldn't investigate, since Sheffield's admitted use of the steroid cream had happened before the sport had any policy regarding steroids. After all, the playoffs were at hand, so the games took precedence. And as the Yankees embarked on what they hoped would be a championship run, they knew Sheffield well enough to be comfortable the distraction he'd created wouldn't stop him from hammering the baseball.

They did have pressing concerns, however, as the playoffs began.

First, though it had been clear in the final weeks that Joe Torre had given up any hope of Jason Giambi making a meaningful contribution in the playoffs, now it was official, as the Yankees left him off the postseason roster entirely, an appropriate way to complete a season that was a disaster from start to finish. Rendered weak and ineffective by what the Yankees diagnosed first as a parasite, then a benign tumor, Giambi couldn't escape speculation that his problems were related to steroids. When questioned again by reporters, he denied ever using steroids. Eventually he would be proven a liar when his testimony to the grand jury in the BALCO case was leaked to the *San Francisco Chronicle* in early December, revealing that Giambi confessed to using various types of steroids during his career.

Whatever the cause of Giambi's problems, the Yankees had long since come to the conclusion that Lou Gehrig he was not. They didn't think he was tough-minded enough when it came to playing through injuries. In George Steinbrenner's vernacular, he wasn't a warrior. For $120 million, which is what Giambi signed for as part of a seven-year contract in December 2001, he was expected to have Derek Jeter's toughness and the Yankees were disappointed to find out otherwise. Giambi's insistence on having his personal trainer, Bob Alejo, with him at all times turned off teammates as well as club executives. But what cost him the most respect in his own clubhouse was his decision to take himself out of the lineup for Game 5 of the 2003 World Series with a knee injury that had been bothering him for much of the season. Giambi said he was worried about his defense costing the Yankees in that game. Teammates and club executives thought he should have been thinking about how much his bat could help the Yankees—indeed, he pinch-hit a home run that night in the eighth inning in what turned out to be a pivotal loss.

Giambi needed a big 2004 season to win back a lot of people, but instead he became Exhibit A for the suspicion that, like other major-leaguers, he'd gotten off steroids because of baseball's drug-testing policy instituted in 2003. He was ridiculed by the media on his first day in spring training for saying he was only four pounds lighter than previous years, when he looked several pounds thinner. If Giambi had come out swinging the way he had in his glory years in Oakland, the steroids issue would have faded. But he didn't, hitting only .208 in 264 at-bats all season, with 12 home runs and 40 RBIs. And while Giambi had never brought any of his old A's swagger into the Yankees' clubhouse, he looked like a lost soul by the end of the 2004 season. He admitted to at least one friend that he regretted ever leaving the A's; he'd done it for the $120 million from the Yankees, sure, but he'd also done it to please his father, John, who had grown up in southern California in the 1950s and '60s idolizing Mickey Mantle. Giambi's rock 'n' roll personality was more suited to the A's, and he never seemed sure how to act around the corporate Yankees. By now he was aware the Yankees thought he was soft, and he was telling people around him that he hoped they could find a way to trade him during the off-season.

In any case, without Giambi, the Yankees felt fortunate to have picked up John Olerud at midseason on waivers from the Mariners. He was a huge upgrade defensively, and still a solid contact hitter, if not the All-Star he'd once been. And since the rest of their lineup was still loaded with offense, the Yankees didn't expect Giambi's absence in the postseason to be crucial. Instead, pitching remained their concern, as it had for most of the season.

Kevin Brown had thrown the rotation into chaos by breaking two bones in his left hand, punching a clubhouse wall in a fit of rage on September 3, in a 3–1 loss to the Baltimore Orioles. The temper tantrum cemented Brown's status as a loner in the Yankee clubhouse, as teammates were furious with him, and because he came back only a week before the playoffs. Getting ripped by the Red Sox in that first start, Brown was a huge question mark going into the postseason. Worse yet, so was El Duque Hernandez, whose unexpected run as ace ended when a tired arm forced him out of the rotation the last couple of weeks of the season.

So the Yankees looked vulnerable as playoffs began, extremely so by the 12th inning of Game 2 against the Twins. Down a game after losing to eventual AL Cy Young Award winner Johan Santana in the series opener, they found themselves trailing 6–5 going to the bottom of the 12th after Mariano Rivera rather shockingly had blown a 5–4 lead in the eighth. Twins' right-hander reliever Joe Nathan was overpowering the Yankees with his 95 mph fastball, working his third inning of relief. With one out and nobody on base, No. 9 hitter Miguel Cairo was due to hit. Right-hander versus right-hander, it looked to be a bad matchup for the Yankees, and most any manager in baseball would have pinch-hit for Cairo in that spot, especially with speedy left-handed hitter Kenny Lofton on the bench.

However, during the championship years, Torre had proven to be a manager who often trusted his instincts—or perhaps just a hunch based on his feelings about a particular player—over statistics or conventional strategy, often with uncanny results. In this case, Torre had come to admire Cairo as a grinder at the plate, a tough out all season who had looked especially good in September, hitting .349 for the month to finish the season at .292. So he decided not to pinch-hit, and it turned out to be perhaps a series-saving decision, as Cairo, after falling behind 0-and-1, refused to bite on three straight sliders off the outside corner, and finally drew a walk that started the game-winning rally. Alex Rodriguez wound up delivering the big hit, an RBI double, and Hideki Matsui's sacrifice fly scored Derek Jeter for a 7–6 victory, but it was Torre's willingness to trust a journeyman such as Cairo that proved pivotal.

"I just felt like he'd give us a good at-bat," Torre said of Cairo. "He's done it all year."

The escape from a potential 0–2 hole had a predictable effect on the Yankees, as they won the next two games in Minnesota to finish off the series, pulling off still another remarkable comeback in Game 4. Down 5–1, they rallied for four runs in the seventh inning, three on a home run by Ruben Sierra to tie the game and give them a chance to win it 6–5 in the 11th. Their total of 63 comeback victories, and 10 now from four or more runs behind, made these Yankees the greatest comeback team of all time, at least by the numbers, and who would dare argue?

"They're relentless," Twins' center fielder Torii Hunter said afterward. "They know that sooner or later, that lineup is going to get you. Sooner or later it gets everybody."

Indeed, by now it was hard not to think of the Yankees as a team destined to win another championship, after a season and now a playoff series defined by late-inning magic. Of course, you could argue that, with all respect to aura and mystique, the Yankees survived the first round mostly because the Twins' relievers choked in Games 2 and 4, and gave away the series.

They knew by now the Red Sox wouldn't be so generous.

All year the Yankees had heard about how the Red Sox were built for October because they had Curt Schilling and Pedro Martinez, so when they beat Boston's aces in Games 1 and 2 of the ALCS, they were doing all they could not to thump their chests and tell the world what they really thought of the Sox. The Yankees had come to think of the Sox as annoying little brothers, trying to bring attention to themselves with their funky appearance, trying to pump themselves up with all of their false bravado. The Sox had talked tough all season about how they knew the Yankees were worried about them. Even after the Yanks essentially locked up a seventh straight AL East title by beating the Red Sox in the opener of a last-chance series in Boston in late September, Johnny Damon was telling reporters how he still thought the Anaheim Angels were the best team he'd seen all year. And then Schilling had told everyone at his pre-series press conference how much fun it would be to shut up 55,000 New Yorkers at Yankee Stadium in Game 1.

"They never shut up," one Yankee player grumbled privately on the off-day in Boston before Game 3. "You'd think they be a little more respectful, since they've never won anything. It's like they're trying to talk themselves into believing they can beat us. I'm tired of their whole act. You see them goofing around in their dugout sometimes, and it just looks unprofessional. Joe [Torre] would never allow that stuff to go on, and I'm glad."

Another Yankee noted that Schilling was fast supplanting Pedro as the face of the enemy.

"At least Pedro can be funny sometimes," the player said. "I was watching Schilling on his press conference [before Game 1] when he was talking about shutting everybody up, and I had to turn it off. He's the almighty Curt Schilling. I thought I was listening to Jesus Christ."

The Yankees weren't saying anything like this publicly, of course, but they were only too happy to answer questions about the contrast in styles between the teams, in their case a style defined by Joe Torre's demand for professionalism.

When Torre came to New York in 1996, fans across America, and people throughout baseball, were actually rooting for the Yankees as they won the World Series. It had been 15 years since the Yankees had been in the Series, and Torre's own lifelong quest to reach the World Series became a poignant story, but fans could also see that his team played the game the right way, with a hustling, team-oriented approach.

By 2004, however, most everyone outside of New York hated the Yankees, baseball people included, because they outspend the world and win every year. Yet his players play for Torre the same way they did in his first year as manager.

"Joe sets the tone and we all follow," Alex Rodriguez said that day in Boston. "To me the Yankees were always very classy with him as the manager, and that's the way I've tried to be throughout my career, so it's been an easy fit here for me."

Rodriguez almost ended up on the other side, of course, during those endless trade negotiations months earlier. But it was hard to imagine A-Rod, always impeccably groomed and dressed, wearing his hair like Manny Ramirez or Pedro Martinez.

"I'd probably be the Lone Ranger over there [in terms of appearance]," he said with a laugh.

It was harder to imagine Torre presiding over the frat-house atmosphere in the Red Sox clubhouse that seemed to invite bold talk.

"Respect is important to me," Torre said. "I'm not just saying that because we're playing the Red Sox. You have to have that. The respect starts in your own clubhouse. And then, even if you're playing a last-place club, respect the fact that somebody can kick your ass at any time. We like to be businesslike. And it has nothing to do with reacting to what other people say or how somebody else behaves. I'm proud to say that these guys have been very professional."

In New York all of this meant one thing: the good guys were winning.

And when Game 3 turned into a 19–8 laugher, Yankees fans were ready to move on to the World Series, almost disappointed that the Sox hadn't at least put up a good fight. But even with a 3–0 lead that no team in baseball history had ever blown, Torre believed it was important to close out the Sox as quickly as possible because he believed that even one win could change the feel and momentum of a playoff series. In addition, the Red Sox themselves had made a lasting impression on him, particularly in the 48 games the teams had played against each other in 2003 and 2004. Even with the three wins in this series, the Yankees barely held an advantage over that two-year span, 25–23. And there had been so many wildly emotional, scratch-and-claw games among those 48, games that left Torre completely drained at their conclusion, searching for ways to describe the agony and ecstasy he felt managing against these Red Sox.

"Every one of these game takes on a life of its own," he'd say afterward, visibly exhaling. "They wear you out."

So Torre didn't want to hear about what it meant to be up 3–0. He didn't want to give the Sox even the tiniest bit of hope, and so he went for the kill when presented with the opportunity in Game 4. With the Yankees leading by a run, 4–3, in the eighth inning, he turned to Mariano Rivera, the man he'd leaned on so heavily in the postseason, going all the way back to 1996.

At age 34, soon to be 35, Rivera was no kid anymore, and the Yankees had paid closer-type money to Tom Gordon as a free agent to be a setup man, at least partly to help preserve Rivera and rescue him from having to deliver two-inning saves as he had so many times in postseasons past. However, after a strong season Gordon had finished poorly in September, and he wasn't great against the Twins. Furthermore the Yankees were concerned that Gordon didn't seem to be dealing with the pressure of the postseason well; he admitted to the press that he got "overexcited" at times and had to work to calm himself down. What he didn't say publicly was that, according to a Yankees official, he was getting himself so worked up during playoff games that more than once he vomited in the bullpen before coming into games.

Perhaps with this in mind, Torre didn't hesitate to skip over Gordon and bring Rivera in for the eighth inning with a 4–3 lead to get the last six outs for a sweep of the series. After all, Rivera hadn't pitched since Game 2, and because of a rainout, he'd had three days off, so Torre wasn't worried about extending him. Nevertheless, it had been an emotionally draining week for Rivera, who had flown to Panama and back as the series was starting to attend the funeral of two people close to his family who had been electrocuted in

Rivera's swimming pool. On his return he had arrived at Yankee Stadium after the game had started, took his place in the bullpen and wound up saving Game 1, the long, heart-wrenching day adding a chapter to the Rivera legend.

There was another factor to consider: the Red Sox had become something of a nemesis to Rivera in recent years. Since 2001 he'd blown seven save opportunities against them, including two during the 2004 season, and the Sox had seen him enough that they weren't intimidated by him. However, Rivera had proven in Games 1 and 2 that he could still dominate them when his trademark cut fastball was crackling, and it's hard to believe there was a Yankee fan anywhere at the time who protested upon seeing Torre bring his closer into the game in the eighth. As it turned out, of course, when Rivera surrendered the tying run in the ninth on a walk to Kevin Millar, a stolen base by pinch-runner Dave Roberts, and a single by Bill Mueller, second-guessers insisted that Torre had no business using Rivera for two innings in that situation, not with such a huge cushion in the series.

In any case, it was the beginning of a rather shocking fall from grace for Torre, who, for once, found himself pushing all the wrong buttons after so many Octobers when most everything he did seemed to turn out right. The Sox went on to win Game 4 on David Ortiz' 12th inning home run, and then the next night the Yankees' late-inning bullpen, such a strength all season, failed again. And for a second straight night Torre suddenly found himself in the line of fire, as his handling of the bullpen again was criticized.

This time the Yankees had a 4–2 lead going to the eighth, and because he'd used Rivera for two innings the previous night, Torre wanted to limit him to just one on this night. So he allowed Gordon, who had relieved Tanyon Sturtze in the seventh and induced an inning-ending double play from Manny Ramirez, to start the eighth. Gordon gave up a leadoff home run to Ortiz to make the score 4–3, and Torre reluctantly had pitching coach Mel Stottlemyre call the bullpen to have Rivera start getting loose. When Gordon then walked Kevin Millar, Torre continued to hope his setup man could escape the inning. But then Gordon gave up a sharply hit single to Trot Nixon, putting runners at first and third with no outs, and a desperate Torre felt he had no choice but to go to Rivera to keep the game from slipping away completely. Rivera got out of the inning with a tie, surrending a sacrifice fly to Jason Varitek, but he wound up pitching two innings again, this time without a realistic chance at saving a victory.

Rivera did succeed in extending the game, giving the Yankees numerous chances to win. But suddenly the lineup that had bombed Sox pitching for 19 runs in Game 3 couldn't get a clutch hit, as the Yankees went 1-for-13 with runners in scoring position, and left 18 runners on base. Finally, the Sox took advantage, when Ortiz delivered the game-winner, a soft single to center in the 14th inning against Esteban Loaiza that scored Johnny Damon for a 5–4 victory.

Now the tiny visitors' clubhouse at Fenway Park had to feel downright claustrophobic to the stunned Yankees, who dressed as quickly as possible and bolted for the team bus. For once the walls were even closing in on Torre, the Teflon manager. Gordon may have cost the Yankees the win, but suddenly Torre was being widely second-guessed. Regardless of his intentions, he wound up bringing Rivera into an impossible situation, so why hadn't he brought him in after Ortiz' home run? Or at least after Millar's walk. At that point Rivera still would have had a legitimate shot at escaping the inning with a 4–3 lead and a second consecutive chance to close out the World Series. Torre was firm in his answers afterward, saying his strategy was dictated by his determination to keep Rivera out of the eighth, and changed it only when he felt he would lose the game right then and there. Nevertheless, as the Yankees returned home, Torre's managing was the talk of New York. The rainout in Boston meant there was now no off-day before Game 6, for which the Yankees could be thankful, as they didn't have an extra 24 hours to consider the possibility of blowing a 3–0 lead, and the newspapers didn't have a day to analyze and reflect on all that went wrong in Boston.

Still, Torre was catching serious heat on the radio, and not just from the callers. Michael Kay, one of the team's broadcasters, lambasted him on his morning show on ESPN Radio, taking him to task for various pitching decisions—particularly not switching the rotation after the rainout to allow Mike Mussina to stay on regular rest and start Game 4, and then for using Rivera for two innings in Game 4 when he had the luxury of a 3–0 lead. Meanwhile, the city's most influential radio voices, Mike Francesa and Chris Russo, were blasting away on their *Mike and The Mad Dog* WFAN afternoon show, on which Torre is paid to do a weekly show with the hosts. For a change, it wasn't Russo, the Yankee hater, barking the loudest. Instead Francesa, the Yankee fan and Torre admirer, was outraged, hammering Torre for the way he used Rivera in Game 5, and also for not stealing a base in the 13th inning against knuckleballer Tim

Wakefield, when Jason Varitek was having so much trouble catching the knuckler that he was charged with three passed balls. Together Francesa and Russo even mused that Torre missed his old bench coach, the always-aggressive Don Zimmer, whispering ideas for strategy moves in his ear. All in all, the level of criticism was unprecedented for Torre as Yankee manager, and surely he was aware of it, but if he was bothered at all, he didn't let it show at his press conferences the rest of the way. That was part of Torre's greatness; he was unflappable in the face of defeat, or criticism from either the media or Boss Steinbrenner. Over the years his teams had reflected that calm, confident demeanor and won championships at least partly because of it.

This was the ultimate test, however, the Red Sox threatening now to make history against them, and for a change, the Yankees responded poorly. They didn't hit against Schilling in Game 6, losing 4–2, and wound up looking desperate when A-Rod was called out for slapping the ball out of Bronson Arroyo's glove on a tag play along the first baseline in the eighth inning. It was a play that once again brought to the surface the hard feelings between A-Rod and the Red Sox players, with Schilling going on ESPN TV and radio to rip the $252 million man for what he called a "junior-high play." Schilling even insinuated that it was a dirty play, saying that A-Rod could have broken Arroyo's arm with his slap, a ridiculous assertion that spoke to the level of animosity between them. A-Rod was furious when he heard of Schilling's remarks the next day, before Game 7. He wouldn't comment on them publicly, but made a point of telling friends that Schilling had made several recruiting calls to him the previous winter during the trade negotiations that nearly brought him to the Red Sox, saying how much he looked forward to playing with A-Rod. The obvious implication was that Schilling was a phony—which, of course, is exactly what the Red Sox thought of A-Rod.

In any case, when A-Rod went 0-for-4 in the Yankees' 10–3 loss in Game 7, and failed to get the ball out of the infield, the play from Game 6 seemed to linger as a symbol of his first season in New York. So much was expected; *this* is what we get? Yankees fans no doubt would have felt better if A-Rod had just veered inside the baseline and run Arroyo over, rather than swipe at the ball with what *Daily News* columnist Mike Lupica called "a purse-snatching move." Still, the idea that the play was somehow beneath major league standards, a notion the media quickly embraced based on the Red Sox players' reaction, was surely an overreaction simply because it was A-Rod. If he'd done it even a few years ago, before umpires began conferring as often as they do now to make sure they get calls right, he might have gotten away with it. First base umpire Randy Marsh was screened on the play, and called A-Rod out only after he got together with the other umpires, at which point Joe West said he saw A-Rod slap the ball away. That he got caught made him look bad, but it didn't make him wrong for trying. At least that's how one Hall of Famer saw it. ESPN broadcaster Joe Morgan, who was part of two World Series winners with the 1970s Cincinnati Reds, went on Michael Kay's radio show after the series and said he couldn't believe the abuse A-Rod was taking for the play.

"I thought it was a great play," Morgan said. "It was a reaction. Every single member of the Big Red Machine would have done the same thing. He was just trying to make a play to avoid being out."

When Kay told him A-Rod was being criticized at least partly because, in slapping at the ball, he looked less than manly, Morgan sounded incredulous.

"So you're more of a man if you stand there and get tagged out?"

Morgan had a point. And had the Yankees come back to win Game 7—with the help of a timely hit or two by A-Rod—the play would have been forgotten quickly. Instead, they not only lost Game 7, they were humiliated in a 10–3 loss that was over in the second inning when Johnny Damon welcomed Javier Vazquez into the game with a grand slam. It was slow torture, perhaps a worse fate than the heartbreak the Red Sox suffered a year earlier, when their hopes died suddenly via the Aaron Boone home run. After all, for a solid couple of hours the Yankees had nowhere to hide, playing out the final innings of a game they knew would leave a permanent stain on pinstriped history as the greatest collapse in baseball history.

In the end, all the fears about pitching proved prophetic. When the Yankees needed someone to rescue the series and their season, all they had to choose between was a broken-down Kevin Brown and a mentally fragile Vazquez. Each wound up proving it wasn't much of a choice at all. Torre and Stottlemyre settled on Brown as the starter, hoping his toughness and experience would get him through five innings or so. The problem was Brown still hadn't learned to adjust to the problems, whether it was the parasite, the bad back, or age, that had robbed him of his dominating stuff. Rather than change speeds and hit spots, Brown again went out and tried to overpower the Red Sox with a sinker than now reached 90, rather than 94, mph on the radar gun, and no longer sunk so hard and late that it felt to hitters like a cannonball on contact. He gave up a two-run home run to David Ortiz in the first inning, and quickly got into trouble in the second. Here Torre made one last second-guessable decision, bringing Vazquez and his starting-pitcher mentality into a bases-loaded situation with no margin for error. Perhaps he would have been better served using a reliever such as Tanyon Sturtze, who had come into such situations for much of the season, and then going to Vazquez to start an inning. At least that was the obvious move in hindsight, after Damon slammed Vazquez' first pitch deep for a 6–0 lead, turning Yankee Stadium as quiet as a confessional booth.

When it was over there were culprits in all corners of the clubhouse. Brown was sure to be remembered for changing the dynamics of October with his self-inflicted broken hand in September. None of the big boppers hit a lick after Game 3. Derek Jeter ran out of postseason heroics. Gordon and Rivera flat let the series get away. And for once Torre made all the wrong moves.

Yet the season ended much the way it started, with everyone in New York talking mostly about A-Rod. His presence was supposed to make a difference in games like these. He was supposed to assure the Yankees of another championship. Only none of it turned out that way. For most of the season A-Rod didn't hit in the clutch, prompting boos from fans. He never did make friends in the clubhouse. He fretted over criticism, to the point where he didn't talk to Jim Kaat for a while after the Yankee TV announcer was critical of his long swing during a game. And finally, A-Rod got caught slapping the ball out of Bronson Arroyo's glove.

When Game 7 was over, he stood at his locker and said he was embarrassed. He said he still didn't believe anyone could beat the Yankees four straight. He said it would make him more determined. He said all the right things. But Yankee fans didn't care. They were left to wonder how the year might have turned out had A-Rod gone to the Red Sox for Manny Ramirez as he was supposed to. Sick as they were of Curt Schilling, they had to wonder if he was right when he rubbed it in after the World Series, saying the Sox wouldn't have won a championship if the deal had gone down and A-Rod had come to Boston.

Maybe it wasn't fair to A-Rod. But then, as the fans in Boston would have been all too delighted to tell him: fair has never had anything to do with the Yankees and the Red Sox.

OCTOBER HEAD-TO HEAD—THE CHOKE'S ON THEM

In the weeks after the 2004 baseball season, I saw the following bumper sticker on the back of a car:

I root for two teams: the Red Sox and whoever beats the Yankees.

For Red Sox fans, finally and gloriously, those teams were one and the same.

So while there was still a World Series to be played in Boston, there was simply no overstating the magnitude of the 2004 American League Championship Series, particularly in the eyes of Bostonians and New Englanders. And while New Yorkers inevitably will come up with some profane argument about the meaninglessness of one October series when their team has won 26 world championships, they must nonetheless live with the reality that their Yankees, *their glorious Yankees*, are now the authors of the most monumental collapse in the history of team sports.

So there, Mr. Harper.

How do you like *them* (big) apples?

In retrospect, after all, it was not simply defeating the New York Yankees that gave the Red Sox and their fans cause for joy; it was *how* they defeated the Yankees. New York led the series, 3–0. New York had a lead and the great Mariano Rivera on the mound in the ninth inning of Game 4. The Yankees had a lead and Rivera on the mound again in the eighth inning of Game 5. And still, the Yankees could not put away a Red Sox team they had dominated for decades, relying on the preposterous concept of *ghosts* to bury a team that finally had the *cojones* to look the Yankees squarely in the eyes and see what had long been suspected.

Nothing.

Emptiness.

Like the New York tabloids said, *The Choke's on You.*

Truth be told, Red Sox followers could not have dreamed up a better scenario in which to inflict as much pain and suffering on the Yankees and their obnoxious fans, to make them understand what it was like to lose. In the minds of the most twisted and devout Red Sox followers, the most torturous scenario would have had the Yankees winning the first three games of a seven-game series, the third contest in a landslide that would manage to fatten up the already obese New York arrogance. (In ancient times, this was called hubris.) Then New York would have its foolproof closer on the mound in Games 4 and 5, only to learn that he was indeed mortal. Then the Yankees would lose Game 6 to a man pitching on one leg. Then the Yankees would get their face kicked in during a humiliating Game 7, at home, in the *House That Ruth Built*, allowing Red Sox fans to come out of the bleachers and the balconies, descending on New York from the upper decks like the vultures that typically pick apart the last remains of the dying Red Sox.

In that way, we offer a modern twist on those infamous words from Marie Antoinette:

Let them eat crow.

In the immediate aftermath of the 2004 American League Championship Series, at least in Boston, there was considerable debate. Did winning the World Series even matter? Wasn't it enough for the Sox to get up off the ground, dust themselves off, and beat the snot out of the smug Yankees? Didn't upending New York make up for Bucky Dent (in 1978) and Aaron Boone (in 2003) and all of the Yankees, in between and before?

The answers, in order:

Yes.

No.

Maybe.

Following the Game 7 victory over New York, even the Red Sox and their owners fell victim to such peculiar theory. Owners Henry and Tom Werner, in particular, suggested that winning the World Series would be no better an accomplishment, and even Red Sox veteran and senior statesman Tim Wakefield put the victory over the Yankees in a historical context. None of them noted—at least in the midst of a glorious clubhouse celebration—that losing to the Yankees would fail to strip New Yorkers of their trump card, that one chant that drunken Yankees fans always resorted to when nothing else worked.

Nine-teen eight-teen!

Of course, the words frequently were slurred.

But still, didn't New Englanders see? To truly overcome the Yankees and everything they stood for, to finally get past the inferiority complex and the feeling of helplessness, the Red Sox and their followers needed to think *beyond* them. They needed to put things not in the context of the Yankees, but of the Red Sox, who were finally moving onto bigger and better things. They needed to learn that the Yankees mystique was nothing more than the hot air blowing from the subway grates and manhole covers on Fifth Avenue—the *Canyon of Heroes*—and that there really was not anything that magical or supernatural or divine about the Yankees and their concrete palace of a home, which were nothing more, respectively, than *just another team* and *just another place*.

In the end, that is what New York was.

Hype.

Perpetuated, of course, by a New York media that was far more blinded by its love for the Yankees than it would ever have you believe.

But seriously, did New Yorkers ever listen to themselves talk? There was, without question, that core of Yankees press that was truly hard on the team, objective and demanding. Yet for all the criticisms that New Yorkers aimed at the Red Sox and the New England media, they were guilty of many of the same quirks. New York had an extended press corps of lightweights that spoke of the Yankees only in reverential tones, that asked opponents questions like *How do you think you will do against the Yankees?* and *Can the Yankees be beaten? What is it like to come in here, to New York, and play against the Yankees, the most storied and decorated franchise in the history of professional sports?*

There was always that implication that New York was best, a measuring stick, top of the list, king of the hill.

You know, *A Number One*.

And all the rest of that crap.

But following Game 7, there was finally that feeling throughout New England that the Yankees were just another collection of baseball players, 25 men who may have looked imposing and intimidating, but who were really no better than anyone else. Don't you see? All along it was *the suits*, those obnoxious, cheesy pinstripes that New Yorkers actually thought *looked good*, the way that Donald Trump must look in the mirror each morning and brush off his lapel, then say to himself: *Damn, my hair looks perfect today*.

For decades, we New Englanders have had to bite our tongues about that sort of thing, only because New Yorkers always seemed to find a way to win.

But that is no more.

So the gloves are off.

In the final games of the American League Championship Series, in fact, even the biggest Yankees shrank in the eyes of America. Alex Rodriguez had one hit in his final 15 at-bats of the series, further proving that while he was indeed a great talent, he still was not a *winner* and had no real understanding of what it was to *fight*. The tough-as-nails Gary Sheffield went 1-for-16 in the final four games, proving once again that the best thing to do against any bully is to stand up to him. And respectable outfielder Hideki Matsui, for whom the Red Sox seemingly possessed no answers, had just three hits in his final 16 at-bats, two of those coming in the final three innings of Game 7, after the Red Sox had built an 8–1 advantage.

"Obviously, I don't have words to describe my disappointment," said Rodriguez. "It's hard any way you look at it, not being able to put them away. It's very frustrating. . . . It hurts bad."

To which Red Sox followers replied:

Good.

During the final three games of the ALCS, in particular, there were signs that the Red Sox had detected a chink in the New York armor, most notable in the Yankees' makeup. It was during Game 5, after all, that Sox bad boy Martinez flattened Matsui with a fastball, a point after which Matsui was a non-factor in the series. A hobbled Curt Schilling did the same to Rodriguez in Game 6, effectively taking Rodriguez out of the fight, too. Sox general manager Theo Epstein, in particular, identified the two pitches as pivotal moments in the final three games, when the Yankees had their confidence shaken and when the Red Sox steadily began to regain their bounce.

In the end, it was impossible even for the Red Sox to ignore the countless moments along the way where things could have been different, the many crossroads in which Boston always seemed to end up on the right path. Prior to the 2003 season, after all, it was the Yankees who had outbid the Red Sox for Cuban defector Jose Contreras, the pitcher who proved such a bust in New York that the Yankees were ultimately forced to trade him for pitcher Esteban Loaiza, who allowed the game-winning hit to David Ortiz in Game 5. It was the Yankees who ended up with Rodriguez, who disappeared in Games 4 through 7, finishing with a

.258 ALCS batting average that was noticeably lower than that of Red Sox shortstop Orlando Cabrera, who batted a sterling .379. It was the Yankees who lost Roger Clemens, who departed the Red Sox following the 1996 season with more wins in a Boston uniform (192) than anyone but the great Cy Young (also 192). And it was the Yankees who replaced Clemens, Andy Pettitte, and David Wells—at least in part—with the talented but unproven Javier Vazquez, whom the Red Sox had similarly coveted and whose performance deteriorated badly in the second half of the season, right up to (and including) a pair of home runs he allowed to Johnny Damon in Game 7 of the American League Championship Series.

Along the way, too, how many chances were there for the Red Sox to end up similarly derailed? During October and November of 2003, what if someone had put in a claim for Sox outfielder Manny Ramirez, whom the team placed on waivers and had such a brilliant regular season that he was a leading candidate for the American league Most Valuable Player award? What if the Red Sox had acquired Vazquez, a move that would have preempted the acquisition of Schilling, the hero of ALCS Game 6? What if Conteras had been a member of the Red Sox? What if closer Keith Foulke had chosen to remain with Oakland rather than sign with the Red Sox, for whom he made five scoreless appearances in the American League Championship Series after a pair of scoreless appearances in the AL Division Series, failing to allow a run (earned or unearned) in nine innings, a performance that was downright *Rivera-esque*?

And what, finally, if Tony Clark's double in Game 5 had clipped the top of the wall and bounded in the corner for a triple, if the umpires had failed to make the correct calls in Game 6 and allowed Rodriguez to cheat while taking away Bellhorn's home run, if Dave Roberts had been out at second base trying to steal against the estimable Rivera in Game 4 instead of successfully placing himself in scoring position and altering the course of the series?

What then?

"If we had lost that fourth game to the Yankees, we'd be saying, 'How do we fix it?'" Red Sox manager Terry Francona noted weeks after the conclusion of the postseason. "Now we're asking, 'How do we keep this thing together?'"

But wait.

We're getting ahead of ourselves.

The Red Sox still had a World Series to play.

The Yankees were the ones who had no choice but to be reflective.

"They were better than us," Derek Jeter, the respected Yankees shortstop, said of the Red Sox. "Bottom line, they didn't give up."

The bottom line?

This time, it was the Yankees who were uttering words all too familiar in the six-state region of New England.

Wait 'til next year.

OCTOBER HEAD-TO-HEAD—HELL FREEZES OVER

Michael Kay has been covering the Yankees as a sportswriter and then a broadcaster for nearly 20 years, long enough to knock the fan out of him. It's what happens to most anybody when the Yankees—or any team—become your job, and you are exposed to all the warts that come with the territory. Kay, who grew up in the Bronx rooting for his hometown team, is still passionate about calling the games on TV, and he'd rather see the Yankees win than lose, but after all these years it's more business for him than the can't-sleep-after-a-loss emotion of a die-hard fan.

Yet for the first time in years, Kay found those old feelings stirring as the unthinkable became reality and the Red Sox completed the historic comeback from 0–3 to win the ALCS.

"Watching the Red Sox celebrating on the field after Game 7," Kay said weeks later, "I honestly felt sick to my stomach. I guess even after all the years in this business, that got to me. I still can't believe it happened."

To some extent or another, all New Yorkers who aren't Mets' fans experienced a similar emotion. After all: it was the Red Sox. *The Red Sox.*

The editors at the *Daily News* summed up the city's feeling best with their back-page headline: Hell Freezes Over.

Personally, I understood the pangs of nausea, having grown up a Yankee fan lucky enough to see Mickey Mantle hit a game-winning home run on my first trip to Yankee Stadium with my father. But all these years later, I can't say I was deeply affected by the Yankees' losing. Too many nights of writing on deadline, I guess, to have anything but a journalistic viewpoint by now.

Actually, I think I stopped rooting for the Yankees in 1978, the year that would make Bucky Dent a four-letter word in Boston forever. It was my first full year as a sportswriter, and it didn't take long to realize that as a fan, you're better off not knowing too much about some of your favorite ballplayers. As a fresh-faced reporter for the *Morristown* (New Jersey) *Daily Record*, I accompanied our Yankee beat writer, Joe Sullivan (now the *Boston Globe* sports editor, ironically enough), to the stadium and was rather shocked to find out that Craig Nettles and Thurman Munson could be so rude and crude in dealing with the press. Those were the days before players worried that anything they said might make them fodder for ESPN or radio talk shows, and Nettles, in particular, wasn't shy about calling a reporter "an asshole," as I heard him do to Sullivan because he didn't like a question that Joe asked. Meanwhile, it took courage for anyone to ask a question of Billy Martin after a Yankee loss in those days, because any little thing was liable to send him into a screaming rage. I only filled in occasionally on the Yankees at that time, but it was an eye-opening experience.

It was also my first up-close glimpse of George Steinbrenner, and he was at his most impetuous at the time. You never knew when he might come storming into the press box to scream to reporters about bad umpiring after a call went against him. You never knew when he would get so mad over an error that he would demote a player on the spot; one night he became so furious with rookie second baseman Bobby Meacham that he sent him down to the minors, past Triple-A, all the way back to Double-A. You never knew when he might fire Billy Martin again, or pick a fight with Reggie Jackson, and then later Dave Winfield. He never forgave Winfield for going 1-for-21 in the 1981 World Series. And when Winfield was having a big offensive game one night in May a couple of years later, Steinbrenner marched all the way down to the front of the press box to vent to the beat writers: "There he is, Mr. May. I used to have Mr. October. Now I have Mr. May."

Over the years Steinbrenner became less demonstrative, less of a visible in-game presence. But his omnipresence around the Yankees remained larger than life somehow, and when he was in New York for a game, watching from behind closed doors in his Yankee Stadium office, he created the sense of being the man behind the curtain, a baseball version of the Wizard of Oz. As a result, in the press box there is still an unspoken surge of energy among the New York writers when the Yankees lose a big one. Years of witnessing the Boss react like the worst kind of sore loser taught us that the real intrigue begins after the final out. So as Game 7 was ending, and the Yankees were suffering the worst loss in the history of the franchise, as the first team ever to blow a 3–0 lead in a postseason series, the sense of anticipation was palpable as we hurried downstairs: what would George do? If not tonight, then tomorrow. Or next week. Or next month.

Because they spend so much money, because they've won so often in recent years, the Yankees are more interesting these days when they lose, at least from a journalistic perspective. That's not the media being nattering nabobs of negativity, as Spiro Agnew once famously put it. That's just the way it is, particularly when the George factor is part of the equation.

On this night, however, Steinbrenner apparently was too distraught to lash out at anyone. Weeks later one Yankees official described the owner as being "in a catatonic state" after Game 7. He didn't venture into the clubhouse or manager's office, all but locking himself into his own loge-level office, watching the highlights, interviews, and analysis on his YES Network as if looking for some revelation as to how it happened. Surprisingly he didn't fire anyone or even order GM Brian Cashman and other Yankees executives to report to Tampa immediately for organizational meetings, as he has after season-ending losses in years past. He even made a point of telling Cashman that his job was safe, that he would be back in 2005. This wasn't the Boss of old; maybe it was a sign of an old Boss. He didn't apologize to the city of New York, as he'd done once after the Yankees lost the 1981 World Series to the Dodgers. Nor did he get into a fight in an elevator with a couple of disrespectful punks, as he claimed to have done after that same World Series, explaining that he was forced to defend the honor of New Yorkers.

Finally, at 1:20 A.M., nearly two hours after the final out was made, George exited the stadium and stopped briefly for the reporters on the Steinbrenner Watch. He was subdued, offering not a single angry word about his own team. Instead he spoke only briefly in praise of the Red Sox.

"I want to congratulate the Boston team," he said. "They did very well and played very well. They are a great team."

And with that Steinbrenner got into his Town Car, ignoring follow-up questions about whether the loss had put anyone's job on the line.

"Good night," he said as he closed the door and the car sped off.

Yankee misery and embarrassment was obviously the main story for any New York sportswriter on this night, yet even on our side of the press box there was an inescapable feeling of being part of something bigger than all of that. As New Yorkers perhaps we can never understand just what it meant to New Englanders to finally beat the Yankees, but it was impossible not to marvel at the sense of history being made.

I know I felt that way. After all these years in sportswriting, I root not for a team but for the best story, and there may never be a better story than this improbable comeback by the Red Sox to finally slay their dragon. Nevertheless, that doesn't mean I didn't feel some aftershocks. I've got three buddies from Boston, Charlie Henry, Skip Carino, and George Papagelis, with whom I played on a national championship fast-pitch softball team in 1983, and they couldn't wait to return all the "your-team-chokes" taunts they've heard from me over the years. They were buzzing my cell phone while I was still working the locker room after the game.

"I don't even care what they do in the Series," Papagelis bellowed into my voice mail. "We beat your damn Yankees. I'd save you some champagne, but you might choke on it. Like your team."

Ah, friendship. My pals also pointed out, along with a few hundred other Red Sox fans who sent an onslaught of nasty e-mails to my *Daily News* address, that I was the real idiot in this series for burying the Sox in my newspaper column after Game 3.

Fair enough. I did hammer the Sox that night. But then, how could you not, the way they ran the bases so recklessly in that 19–8 debacle? With a century of major league baseball history on my side, I liked my odds of declaring the series over at 3–0. But the Sox were grittier than anybody knew, so I'll take the abuse—even from Massarotti, who had this goofy grin on his face when I saw him downstairs in the Sox locker room, and couldn't wait to zing me:

"The great Yankees," he said, in a theatrical tone. "Will New York ever be the same?"

What could I say? I'd razzed him enough over the years, so all I could do was laugh good-naturedly and tell him: "Go write your friggin' column, and don't make it too sappy."

I had to hurry upstairs and write my own column, so it wasn't until later, when the exhilaration of making deadline on such a memorable night had worn off, that I considered the ramifications. Life as we knew it in New York *had* changed forever. Even for sportswriters, there *was* a certain satisfaction in knowing the Yankees always found a way to put the Red Sox in their place all these years, and now that was gone. In the press box it had always afforded us a certain smugness about the rivalry that we could lord over our Boston colleagues, even if it was just for laughs. Now, by extension, we were the chokers.

Ah, but then I remembered. At least we still had the media-game bragging rights. Once a season the Yankees and Red Sox are each kind enough to give us their ballfield for a couple of hours, and Boston and New York writers play a home-and-home series. It's not pretty, and nobody is thinking the GMs are watching from an office somewhere, ready with a contract for the best player. Well, nobody but Bob Klapisch of the Bergen *Record*, our 40-something pitcher who brings his own radar gun to check on his velocity. In any case, the games are competitive and we take them seriously, if only so we don't have to hear about it from the other side of the press box that night. It's fair to say that we New Yorkers have dominated the series in recent years, though we had to hold off a last-inning rally in Boston earlier this summer to sweep the season series. It got a little hairy before we finally held on to win by one run, but when the game ended it felt like business as usual. An extension of the real rivalry, if you will. Little did we know at the time that with the win we would wind up defending the honor of New York in 2004. Somehow, I don't think Yankee fans will find much solace in that.

Good thing it's not every year that hell freezes over.

EPILOGUE: THE WORLD SERIES

UNLIKE THE 2003 NEW YORK YANKEES, WHO WILTED IN THE WORLD Series following an emotionally-draining American League Championship Series, the 2004 Boston Red Sox had no such difficulty. The Red Sox scored four runs against the St. Louis Cardinals in the first inning of World Series Game 1, three of them coming on a home run from the unrelenting David Ortiz, who would finish the playoffs with 19 RBI, tying a major-league record for one postseason. Red Sox starter Tim Wakefield and a handful of relievers proved incapable of holding leads of 4–0, 7–2 and 9–7, but the Red Sox ultimately claimed an 11–9 victory when, in the bottom of the eighth inning, second baseman Mark Bellhorn hooked a two-run home run that struck the top of the right field foul pole.

Going back to game of the AL Championship Series, Bellhorn had homered in three consecutive games. In the last two, the ball had struck the right field foul pole, coming within inches of going foul.

The Red Sox simply could do no wrong.

In Game 1, in fact, the Red Sox won despite making four errors, a feat they duplicated in Game 2, which nonetheless produced a lopsided 6–2 victory behind the sewn-up Schilling, who once again took the mound with his ankle featuring the kind of stitches that similarly held together a baseball. Once again, the Red Sox scored early—catcher Jason Varitek hit a two-out, two-run triple in the first—and this time coasted to an easy victory that was never really in doubt thanks to the grittiness, effectiveness, and efficiency of their one-legged staff ace.

All in all, after making just two errors combined in 10 games against the Anaheim Angels and New York Yankees, the Red Sox made a whopping eight in the first two games against the St. Louis Cardinals.

And not only had the Red Sox won, but they had never even trailed.

"You've got to feel fortunate," said pitcher Bronson Arroyo, who pitched in relief of Wakefield in Game 1. "But you've got to look at the good things also. We scored some runs and we feel we can hit their pitching a little bit."

In fact, while the Cardinals had finished the 2004 regular season with a major-league-leading 105 victories—St. Louis owned the best record in baseball—a shortage of pitching left St. Louis vulnerable against a Red Sox lineup that had led the majors in runs scored. And while the Cardinals had, in fact, finished second in all of baseball in team pitching with a sparkling staff ERA of 3.75—only the Atlanta Braves were a whisker better at 3.74—the Cardinals did so in a league that operated without the designated hitter (in this case, Ortiz) and had the misfortune of playing through the postseason without their staff ace, injured right-hander and New England native Chris Carpenter.

Once again, this time it was the *other team* that suffered from a simple case of bad luck.

For the Red Sox, St. Louis was a fitting opponent, though the same could have been said of the Houston Astros, whom the Cardinals had defeated in seven games of a stirring National League Championship Series. But while a meeting with the Astros would have allowed the Red Sox to square off against Houston pitcher Roger Clemens, whose 192 career wins in Boston tied him with Cy Young for first in Red Sox history, the series with the Cardinals allowed the Red Sox to face the *second* most successful franchise in baseball history, a timely opportunity given that the Sox had just come from dethroning the mighty Yankees.

Behind the Yankees, after all, the Cardinals' nine world championships ranked second in baseball history. St. Louis also had defeated the Red Sox in the 1946 and 1967 World Series, Boston's first two trips back to the Fall Classic since the city's last title in 1918. And so if the Red Sox finally were to win the title that had eluded them for the majority of the 20th century, they would have to do so by defeating the two most decorated franchises in baseball and the two most sizable obstacles on their seemingly endless road back to glory.

While the Cardinals hardly looked like a formidable opponent after the first two games of the Series, any lingering doubt was fully and formally exhausted during Game 3, when St. Louis effectively committed suicide. After the Red Sox had staked yet another starter to a lead in the first inning—this time, Pedro Martinez had a 1–0 advantage *before throwing a single pitch*—the Cardinals threatened against Martinez in the bottom of the first. St. Louis had the bases loaded with one out when Jim Edmonds lifted a soft fly to short left field, a play on which baserunner Larry Walker curiously tagged from third base. The decision proved downright foolish when Walker was thrown out at the plate by, of all people, Manny Ramirez, and after the game Walker indicated that he ran only because teammate Albert Pujols had inexplicably broken from second, leaving himself open for an easy double play.

While television replays confirmed Pujols' blunder—Ramirez, in fact, could have had an *easier* double play by simply throwing to second base—Walker's postgame remarks indicated a frustration and desperation in the St. Louis clubhouse that was undetectable when the Red Sox faced an identical 3–0 series deficit to the New York Yankees roughly a week earlier. The obvious message was that the St. Louis Cardinals were in no shape—mentally or physically—to come back from a 3–0 deficit against a Red Sox team that had won seven postseason games in a row.

Still, while Walker's mistake was critical in an eventual 4–1 Red Sox win—Martinez pitched seven shutout innings—it was hardly the signature moment of Cardinals ineptitude. That came two innings later—in the third—when St. Louis pitcher Jeff Suppan (another former member of the Red Sox) demonstrated previously unseen indecision on the basepaths, failing to score from third base on a ground ball to second base. The Red Sox, in fact, had conceded a run on the play, but a confused Suppan inexplicably changed direction three times—he broke back to third base, then to home, then back to third base—before the Red Sox put him out of his misery and mercifully picked him off.

"Basically, I screwed up. Period. I got hung up," said Suppan, a likeable southern California native who was originally drafted by the Red Sox. "I really don't know how to describe it or explain it."

Nor could anyone else.

Nonetheless, in the Boston clubhouse, the Red Sox were taking nothing for granted. Rock-jawed Sox catcher Jason Varitek was among those stressing that the Sox needed to maintain their focus entering Game 4, but the reality was that the Cardinals were cooked. Even the Red Sox knew it, though to admit as much would have been to take the Cardinals lightly, and the Red Sox were not about to do that.

Not after 86 years of waiting.

Not after enough heartbreaking finishes to extinguish the spirit of the most die-hard loyalists.

Not after the Sox had just overcome a 3–0 deficit against the Yankees.

At this stage, everybody in Boston knew enough to take nothing for granted, though there was an obvious air of inevitability in the Boston clubhouse.

"I know a lot of times they're waiting for us to stumble and fall," Red Sox pitcher Derek Lowe said of pessimistic Sox followers. "I hope they're not waiting for us to stumble and fall now. This team has a lot of confidence. I hope they're excited. We're one step away."

As luck would have it, that final step would be the responsibility of Lowe, who had been reinserted into the starting rotation following the ALCS victory over the Yankees. Going back to the 2003 season, in fact, Lowe had saved the Game 5 clincher against the Oakland A's in the AL Division Series, then won decisive Game 3 against Anaheim in 2004 and penultimate Game 7 against the Yankees. Now he was getting the ball with a chance to close out the Cardinals, afforded an opportunity to become the first pitcher in baseball history to win three series clinchers in the same postseason.

Continuing the trend that had been set in Game 1, Lowe was entrusted with an early lead. Wild man Damon led off the game with a home run and, two innings later, Nixon belted a two-out, two-run double off the center field wall to give the Red Sox a 3–0 lead. In the latter instance, manager Terry Francona actually had ordered Nixon to take the 3–0 pitch, but the Sox got their signs mixed up and Nixon swung away, delivering what would be the final run-scoring hit of the 2004 baseball season.

Even when the Red Sox saw things that weren't there, it seemed, they were landing on their feet.

As for Lowe, he was nothing if not positively robotic, mowing down the Cardinals on a seemingly endless succession of ground balls, weak flies, and strikeouts. In seven innings, he allowed just three hits and permitted only two runners to advance as far as third base. Manager Francona employed Arroyo and left-hander Alan Embree in the eighth before turning the ninth over to Foulke, whose final pitch of the game resulted in a one-hopper off the bat of St. Louis shortstop Edgar Renteria that bounced directly back to the pitcher, who fielded the ball and seemingly came to the realization that, in his hands, he possessed the World Series championship that Red Sox fans had so long waited for. Handling the ball with appropriate delicateness, Foulke jogged toward first baseman Doug Mientkiewicz and *underhanded* the ball to his teammate, touching off a celebration on the field, in the clubhouse, and throughout all of New England, or wherever Red Sox fans were.

And while even the most experienced baseball observers shook their heads in awe of a Boston team that had responded to a 3–0 series deficit to the Yankees by winning *eight in a row*—"Unbelievable," commissioner Bud Selig said as he emerged from the Red Sox clubhouse celebration after the game—the Red Sox were able to put the accomplishment into perspective.

"We'll never hear the '1918' chants again," said Wakefield. "It's huge for the franchise. Ever since Mr. Henry and Mr. Werner and Larry (Lucchino) took over, they've pointed us in the right direction. People that have lived there longer than I have had too many sad days. Now they can rejoice in the city of Boston."

Said catcher Varitek: "I can't explain the great feeling we have for the whole New England area. They can finally rest. They can finally take a nap. Some people that have suffered a long time can finally go to sleep."

In New England, finally, it would be a peaceful winter.

In the end, if the Red Sox and their followers did not know it already, here is what they learned: the New York Yankees made them better. The World Series against the St. Louis Cardinals did not simply seem anticlimactic. It *was* anticlimactic. In the four-game sweep of the Cardinals, the Red Sox never trailed. They outscored St. Louis, 24–12, and outhit the Cardinals, .283 to .190. Red Sox pitchers posted a 2.50 ERA while St. Louis pitchers came in at an unsightly 6.09, and none of the numbers were deceiving.

The Red Sox had dominated.

But really, how could it have been any other way? While the Red Sox and Yankees had shared more than 100 years of history, the most recent seasons, especially, had proven once again that the teams competed at the highest level. During the course of the 2003 and 2004 seasons, the Red Sox and Yankees played 52 times in the regular season and playoffs. Boston won 27 games and New York won 25, only Boston's victory in Game 7 of the 2004 ALCS preventing a 26–26 split. Each team won an American League Championship. And during the 2004 season, in particular, the Red Sox outscored the Yankees 149–146 over the span of 26 meetings, a margin of just three runs.

Overall, over the course of 52 baseball games in two years, the Red Sox scored 287 runs and the Yankees 270, a difference of just 17 runs that translated into less than one-third of a run *per game.*

In two extraordinary years, from Aaron Boone's home run to Johnny Damon's grand slam, that was the difference between the Red Sox and Yankees.

A *fraction.*

And make no mistake: the Yankees were better for it, too.

"It's like a World Series playing those guys in the *regular season,*" Red Sox outfielder Trot Nixon said in a private moment while standing near the bat rack in the visitor's dugout at Busch Stadium in St. Louis before Game 4 of the World Series. "Against the Yankees, when you get a three-game series or a four-game series, that could swing the division. Whether it's the first week of April or the last week of September, those games—nothing can compare. I don't know what it's like in Los Angeles or San Francisco, but those games [against the Yankees] mean something. Nothing can compare. Nothing prepares you more than that."

Weeks later, following the 2004 World Series, the Red Sox and Yankees were at it again. Sox pitcher Pedro Martinez was among the many Boston players who filed for free agency, ultimately choosing to leave the Red Sox for a four-year contract with the New York Mets. The Red Sox all but officially had cut ties with Lowe, who would similarly end up elsewhere. And while the Yankees had reinforced their pitching staff by finally acquiring Randy Johnson and right-hander Carl Pavano (a former Red Sox farmhand who had been traded for Martinez in December 1997) as well as right-hander Jaret Wright, the Red Sox had signed former Yankees left-hander David Wells, pitchers May Clement and Wade Miller, and shortstop Renteria, who had made the final out against them in the World Series.

And so, as fall turned to winter and winter moved toward spring, the Red Sox and Yankees reminded us all of a long-standing truth.

In Boston and New York, the baseball season does not end so much as a new one begins.

INDEX

N

S

W

Y

Z